LEARNING CENTERS

CENTERS
development and operation

LEARNING CENTERS
development and operation

Frances Bennie

EDUCATIONAL TECHNOLOGY PUBLICATIONS
ENGLEWOOD CLIFFS, NEW JERSEY 07632

Library of Congress Cataloging in Publication Data

Bennie, Frances.
    Learning centers.

    Bibliography: p.
    Includes index.
    1. Open plan schools.   2.   Individualized instruction.
I.   Title.
LB1029.06B46   371   76-58528
ISBN 0-87778-097-8

Printed in the United States of America.

Library of Congress Catalog Card Number:
76-58528.

International Standard Book Number:
0-87778-097-8.

First Printing: March, 1977

12/1/78 Rel. 14.95

This book is dedicated to
my daughter Lisa

Acknowledgments

Recognition is due to the many classroom teachers, administrators, college professors, and students who contributed to this work either directly or indirectly. Among those deserving of special recognition are: Dr. Ben Wallace, former Superintendent of the Mineola Public Schools in New York, an outstanding educator of vision under whom I had the privilege to work, to innovate, and to learn for eight years; Dr. H. Alan Robinson and Dr. Sidney Rauch, Professors of Reading at Hofstra University, for their guidance and suggestions in the development of my doctoral dissertation upon which this book is based; Dr. John Van Buren, Dean of the School of Education at Hofstra University, for the insights I gained from him about teaching, learning, and the individual while I was a graduate student in the Counselor Education Program at Hofstra; Mr. James Reilly and Mr. George Bretton, Assistant Superintendents of Schools for the Plainedge Public Schools, for their personal support and encouragement as I introduced to that district and implemented learning centers.

My appreciation is also extended to Dr. Pauline Perahia, Director of the Learning Center at Farmingdale College, Long Island, New York and former Coordinator of the Reading Laboratory at Queens College, New York for sharing with me her experiences and expertise related to the development and operation of learning centers at the college and university levels. I am similarly grateful to Mr. Richard Tropp, Director of Instructional Television Service for the Long Island Educational Television Council, for sharing with me his technical expertise. Credit for the photography appearing in this book is owed Mr. Edward Wachtel, media lab assistant at the Center for Instructional Development, Queens College, and Mr. David Brinson, teacher in the Plainedge Public Schools. The photograph appearing on the book jacket is by Mr. Brinson. Last, but by far not the least, my appreciation is extended to Mr. Lawrence Lipsitz, my editor, for his many valuable and insightful editorial suggestions.

Preface

Individualization of instruction has long been a goal of American public education. Although it is not a new concept, it is one that has been subject to more interpretations than perhaps any other major idea in education. Educators have frequently agreed upon the definition and purposes of individualized instruction; yet there has been little consensus with respect to the methodologies for best achieving this goal.

As a result, a wide gap has persisted between theory or intent and actual practices in the schools. This failure to provide for the great diversity of pupil needs, a responsibility rendered mandatory by universal compulsory public education, has been harmful to both the academic achievement and the personal growth and development of students.

The effects of this failure have been manifold and far-reaching. It has resulted in large numbers of pupils failing to achieve basic literacy. It has resulted in students failing to acquire life-relevant skills and to develop realistic career goals even after a dozen years of schooling. It has resulted in pupils developing negative attitudes toward school and toward learning in general and, consequently, in the failure of many pupils to complete high school. Lastly, it has resulted in the stigmatizing of and consequent damage to the self-esteem of children whose patterns and rates of learning deviate from those normally provided for in the public schools.

Over the past two decades, advancements in technology, improvements in the quantity and quality of educational research, refinement of methods and instruments for assessing individual needs, additional instructional resources, and dramatic social and economic changes have set the stage for change in education. A steady trend toward the infusion of the precepts of more flexible education into the public schools has been evidenced by the increasing numbers of and growing interest in "open" classrooms, "schools without walls," alternative schools, and learning centers. Without doubt, learning centers have developed with greater rapidity than any of these approaches.

Predicated on the belief that children learn in different ways and at various rates, learning centers have come to be viewed increasingly by educators as an economical and viable strategy for accommodating diverse learning styles and a wide range of learning needs at every level.

Today, educators throughout the country are attempting to provide learning centers for their schools. Many are planning to initiate learning centers in the future. For others, the conceptual framework, underlying philosophy, and methodologies required for the establishment and successful implementation of a learning center remain illusive.

It is the purpose of this book to provide the educator with an understanding of the learning center concept, its origins, present manifestations, and potential—through proper implementation—for achieving true individualization of instruction.

Chapter 1 traces historically over a 200-year period those trends, developments, philosophies, and research occurring in education within the social, political, economic, and scientific contexts of the times that led to the emergence of learning centers.

Chapter 2 offers an overview of existing trends in the development of learning centers, focusing upon the various facets of the learning center and its functioning.

Chapter 3 sets forth a conceptual framework for learning

centers and is the basis for the operational model developed in Chapters 4, 5, and 6. The model itself is divided into three parts, and focuses upon (1) processes: approaches to individualization of instruction as implemented through the learning center; (2) the properties of a learning center, including physical facilities and instructional and non-instructional resources and equipment; and (3) the people associated with the learning center. Reading and language arts has been selected as the instructional area to which the model is applied. This selection was made due to the vital importance of reading, writing, speaking, and listening skills to academic success and effective functioning in daily living.

Chapter 7 describes a "typical" day in the operation of a learning center. This chapter puts into a practical context the philosophy, ideas, concepts, and procedures discussed in the preceding chapters.

The learning center as a catalyst for change and vehicle for continuous professional staff development is discussed in Chapter 8.

The educator interested in or presently involved with learning centers should keep in mind that implementation of a new center is a continuous and constantly evolving process that takes place over several years. Only after the doors to a new center open does that center begin its journey toward maturity. The errors, experimentation, uncertainty, and frustration that characterize the functioning of a new center are to be expected. As with a young child, it is in these ways that learning takes place, confidence grows, and new skills are developed.

With the encouragement and understanding of a sympathetic building administrator, and the teamwork and perseverance of a professional staff committed to its students, this book can be a guide to developing a dynamic learning center that ultimately will become the instructional *heart* of the school.

Frances Bennie
September, 1976

Table of Contents

Glossary

Assessment of learner needs: the collection and recording of data regarding the status—physiological, socio-psychological, and perceptuo-cognitive development—of each individual.

Cognitive style: (see learning style).

Criterion-referenced testing: tests linked to a set of specified instructional objectives which describe the developmental instructional program. The tests are designed to measure only what is stated in the objectives. They are not standardized. Test results state what a student can demonstrate, not the percentage of demonstration or how a student performs compared to other students.

Diagnosis of learner needs: the organization, analysis, and interpretation of the data recorded about the development status of the individual.

Expressive communication modes: modes of communication involving language or the creative arts for the purpose of production. Examples would include production of films, filmstrips, tape recordings, graphics, self-directed photography, dance, drama and art, and sculpture.

Evaluation: determining the degree and/or extent of success of the individual in the achievement of a particular learning objective or in the development of a desired behavior.

Humanities approach: integration of the language arts, poetry, drama, the creative arts, and literature.

Individualization of instruction, process approach: an approach aimed at meeting individual needs and including six main processes which are sequential. These include: (1) assessment, (2) diagnosis, (3) prescription, (4) interaction, (5) evaluation, and (6) reassessment, follow-up, and recycling.

Individualized reading program: a reading program which employs a diagnostic-prescriptive approach to skills instruction and in which a wide range of print and nonprint materials are used for learning, such as books, multi-level self-directing and self-correcting kits, media materials, magazines, etc. Pupils self-select books to read based on interests, and individual pupil-teacher conferences are regularly scheduled to assess comprehension, identify need for specific reading skills instruction, make suggestions, and provide instruction. Pupils are grouped flexibly in continuously changing groups for specific skills instruction.

Instructional materials resource center: a center in which instructional materials are housed for loan to teachers and pupils for use in the classroom.

Integration/application of learning: the provision for cognitive transfer and application of learning and behaviors developed into environmental contexts.

Interaction process: the activity of the pupil in accomplishing the learning objectives. *Interaction setting*: the environment/s in which the pupil works to accomplish the learning objectives. Important characteristics of the interaction setting include the social contexts, instrumentations, time modules, and physical setting in which the interaction takes place.

Learning center: an area or complex of areas equipped with a diversity of print and nonprint media materials, types of audio-visual equipment, and programmed instruction, and designed to accommodate various learning styles and needs both through physical design and through the application of a systematic process approach to individualization of instruction.

Learning module: a series of interaction alternatives focusing on specific behaviors to be developed. A module includes the behavioral objectives, learning set (social context, environmental setting in which the pupil will work, materials to be used, etc.), criterion performance, a series of sequenced interaction alternatives, and appropriate evaluative instruments.

Learning style: those significant pupil characteristics which in combination suggest ways of manipulating the learning environment so as to facilitate and enhance the development of a given behavior, skill, or body of knowledge.

Life-relevant skills: needs—gratifying skills or behaviors. These include: (1) the instrumental skills of reading, writing, speaking, listening, mathematics, and visual literacy; (2) analytic thinking skills; (3) social interactive skills; (4) creative and expressive behaviors; and (5) self-process skills.

Media materials (nonprint): filmstrips, films, slides, audio cassettes, record discs, filmloops, study prints, artifacts, models, dioramas, photographs, video cassettes, etc.

Media materials (print): books, magazines, booklets, charts, diagrams, multi-level kits containing reading selections on cards, etc.

Open classroom: a learning environment which provides for choice by designing the classroom into interest and/or learning centers and where the teacher helps children direct their own learning.

Prescription, prescriptive programming: a work assignment for the development of a behavior based upon data known about the individual and the relationship to the behavior to be developed.

Process education: education that focuses on development of process skills, such as the analytic thinking skills, social interactive skills, creative and expressive behaviors, self-evaluation skills, and instrumental skills, such as those of reading and the language arts. Proponents of process education believe that the process skills should be the goals of education, and the curriculum or content the vehicle through which these are developed.

Receptive communication modes: sensory intake which may

be visual, auditory, tactile, olfactory. Listening, viewing, and touching are forms of receptive communication models.

Self-directing/self-correcting instructional materials: instructional materials which may be used by the learner with minimal teacher direction or assistance and which are designed to allow the learner to evaluate and correct his or her own work by providing the criteria for self-evaluation.

System: a set of interrelated factors that are used together to produce an output. A system is comprised of people, properties, and processes. A systems approach to individualization of instruction would require the development of sub-systems as follows: (1) assessment of learner needs (collection of data); (2) diagnosis of learner needs; (3) prescriptive programming; (4) monitoring of interaction process; (5) pupil evaluation; and (6) reassessment, follow-up, and recycling.

Systems approach: organized means of carrying out some function when those means are complex and comprise a number of interrelated elements.

Teaching machine: a device designed to present a body of information to a student to which the student may respond. The machine must recognize the nature of the student's response and behave appropriately. The device frequently consists of four units: an input unit, an output unit, a storage unit, and a control unit. Teaching machines usually require the active participation of the learner at every step.

LEARNING CENTERS

CENTERS
development and operation

1.
The Emergence of Learning Centers

Introduction

The emergence of learning centers has resulted from a wide variety of trends, developments, and research in education, psychology, and sociology. These have been influenced by the social, economic, political, scientific, and technological contexts of the times in which they occurred. Learning centers did not suddenly appear on the educational scene, and they are not a mere fad.

Learning centers represent the attainment of a highly sophisticated level of integration of people, processes, and resources. As a result, they have enabled educators to achieve the flexibility required to manipulate the teaching-learning environment to the advantage of individual learners.

An historical perspective of learning centers reveals that they may never have developed without the necessary advancements in technology, the acceptance of certain views about the individual and individual differences, and the enactment of key federal aid-to-education legislation.

Historical Perspective of Learning Centers

Late 1700s to 1900

Interest by educators in providing for the needs and interests of individual pupils is not new. Between 1746 and 1841, educators such as Pestalozzi and Herbart focused not only upon the needs and interests of pupils, but also upon respect for individuality. However, universal compulsory education subsequently created great difficulties for schools which considered meeting diverse student needs.

Emphasis upon child-study was an attempt to deal with this problem (1885-1895), and it led to a focus upon the concept of identification of individual learner needs. This concept of assessment and diagnosis of individual needs was to become a key idea in later concepts of individualization, and basic to the learning center concept.

Along other lines, experiments between 1824 and 1896 with photography, motion pictures, electricity, radio, and the phonograph would later have significant implications for the development of a media technology in education and the emergence of learning centers which utilized this technology.

From 1900 to 1960

During this period, dubbed the Manufacturing Era, urbanization, immigration, and industrialization had an impact upon every facet of the social, political, and economic structure of the nation. Schools were characterized by institutional rigidity, standardized curricula, the authoritarian role of the teacher, and behavioral conformity. Little attention was paid to individual needs or differences of students. These adverse conditions during the early 1900s gave rise to the "Progressive Movement" led by Dewey. This movement attempted to shift the schools to a new child-centeredness, emphasizing creativity and pupils' interests. However, the movement died for lack of capable practitioners, though Dewey's concepts were to persist during the quest to achieve individualization, reappearing almost intact with the emergence of the open classroom in the 1960s.

Binet, a contemporary of Dewey, in 1905 focused attention upon individual differences related to pupil achievement in school. This gave rise to the testing movement, producing through the years increasingly refined instruments to identify individual needs in all areas of child development.

Although seemingly unrelated to the endeavors in education at the time, advancements were being made in technology that would have implications for the development of an educational technology. In 1926 talking movies revolutionized the industry, and the basis for applied systems work had already begun by the early 1920s in the laboratories of the Bell System.

The late 1920s and early 1930s were a time of world-wide economic and social crisis. Emphasis shifted from knowledge gain to the question of what education should do to play its part in solving social crises. Curriculum was modified to provide for individual and community differences. "Meaningful experiences" and "learning-by-doing" were emphasized by some educators, though this concept was not ready to be widely accepted. Ability grouping as a means of providing for individual differences was first introduced, and prevailed for nearly 40 years, despite the fact that it was not found to be consistently effective. During the mid-1920s another sort of response to the problem of meeting diverse learner needs was introduced by Pressey's first automated teaching machine.

In the 1920s and early 1930s, social science in America and England became rigidly environmentalist, in contrast to theories of heredity that still predominated in Europe. Piaget, whose first observations of children occurred during this period, viewed nature and nurture as always relative to each other, convinced that this relativism extended to the development of intelligence as well.

His research, which was to greatly influence American education and lead to the development of the concept of open education, would not be widely known or accepted until the late 1950s. Meanwhile, his research conducted in the 1930s and 1940s suggested that the child's ideas about the world involved both mental structures and experience. He emphasized the element of "readiness," which suggested that a child must reach a necessary level of maturation before he or she could learn particular skills.

Piaget's findings demonstrated two levels of distinction between appearance and reality; one was concrete, the other symbolic. In early childhood, children learn through discovery by dealing with concrete experiences in the environment. At adolescence the child becomes ready to deal at the symbolic level, understanding subtleties of language and mathematical abstractions.

Piaget's work indicated that we must expand our view of knowledge to include not only facts that are correct but also concepts that may be the same or different from ours without being either right or wrong. He pointed the way to the principle of helping children to "learn how to learn," which would become the basis for open education, process education, and learning centers during the 1960s and 1970s.

Despite attempts to provide for individual needs, by the 1930s the problems caused by universal compulsory education became overwhelming. Delinquency, failure to control student behavior, moral confusion, deterioration in achievement of basic skills, lack of overall curriculum, and excessive non-instructional responsibilities of teachers were but a few of the troublesome areas which in effect reflected the state of turmoil in the country brought on by the Great Depression. The attempt to have "something for everyone" and still maintain quality of instruction gave rise to the beginning of a continuous stream of experiments aimed at providing for individual needs.

In 1930, the first self-scoring immediate feedback device was developed. Meanwhile, Pressey continued with his work, which was destined to pave the way for later development of the concepts of item-analysis, criterion-referenced testing, and self-directing and self-correcting instructional materials. Other researchers experimented with Pressey's devices during this period, and the results favored the use of the automated means of instruction in contrast to regular classroom techniques.

During the latter half of the 1930s, many psychologists became particularly interested in the study of the consistency and predictability of personality. In the early 1940s, Allport suggested the concept of "style," which he defined as the consistency and pattern of expressive behaviors that individuals manifest in performing various types of activities. This was the first conceptualization of learning style, a concept that would grow in importance during the late 1960s and more so during the 1970s in the quest to meet individual learning needs.

During this period, the first experimental designs on the uses of the educational media for reading and language arts skills development appeared. It was found in 1933 that below-average students were able to acquire significantly more factual information when film materials were made a part of their instruction.

Similarly, researchers reported in 1939 that in an experiment using a sound film in a special class for boys, those in the experimental group surpassed the control group in vocabulary and word recognition after a period of four weeks of study. Also, using sound films, Eads (1938) and Gray (1940) each found this media form to be effective at the elementary level for concept development and vocabulary improvement.

In 1938, the first research on the use of visual aids in teaching beginning reading was reported. Research at this time investigated the use of a visual technique which consisted of preparation of slides containing the text of a story or simple sentences which were used to teach beginning reading in the first grade. Based on these findings, it was concluded that considerable improvement may be expected when this method replaces the traditional procedure, particularly with slower children.

In 1942, ten papers on the administration of mass communications in the public interest were read before the Sixth Annual Institute of the Chicago University Graduate Library School to a group actively involved in communication research. They dealt with the problems inherent in the uses of print, radio, and film to develop and express public opinion.

Along these same lines, in 1948 a study was conducted

comparing elementary school children who attended motion pictures, read comic books, and listened to serial radio programs to excess with those who indulged in these activities seldom or not at all. It was found that those elementary and junior high pupils who made excessive use of these media forms did significantly better on the Stanford Achievement Test than the group not using the media. The difference in the two groups was greatest at the primary level, less at the intermediate level, and insignificant at the junior high school level.

During World War II, further advancements were made by the military in intelligence testing, the use of automated teaching, and in the development of teaching films, television, and other forms of media technology. Immediately following World War II, television facilities in the United States expanded rapidly, ultimately finding their way into the public schools by the late 1950s and on a much larger scale during the 1960s.

The late 1940s saw general systems theory beginning to emerge in many disciplines, along with information regarding the discipline of cybernetics. During the early 1950s, systems theory became of interest to behavioral scientists as a basic approach to providing frameworks of concept organization in the behavioral sciences and related applied fields of knowledge such as education.

The 1950s saw the development by Maslow of a needs hierarchy where basic needs common to all people were described as the motivating forces of behavior in each individual's quest for self-actualization. Maslow's work was to serve as the conceptual framework and foundation for behavioral researchers and subsequently for theories of process education. These theories focused upon the importance of developing in students skills and behaviors that would enable them to gratify basic survival needs and to become progressively more self-actualizing individuals. Behavioral researchers later translated Maslow's basic needs hierarchy into life-relevant skills and behaviors the development of which would become the goals of process education.

Along other lines, in 1954 Skinner published an article, "The

Science of Learning and the Art of Teaching," which provided the basis for the development of programmed instruction and teaching machines.

In 1959, in a series of experiments, researchers found that learning was significantly enhanced by immediate knowl-edge of results, and higher scores were produced on a criterion test when indication of an incorrect response was accompanied by an explanation. This research highlighted the beginning of a concern with the possible effects of specific variables and their interaction on learning, which would later suggest the im-portance of manipulating variables in the learning environment to accommodate individual needs.

In addition to the experimentation with programmed teaching devices, research with audio-visual media continued during the 1950s. However, unlike the work with programmed devices, which was geared toward meeting individual learning needs, uses of the instructional media remained pointed toward large-group instruction. In 1953, Witty and Fitzwater explored the relationship of film experience to the acquisition of skills in silent reading in what was one of the first attempts to individualize learning through non-print media. For the study, Encyclopaedia Brittanica Films provided four films and a special magnetic sound track recording projector which allowed the child to hear the regular sound track of the film and also on another track to record whatever he or she wished. Pre- and posttesting showed that the 27 second grade children in the study made greater gains during the experimental period when the film was used along with the basal reader than they did during the period when only the basal reader was used.

Another study focusing upon beginning reading instruction through the non-print media, conducted by McCracken, and reported in 1956, was a series of longitudinal investigations which came to be known as the New Castle Experiment. McCracken's study, like earlier work, involved the preparation of filmstrips to accompany a particular basal reading series so that there would be at least one filmstrip frame for every lesson in the basic books. In this program all initial teaching occurred at the projection screen, the textbooks being used only for extended reading practice and to test the learning. McCracken reported that between 1949 and 1956 more than 600 pupils in all IQ ranges participated in this program with none achieving lower than medium progress. Although McCracken was criticized for never reporting fully all of his results, his work stirred much interest in the use of this media form for beginning reading instruction, and the method was generally viewed as worthy of further study. McCracken could hardly foresee the flood of audio-visual programs that would emerge a decade later utilizing his general approach and becoming basic equipment for learning centers.

Another development important to learning centers occurred during the latter part of the 1950s. A group at Wayne State University began formalized work on the development of a set of disciplines called the "educational sciences." From this work was derived research leading to the formulation of the concept of cognitive learning style and cognitive mapping procedures.

Perhaps the most significant development for learning centers occurred in the late 1950s. Even before the Soviet Sputnik, critics of education in America had begun to demand that educators abandon the goal of achieving "personal adjustment for the whole child" and devote themselves to teaching children how to think. This new emphasis led to a search for new curricula, instructional materials, and approaches. When curriculum builders turned to psychology for information about how the mind grows and how children think, they found that psychologists had little to offer.

It was at this point that Piaget's work first came to the attention of American educators. The concept of open education would develop from Piaget's research and theories, having influence upon the development of learning centers during the 1960s.

The research and advancements in technology of two hundred years, along with the development of certain trends and philosophies in education, psychology, and sociology, had paved the way for new approaches in education. The time was nearly ripe for the emergence of the learning center.

The Period from 1960 to the Present

The period beginning in the early 1960s was one that would focus upon the individual's creative adaptive potential as required by an increasing technological sophistication. The high level of educational achievement and mental development needed to meet job requirements brought into sharp focus the relevance of reading. Achieving basic literacy, providing for future manpower needs, dealing with problems of personal alienation, and making relevant the education that the schools provided were key problems to which innovators during the 1960s addressed themselves.

The development and experimentation with principles of open education were infused into the public schools. Open education emphasized the interaction of the child with his or her environment for learning; children learning from a total experience rather than successive discrete steps; the rich availability of manipulative materials; the learning process of each individual as something unique; observation and diagnosis of individual needs; the role of the teacher as a guide, counselor, diagnostician, and manager of learning environments; the competence and right of children to make significant decisions concerning their own learning; the natural desire of children to share with others new learnings which are important to them; self-selection by children of the materials with which they wish to work and the questions they wish to pursue; the gradual nature of the process of concept formation; the idea of readiness for a particular type of learning; the importance of experience preceding verbal abstractions; the interdisciplinary nature of integration of experience; and, finally, an emphasis upon learning *how to learn*. Open education had significant implications for the design of the instructional environment. It suggested that the spatial organization of the learning environment reflects beliefs about children's learning and about the nature of knowledge. Open classrooms were divided often by moveable screens or furniture into "interest areas," each perhaps ten square feet. Children had the opportunity to move from area to area to explore materials in their own ways. Many of these principles and approaches would be incorporated into the philosophy and methodologies of learning centers.

The 1960s also ushered in vast increases in knowledge, dramatic advancements in technology, and major social changes precipitated by civil rights legislation, the Feminist movement, and the "new morality." In addition, the 1960s saw a significant improvement in both the quality and quantity of experimental and exploratory designs in educational research. Now available to education with the enactment of the federal Elementary and Secondary Education Act, the National Defense Education Act, and through private foundations was major funding to encourage and support systematic approaches to educational innovation, research, and redesign.

Much of this funding was directed toward furthering individualization of instruction, with specific provisions made for the infusion of new audio-visual equipment into the schools, frequently accomplished through the expansion of library facilities, the development of learning centers, and the expansion of reading labs.

Although educators defined individualization in many different ways, the underlying commonality that pervaded all the popular definitions was the premise that children differ and that the school must provide for these differences. New emphasis was placed upon the pupil and the teacher as persons, and upon the interaction that takes place between them. An individualized approach was viewed by many educators as one that would provide an environment to stimulate exploration, provide opportunities for self-selection of materials, and offer guidance which would allow growth at the individual's own rate and interest.

Interest in individualized reading grew rapidly in the late 1960s and the early 1970s, and influenced instructional practices by making teachers more aware of pupil differences and broadening their approaches. Individualized reading had an influence upon the types of instructional materials being published and upon the increased diversity of books brought into elementary and secondary school libraries. During this period, publishers produced reading centers for grades one through six, making the individualized reading approach more manageable for teachers. Using a wide range of paperback books, these centers included the concepts of self-selection, self-direction, self-pacing, the individual teacher-pupil conference, flexible grouping for specific skills instruction, involvement of pupils in creative activities, and personal response activities to books read.

Besides individualized reading, innovations which gained the most attention during the 1960s and through the early 1970s were: (1) flexible modular scheduling, (2) differentiated staffing, (3) team teaching, (4) central/subject area resource centers, (5) large-group/small-group/independent study, (6) interdisciplinary programs, (7) curriculum alternatives, (8) learning packages, (9) behavioral objectives, (10) short-term courses, and (11) career education.

Many of these innovations found their way into the reading and language arts programs and were employed to attack the critical problem of basic literacy. Right-to-Read programs increasingly became characterized by their use of these and other innovations, such as large scale use of volunteer tutors, use of listening and learning centers, multi-level and multi-media instructional materials, diagnostic-prescriptive approaches, careful record-keeping of individual pupil progress, and emphasis upon professional staff development and in-service training. All of these innovations helped to establish a climate in which learning centers could flourish.

With the advent of the open classroom and other types of individualized approaches, the teacher came to be viewed as a guide, diagnostician, and manager of the learning environment. This was no less the case in the new reading labs, which also employed paraprofessionals, teacher aides, and community volunteers. Plans for differentiated staffing emerged as paraprofessionals and aides came on the scene, and the role of the teacher began to change.

The value of the concept of full utilization of all resources for learning gained increasing recognition by educators. In response to the need for instructional materials better suited to meet individual learning needs, by the mid-1960s, a few companies began producing media materials such as tape programs, controlled reader programs, and multi-level study skills libraries. Similarly, publishers produced multi-level reading kits in the field, and by the late 1960s marketed multi-level materials for specific skills instruction in reading. Diagnostic inventories and behavioral objectives were frequently basic to the materials, and later in the 1970s criterion-referenced tests became incorporated as well.

By the early 1970s, the educational marketplace was flooded with diverse, good quality media materials, multi-level and specific skill materials, and teaching machines. Computer-assisted instruction and other educational uses for computers were emerging and being applied, along with educational television. Throughout the 1960s, professional educators began to employ techniques of the systems approach, with some of these efforts financially supported by the U.S. Office of Education.

During the period between 1961 and 1976, interest in and investigations into the concepts of cognitive learning style, modality preference, physical environment and learning style, psycho- and sociolinguistics, the language experience approach, and open education surged. By the early 1970s, the emphasis upon meeting individual needs, and the introduction of and expansion of multi-media sources of information had rendered the services of a well-conceived and well-managed learning center imperative in the modern school.

Research on Educational Media

The nonprint media are the principal types of resources used in the learning center, along with multi-level kits and various types of programmed instruction. After 1960, educators began looking increasingly to audio-visual techniques as a means of individualizing instruction, particularly in reading and the language arts. By 1970 it was apparent that the media could be used as integral parts of a systems approach to instruction rather than as occasional aids in the educative process. The rapid growth of learning centers in the late 1960s represented a major step toward this end.

After 1960 investigations of uses of the educational media for reading and language arts instruction increased in diversity, quantity, and quality. Whereas most investigations into the uses of the media for instruction focused upon films prior to 1960, studies conducted after 1960 suggested the dramatic increase in the types of media being used and their potential value. These media included sound filmstrips, television, film loops, controlled reader films, overhead transparency projectuals, audio-cassettes, audio-card readers, and manipulatives. This variety gave the new learning center managers a vast range of media resources from which to select appropriate instructional media for individual learners.

Research on Expressive
Communication Modes

Many different approaches were developed after 1960 in which audio-visual techniques were used to involve students in actual production. Pupils were now producing their own TV shows, making films and filmstrips, and developing tape recordings. Invariably, studies reported such approaches to be significantly more successful than traditional methods for developing reading and language arts skills and in fostering positive pupil attitudes toward reading and the language arts—and learning in general. One such study, reported in 1973, involved first and second grade children in tape recording their impressions, stories, or experiences. These recordings were then typed by an aide and returned to the pupil, who might choose to share it with his teacher, his peers, or simply read it to himself. The study was longitudinal and was replicated by other research efforts in subsequent months. Each of these investigators found that the children in the experimental groups did significantly better on the three forms of the Stanford Achievement Tests used in the study. The New York State Education Department published the results of a study first conducted in Uniondale, New York, in which fifth and sixth graders produced their own TV shows doing their own research, scripting, and taping. Findings indicated that this approach increased reading levels of retarded readers by as much as two years and had an impact upon fostering positive attitudes toward learning and bolstering the self-esteem of pupils who have had patterns of school failure.

Chapter Summary

The advantages of systematic approaches to the use of the new media became apparent to many educators with the turn of the decade in 1960. The potential of the new media for developing a technology of individual instruction was realized when the first learning centers began to be developed. Even these early centers focused upon diagnostic-prescriptive methodologies and were grounded firmly in the beliefs that pupils learn in different ways and at different rates and that they are capable of assuming responsibility for much of their own learning.

Although learning centers were developed early in the 1960s, most did not appear until after 1965, with the greatest numbers of new centers emerging between 1968 and 1973. Today learning centers continue to be developed across the country despite the economic crisis confronting public education. An important reason for this phenomenon surely rests on the fact that, in the final anaylsis, learning centers are an economical and efficient way of facilitating individualization of instruction. Properly equipped, staffed, and operated, a learning center enables teachers to accommodate a great diversity of learning styles and needs, because it offers teaching-learning options not normally provided in the classroom.

Despite the rapid growth of learning centers and the continuing interest in them by educators, there have been few books written on the subject. To date, the principal method for an interested educator to gain information about learning centers has been to visit existing centers and to talk to the professionals and pupils using them. Although there are some real advantages to this method, there are also many drawbacks when it is used as the sole approach.

One such drawback rests in the fact that many learning centers have been mere adoptions of the *physical trappings* of centers seen elsewhere. Often these centers have been developed without a clear understanding of the underlying beliefs about education upon which learning centers are built, and without a clear understanding of how the methodologies and staffing patterns employed should reflect these beliefs. A second drawback of visitations rests in the fact that they can be costly to school districts when many substitute teachers must be hired to free the visiting teachers. A third limitation of the visitation is that if it is to be of significant value, the visiting teachers must know what to look for and be able to ask the right questions. These abilities presume some prior knowledge and experience with the subject. This is often not the case, and for this reason many important questions may be left unanswered during a visitation.

Few could honestly dispute the fact that first-hand observation is nonetheless a valuable learning technique. However, there still exists a need for much more written information than is presently available about learning centers. It is hoped that the subsequent chapters of this book will help to fill this gap.

The historical perspective of learning centers provided in Chapter 1 is the first step in this direction. It makes evident the fact that a variety of trends, developments, and research in education, psychology, and sociology have set the stage for the emergence of learning centers. Some of these trends began as far back as the 1700s, although the most significant developments occurred in the late 1950s and early 1960s. The historical perspective reveals that learning centers may never have developed without the necessary advancements in technology, the development of educational media and programmed instruction, the acceptance of certain views about the individual and individual differences, and the enactment of key federal aid-to-education legislation such as the National Defense Education Act and the Elementary and Secondary Education Act. The influence of Piaget's theories, as reflected in concepts of open education and process education, have also had a profound influence upon the development of learning centers. Other important developments have included Allport's first conceptualization of learning style, the development of the "educational sciences," and Maslow's formulation of a needs hierarchy and focus upon the individual's quest for self-actualization.

2.
Trends in the Development
of Learning Centers

Learning centers have grown rapidly in popularity since their appearance on the educational scene in the early 1960s. Although most often introduced into public schools by central office and building administrators, the responsibility for the actual development of most learning centers has been given to school librarians and media and reading specialists, and often has been a shared responsibility.

Undoubtedly, the abilities, skills, and interests of these key professionals have been the most important factors affecting the types and quality of services provided by learning centers. This fact, combined with the paucity of written ideas about learning centers, has resulted in wide variations in their development despite certain basic commonalities. It is the purpose of this chapter to examine trends in the development of learning centers, identifying those characteristics and practices which are common to all or nearly all centers, and those facets of learning centers which have been subject to varying interpretations and practices.

Beginnings

In 1961 the American Association of School Librarians published media standards for school libraries. Within less than a decade, these standards became obsolete and were replaced by new ones published in 1969 jointly with the Department of Audiovisual Instruction of the National Education Association (now the Association for Educational Communications and Technology—AECT). The infusion of the new media into the public schools was rapid and pervasive. The National Defense Education Act of 1958 and the Elementary and Secondary Education Act of 1965 gave impetus to this movement and toward furthering individualization of instruction. With NDEA and ESEA funding, the first library-media centers, resource rooms, reading labs, and learning centers were developed beginning in the early 1960s.

In many schools the learning center concept developed in phases. Often a library-media center or a resource room was developed first, the initial focus being upon newer instructional resources. Then, as the media found their way into reading clinics and reading rooms, diagnostic-prescriptive methodologies normally used by reading specialists were applied to govern the uses of the media in ways that would better meet individual learning needs and cognitive styles of pupils with reading deficits.

The advantages of combining diagnostic-prescriptive methodologies with the use of the highly motivational non-print media became apparent very quickly. It subsequently resulted in the extension of this approach to meet the needs of the general school population through learning centers. These centers were much more than mere repositories for instructional materials. They developed into dynamic teaching-learning settings which applied systems for identifying individual learner needs, providing for these needs, and evaluating the results of instruction.

In many schools, the professional staff at the time the learning center was developed had had little or no prior training or experience with individualized instruction. The new center, in effect, served as the catalyst and vehicle for professional staff development in individualization. Learning center directors, teacher aides, classroom teachers, and building principals learned by doing and often through trial and error. Later, visitations to already developed learning centers became and remain a principal means of learning about how to develop and operate a learning center.

Underlying Philosophy
of Learning Centers

Learning centers are based on the philosophy that the individual pupil is capable of assuming responsibility for much of his or her own learning. They are based, also, on (1) the understanding that children learn in different ways and at varying rates, and (2) the belief that it is incumbent upon educators to provide for these differences.

Objectives for Pupils

Remediation in reading and reinforcement and extension of classroom learning activities have been the main roles for learning centers. In addition to these, other objectives have included providing enrichment and teaching-learning options not available in the regular classroom. Focus upon the processes through which these objectives are achieved has been an important concern in learning centers. Accordingly, learning centers have attempted to develop in pupils such characteristics and abilities as initiative, self-direction in learning, independence, a sense of responsibility, problem-solving techniques, and inquiry, research, and self-evaluation skills. In addition, stimulating interest in learning itself has been a major focus of the learning center.

Instructional Areas Served
by the Learning Center

Skills developed in learning centers have included, in order of frequency cited, (1) reading; (2) research and information retrieval; (3) mathematics; and (4) language arts. Instructional areas served by most centers have included, in order of frequency cited, (1) reading; (2) language arts; (3) mathmatics and science; and (4) social studies and the arts and humanities.

Staffing and Role Definitions

Patterns for staffing learning centers have varied widely and have been closely tied to the specific goals of a given learning center as determined by pupil and teacher needs. Economic factors also have been a consideration. It appears that in many schools the learning center director or teacher has been someone other than the librarian or reading specialist in the building.

In some instances, this person has been referred to as a "master teacher," learning center director, learning center teacher, or a programmed instruction specialist, each title suggesting a somewhat different emphasis in the role. Nonetheless, in all instances, the person charged with coordinating and operating the learning center and its services has had to combine skills in assessment and diagnosis of pupil needs with knowledge of diverse instructional resources and their educational application for meeting individual needs.

A principal function of the learning center director has been to place the best materials in the right hands at the most opportune time to facilitate maximum individual learning. This function suggests the need for the learning center director to possess a variety of skills and abilities. Some of these have included human relations skills; the ability to demonstrate the uses of new instructional resources and techniques in effective ways; willingness to take risks associated with innovation; and the ability to encourage and support teachers as they experiment with previously untried and unproven instructional methodologies and techniques. Most successful learning center directors have been both flexible and extremely well organized.

On-the-job training and learning-by-doing have been the most common methods for training learning center directors. College and university courses in related areas, such as diagnostic techniques and individualization of instruction, have also been helpful.

Teacher aides have been employed in most learning centers to assist with both instructional and clerical tasks. Again, training for the teacher aides has been mostly on-the-job, though some schools have provided more formal types of in-service training as well.

In addition to teacher aides, some schools have successfully used community volunteers to assist in their learning centers. When the functioning of the center has not rested solely upon the reliability and skills of volunteers, and an initial screening has taken place, these people have proven to be valuable assets to the learning center.

Sizes and Designs of
Learning Centers

Learning centers have usually ranged in size from 600 square feet to 3,600 square feet. Some, though, particularly at the junior high school level, have assumed greater proportions. In most instances, the size and design of the learning center has affected the scheduling and services provided.

Study carrels have been used almost universally in learning centers, with the number of carrels available usually having a direct bearing upon the amount of independent study, using the non-print media, that will be feasible. Often these carrels have been constructed by district custodial staffs; however, at the high school and university levels, carrels have more often been purchased commercially.

Most learning centers are carpeted for acoustical reasons as well as to enable pupils at the elementary levels to comfortably sit on the floor for many instructional activities.

Room divider types of shelving are often used to section off learning areas. The height and length of these dividers often depends upon the size of the physical facility, the age groups of the pupils to be served, and the desired effect from an aesthetic point of view.

Instructional Equipment
and Resources

The most common types of audio-visual equipment and media found in learning centers, in order of the frequency listed, have been, (1) cassette players, filmstrip viewers, and books; (2) multi-level kits; (3) typewriters, overhead projectors, and manipulatives; (4) filmloop projectors and slide projectors; and (5) cassette player recorders, controlled readers, slide previewers, 16mm sound movie projectors, magazines, laminated activity cards, study prints, and games.

Other equipment used in learning centers has included filmloop viewers, filmstrip-makers, audio-card readers, closed circuit television and video recording and playback devices, sound-slide viewers, and various programmed teaching machines.

Learning center resources and equipment, except teaching machines, are generally on loan to classrooms. A sign-out loan system is usually employed to keep track of where equipment and materials are in the building at any given time. Some schools have also permitted pupils to borrow, for use at home, cassette players and player-recorders, filmstrip viewers, and media materials.

Diagnostic-Prescriptive Approaches

Diagnostic-prescriptive approaches to the teaching-learning process have been used in virtually all learning centers, with varying degrees of sophistication, formality, and expertise. In some schools, much time is devoted at the beginning of each school year to assessment and diagnosis of individual pupil needs; some schools even keep up-to-date diagnostic profiles on pupils.

Some of the more common techniques used for needs assessment have been standardized exams, pupil performance, criterion-referenced tests, pupil interviews, and teacher judgment. The classroom teacher has generally assumed some or all of the responsibility for diagnosing his or her pupil needs.

On the other hand, responsibility for developing prescriptive strategies to meet individual needs has varied. In most instances, though, it has been a shared responsibility of the learning center director and the classroom teacher.

Scheduling Procedures

The types of scheduling used in learning centers has varied

widely and has been affected by the size, staffing, resources, and objectives of a given center. The size of the pupil population in relation to these factors has been an important consideration and sometimes a limiting factor.

In most centers, pupils visit individually or in small groups. However, many centers—particularly at the elementary level—make provision for whole-class visits as well. Such visits with the classroom teacher in attendance have been used for demonstration teaching, to help teachers learn about the resources in the center, to observe pupils' responses to and interaction with particular resources, and to enable the classroom teacher to work with individuals and small groups of children while the remainder of the class is employed in activities geared to meeting individual needs and styles of learning.

In most cases, there has been an attempt to provide an open, flexible schedule which permits pupils to come and go according to need. Nonetheless, most centers also provide for scheduled visits.

The learning center schedule has most often been developed by the center's director working in consultation with the classroom teachers.

Record-Keeping and Feedback
to Classroom Teacher

Centers have employed a variety of techniques to keep track of individual pupil progress and to communicate with classroom teachers about this progress. Some of these techniques have included individual progress cards, logs, charts, and scheduled conferencing between the learning center director and classroom teacher. Such conferencing has also been used to identify needed changes and modifications in prescriptive programs and strategies being employed.

At the secondary and college levels, computer terminals have sometimes been used to provide assistance with prescriptive programming and to help with the monitoring of individual pupil progress in skill areas such as reading and mathematics.

Concept of Learning Style

The concept of learning style has been viewed by educators involved with learning centers as being very significant and basic to the learning center concept. For the most part, though, methods of identifying individual variations in learning styles have been informal and not very systematic. Like individualization of instruction, the concept of learning style has come to mean different things to different people.

In the area of reading skills development, the greatest attention has been given to certain facets of learning style, such as the following: (1) organization and sequencing of units of learning; (2) pacing of units of learning; (3) modality preference;* (4) analytic and synthetic methods of decoding and encoding; (5) instrumentation for learning such as use of books in contrast to audio-visual approaches; and (6) social context, such as peer tutoring, independent individual study, small-group remedial work, "individualized" reading approaches, and achievement groupings.

The most substantial research and application of cognitive learning and cognitive mapping procedures has been done at Oakland Community College in Michigan under the guidance of Dr. Joseph E. Hill. Hill suggests that an individual's cognitive style is determined by the way he or she takes note of his or her total surroundings—how he or she seeks meaning and becomes informed. For example: Is the student a listener or a reader? Is he or she concerned only with his or her own viewpoint or is he or she influenced in decision-making by family or associates? Does the student reason in categories as a mathematician does, or in relationships as social scientists do? Hill's research indicates that student traits may be organized into several sets and a cognitive map developed that provides a complete picture of diverse ways in which an individual acquires meaning. It identifies the student's strengths and weaknesses as the basis upon which to build an individualized program of education.

*See work of Dr. Joseph M. Wepman, University of Chicago, on modality preference and beginning reading instruction.

Although the applicability of Hill's conceptualization of learning style has not yet been experimented with at the elementary or junior and senior high school levels, educators will generally agree that students do, in fact, learn in different ways and at different rates even at these levels. Learning factors include habits of attention, personality traits, instrumentation preferences (e.g., television, films, audio-tape cassettes, etc.), and other learner characteristics. There is a need at present for an integrated concept of learning style that might be applied to the elementary and secondary school levels.

Social Contexts in Which Pupils Work

Learning centers have generally provided students with opportunities to work in a variety of social contexts. The most common have been (1) independent study with adult assistance as needed; (2) individually and in groups of three to seven pupils; and (3) pairs. Adult assistance may be provided by a teacher aide, a volunteer, or professional educators such as the learning center director, the librarian, or the classroom teacher.

There has been a tendency for pupils in the primary grades to work in small groups, with frequent teacher-pupil interaction. At the higher grade levels, pupils work independently to a greater extent. Thus, in elementary school learning centers, pupils will more often be found working cooperatively in small groups with projects or activities in which a common goal is shared, thus facilitating the development of socializing skills and oral language development, which are important objectives in the early grades.

Evaluation Designs

Methods used for evaluating learning centers have been largely informal. These have included observations, at times using not very clearly defined criteria. They have also included teacher and pupil attitudinal assessments, both of the formal and informal types.

One of the problems in evaluating learning centers has been the difficulty of controlling certain important variables. Some of these critical variables include:

1. Skills and abilities of the learning center director.
2. Quality of the software programs.
3. Accuracy of diagnosis and diagnostic procedures.
4. Accuracy of prescriptive programming procedures, knowledge of which media would be most effective in achieving particular learning objectives, and knowledge of the appropriateness of various materials for different learners.
5. Quality of supportive services provided by teacher aides, paraprofessionals, and volunteers.
6. Degree of support to audio-visual program with respect to maintenance and repair of equipment.
7. Experience and attitudes of teachers, students, learning center director, and other persons involved in or affected by the learning center.
8. Channels of communication and interpersonal relations.
9. Administrative support.
10. Community support.
11. Adequacy in the quantity and quality of audio-visual hardware.
12. Adeptness at scheduling use of the center and frequency of sessions per pupil in the center.
13. Previous experience of teachers with individualized instruction and resultant attitudes, perceptions, skills, and abilities.
14. Organizational skills of those involved in the operation of the learning center.
15. Adequacy of the size and design of the physical facility of the learning center.

At some point, both educators and community will raise these questions: "Are we achieving what we set out to achieve?" "How well are we doing?" and "What changes must be made to do it better?" In order to answer such questions, a well constructed and systematically implemented design for evaluation is generally required.

Chapter Summary

Learning centers appeared on the educational scene in the early 1960s, and their development has been greatly influenced by school librarians and media and reading specialists. Librarians have contributed to learning centers the concept of wide utilization of all resources for learning through independent study; media specialists have contributed the concept of multi-media approaches to learning, replacing the traditional lecture-and-book technique; reading specialists have contributed diagnostic-prescriptive methodologies and the concept of learning style, which they applied to the new non-print media to better meet individual pupil needs. Because so little has been written about learning centers, their development has often been influenced in large measure by the interests, skills, and abilities of the specific professionals charged with their development at the local level.

Existing staffing patterns in schools have required some redefinition of roles in order to staff learning centers. In many schools it was either the reading specialist's or librarian's roles that were redefined and expanded so that they might assume responsibility for the learning center. However, in some schools the learning center director or teacher has been someone other than the reading specialist or librarian, and coordination of the various roles has been necessary.

Similarly, physical designs and sizes of learning centers have varied widely and have often been determined by the availability of space in an already established building. Nonetheless, many school administrators have embarked upon both minor and major remodeling to provide suitable facilities for their learning centers, usually opening archways between previously discrete areas and adding carrels and carpeting.

Philosophy, goals, and objectives of learning centers have been similar from school to school. With a shift in emphasis from teaching to learning, these centers have focused upon the fact that children differ in their needs and styles of learning and that the learning environment can be manipulated to the advantage of the attributes of each individual.

Despite a concern with learning style, most learning centers lack systematic and clearly defined procedures for identifying individual styles. There appear to be many different interpretations of this concept. Ironically, learning centers tend to provide a diversity of instructional resources and equipment and tend to be designed and staffed in ways that would make possible the accommodation of numerous learning styles. The flexibility thus achieved would tend to enhance the chances of a pupil's being able to find his or her best way of learning through experimentation with the options available.

These instructional resources have included a wide range of print and non-print media materials, programmed instruction, and multi-level kits. All types of audio-visual equipment and teaching machines have been utilized in learning centers. Most work has been geared for individual and small-group learning.

Staffing patterns have similarly been diversified, often requiring redefinition and expansion of existing roles to provide staffing for the center.

Although record-keeping systems have varied, all centers have developed some sort of system for monitoring pupil progress and achievement on an individual basis and for coordinating learning center and classroom activities. Computer terminals have been useful in this area.

Learning center schedules have varied widely depending upon the objectives of the center, the size of the pupil population in relation to the size and staffing of the center, and the desires of classroom teachers.

Although schools with learning centers have been endeavoring to evaluate their centers, designs for evaluation have been largely informal, where they exist at all. Two important factors have accounted for this. One has been the difficulty in controlling the numerous important variables associated with the operation of a learning center. The second has been the absence of on-staff personnel with either the expertise or the time to devote to the evaluation of learning centers.

In conclusion, though there are basic commonalities that characterize learning centers, there are also wide variations in the designs and operations of these centers. At this point, more than a dozen years of schools' experiences and experimentation with learning centers has provided sufficient information to make possible the design of a comprehensive model for their future development and operation. Such a model is offered in the subsequent chapters of this book.

3.
Conceptual Framework
for the Model

Underlying Philosophy
and Beliefs

The learning center concept is based upon the understanding that children differ. They differ in their developmental patterns—physiological, psychomotor, socio-psychological, and cognitive. They differ in the ways in which they approach tasks. They differ with respect to interests, aptitudes, talents, abilities, attitudes, and values. They differ in how they perceive and interact with their environments, both external and internal.

The learning center concept is predicated, as well, upon the understanding that all human beings share certain basic needs. These include physiological needs; security needs; the needs for belonging, self-esteem, and love; the need for understanding of one's environment; the need for beauty; and the need for self-actualization, or the exercise of one's potentials which results in self-fulfillment.

In every society, there exist both cultural and social sanctions and customs for ways in which these basic needs might be gratified. Accordingly, behavioral researchers have identified those skills and behaviors which an individual must acquire in order to be able to function effectively in life. These life-relevant skills have been described by Cole in his book titled *Process Education* as including: (1) instrumental skills of reading, writing, speaking,

33

listening, and mathematics; (2) productive-thinking or problem-solving skills (analytic thinking skills); (3) creative and expressive behaviors; and (4) social interactive skills. For proponents of process education, the development of these skills is the main goal of education.

These skills are developed through and applied to the arts and humanities, the natural sciences, the social sciences, and the applied sciences as these are integrated and patterned into curriculum configurations.

**Process Education and
the Learning Center**

The goals of the learning center are not unlike those of process education. Learning centers focus upon developing in pupils skills and abilities that will ultimately enable each to become an independent, life-long learner and to exercise his or her fullest potential. In other words, helping pupils to become self-actualizing adults should be the principal goal of education and is, indeed, the principal goal of learning centers.

Accordingly, learning centers focus upon the development in pupils of life-relevant skills. To the skills previously cited, this writer has added one more instrumental skill and a fifth process skill. McLuhan has suggested in *Understanding Media: The Extensions of Man* that movies as a nonverbal form of experience are, like photography, a form of statement *without syntax*. He illustrated that the photo and movie, like print, assume a high level of literacy in their users and prove baffling to the nonliterate. In a world of mass media it is as essential that the individual acquire nonverbal, visual literacy as it is for him or her to acquire verbal, visual literacy. For this reason, visual literacy skills have been added to the five instrumental skills already cited. In addition, the self-process skills have been added to the process skills cited by Cole. These would include self-awareness, self-exploration, and self-evaluative skills, self-conception, values clarification, and the information processing skills that would enable the individual to relate himself or herself to the world of work and play (vocation and avocation). There has been much evidence to support the importance of these skills to self-actualization. For this reason, they have been critical to career education and are included here as the fifth of the process skills.

Thus, the complete list of those life-relevant process skills, the development of which will be the focus of the learning center, includes:

1. Instrumental skills of reading, writing, speaking, listening, visual literacy, and mathematics.

2. Productive-thinking and problem-solving skills (analytic thinking skills).

3. Creative and expressive behaviors.

4. Social interactive skills.

5. Self-process skills of self-exploration, self-evaluation, self-conception, values clarification, and those information processing skills required for the individual to relate himself or herself to the world of work and play.

This process education basis will have significant implications for the design, staffing, resources, and procedures employed in learning centers.

Learning Style

Whereas process education focuses upon the skills to be developed, and curriculum focuses upon the content through which these skills will be developed, learning style has as its focus those environmental conditions that might be manipulated to facilitate learning for the individual student. These environmental factors include the following:

1. Social context: This refers to persons with whom the pupil is working toward the achievement of a given learning objective (for example, independently and alone, independently in a small group, in a tutorial with an adult or a peer, etc.).

2. Modality-medium-instrumentation (for example, visual-pictorial animation-silent filmloop).

3. Content features: This focuses upon the appropriateness of the content to the maturity level, interests, and experiential background of the learner. (Material that depicts six- and seven-year-olds at play on a farm in a basal reader may be appropriate content for primary children who have some understanding of or interest in farm life; it may not be appropriate for non-English-speaking teenagers learning to read, or for inner-city ghetto children.)

4. Reward system: This refers to that which a pupil values and which might serve as motivation for learning. These rewards may be of three types, as follows:

a. people-related rewards, such as peer praise, public recognition, self-esteem, and pleasure taken in interaction with others;

b. property-related rewards, such as grades, tokens, money, position or job, and privileges;

c. process-related rewards, such as an intrinsic interest in the task or activity, challenge, or need for creative or expressive outlets;

5. Time factors: These relate to a pupil's rate of learning; the number of, frequency of, and intervals between repetitions of a new concept or skill required before learning takes place.

6. Organization and sequencing of units of learning: This aspect focuses upon such factors as divergent and convergent modes of organization, prerequisite skills assumed, number of new concepts introduced simultaneously, opportunities for development of each of the cognitive levels with respect to the new learning (knowledge, comprehension, application, analysis, synthesis, and evaluation).

7. Perceptuo-psychomotor peripheral stimuli: These refer to potential sensory distractors or enhancers of learning that may be present or absent in the learning environment at a particular time. There are four types as follows:

a. auditory, such as noise, speech, music, etc.;

b. olfactory, such as scents, ventilation, etc.;

c. visual, such as decor, motion, activity, lighting, etc.;

d. tactile-kinesthetic, such as furniture, seating, temperature and climate, size of room, freedom of physical movement, etc.

By providing broad and varied options for manipulating the teaching-learning environment, the flexibility required to accommodate diverse styles of learning can be achieved. Accordingly, the concept of learning style has significant implications for the design, staffing, resources, equipment, and procedures employed in learning centers.

Assumptions Underlying the Learning Center Concept

1. Children learn in different ways and at different rates, and it is incumbent upon educators to provide for these differences.

2. Children differ with respect to interests, attitudes, aptitudes, talents, abilities, and values; these differences will have a bearing on the learning process.

3. Children need to be assisted in developing life-relevant skills which will ultimately facilitate their being able to gratify basic needs and become self-actualizing individuals. Process education focuses upon development of life-relevant skills and behaviors.

4. An individual's learning style can be identified and the learning environment manipulated to accommodate it.

5. Individualization of instruction is a process, not a program nor a curricular strategy. This process is comprised of six subsystems, as follows: (a) assessment of learner needs; (b) diagnosis of learner needs; (c) prescription; (d) interaction process; (e) evaluation; and (f) follow-up, recycling, and reassessment.[1] These subsystems are described at length in the following chapter.

6. Professional roles in education should conform to the tasks to be performed in implementing a process approach to individualization of instruction.

Experiences may be direct or mediated and vicarious. Filmstrips with or without audiotape cassettes can take the student back in history or across the globe to experience visually lives and events in other times and places.

7. The learning center is the focal point of the educative process when a process approach to individualization of instruction is implemented.

8. At every stage of development, children are capable of participating in goal-setting, decision-making, and the exercise of options related to their own learning.

9. When offered options and alternatives with respect to what will be learned and how it will be learned, the individual will generally select those objectives and strategies that will best meet his or her needs at the time of the choice.

10. Children are capable of self-directing much of their own learning.

11. Education is learning to learn; therefore, movement toward independence in learning should be encouraged in pupils.

12. Print and non-print media are essential to the accommodation of learning styles and individualization of instruction.

13. Children's feelings about what they are learning are as important as the skills and knowledge being learned.

14. Children can learn most subject matter content, and especially factual material, directly from educational media, with minimal teacher intervention.

Goals and Objectives of the Learning Center

Goals

1. To develop independent, life-long learners.
2. To develop self-actualizing individuals.

Objectives

1. To accommodate diverse learning styles.

2. To provide teaching-learning options not available in the self-contained classroom.

3. To provide opportunities for mediated experiences when first-hand experiences are not feasible nor as satisfactory as the mediated experience, e.g., use of slow motion camera to observe a natural phenomenon; use of film to recapture historical events.

4. To provide opportunities for independent, self-directed study.

5. To provide opportunities for pupils to share in the decision-making involving their own learning.

6. To develop process skills and instrumental skills using the media.

7. To develop initiative, self-direction, independence, re-

sponsibility, decision-making, positive self-concept, confidence, and organizational skills in pupils.

8. To develop library research skills, inquiry skills, and information retrieval skills using print and non-print media and all other types of information resources.

9. To serve as a catalyst for change and the vehicle for continuous professional staff development.

10. To facilitate implementation of a process approach to individualization of instruction.

The Learning Center and the Development
of Reading and Language Arts Skills

The acquisition of language is a developmental process that begins in infancy and continues throughout an individual's entire lifetime. Language, as a communication mode, is both receptive and expressive. It is the medium through which the individual makes his or her needs, feelings, and thoughts known to others and through which others make theirs known to him or her.

Language is the principal instrument of social interaction. Language is also the principal instrument of thought and consequently of learning.

Dewey has suggested that experience cannot stand alone as learning but that it must be interpreted through a process of reflective thinking to be made consequential. He described *knowing* as a transaction between the individual and the environment involving actions and word meanings.[2] Dewey suggested the importance of experience as the starting point for language development, and language as the instrument for interpreting experience so that learning may occur.

It follows that there is a need for much language interplay in the school. This interplay can be between teacher and pupils, between peers, or between older and younger children. It also points up the need for an environment rich in objects and experiences that may serve as stimuli for this language interplay and, thus, for learning.

Experiences may be direct or they may be mediated and vicarious. A field trip to the firehouse or to an airport when studying the kinds of work people do is a direct experience which may serve as the catalyst for language activities and for learning. However, during a study of world cultures or volcanic activity, field trips may not be feasible. In these instances, mediated experiences may serve as the stimuli for language development and for discovery. Through films, recordings, models, artifacts, books, study prints, and other types of mediated presentational modes, the child can experience richly and widely.

Smith, Goodman, and Meredith have suggested that "the world can be brought to the class or the class can be taken to the world in such a way as to promote or enrich symbolic transformation of experience into knowing."[3] They point out that the student can extend his world of knowing through mental dialogue between individual conceptions and public and scientific concepts found in books and in films. The role of the teacher in this process of bringing established and personal knowledge together has been described by Bruner as that of "orchestration."[4] Essentially it is this concept of orchestration that transforms the physical facility that is called the "learning center" into a dynamic teaching-learning environment in which pupils and resources are brought together in ways that will stimulate thought, language, and learning.

Chapter Summary

Learning centers have as their goals the development of skills and behaviors that will enable the individual to fulfill his or her creative, adaptive potentials and to survive in a world where change is so rapid that all knowledge must be tentative. Process education with its emphasis upon life-relevant skills provides the basis for achieving these goals. Accordingly, learning centers focus upon the development of (1) the instrumental skills of reading, writing, speaking, listening, visual literacy, and mathematics; (2) productive thinking or problem-solving skills (analytic thinking skills); (3) social interactive skills; (4) creative and expressive behaviors; and (5) the self-processes, including development of self-awareness, self-acceptance, self-conception, self-evaluation, and self-esteem. Development of inquiry skills, information retrieval skills, and research skills are also goals of the learning center.

Piagetian theory as it has been reflected through open education practices has provided the basis for an approach to learning that has greatly influenced learning centers. This influence has manifested itself in the physical designs, instructional resources, equipment, and practices of learning centers. Through the use of the non-print media, concrete experiences may be provided where they might not have otherwise been possible, and these can serve as the stimuli for the development of language and the cognitive processes when used in small-group situations or individually. Focus upon involvement of the learner in decisions affecting his or her own learning, self-selection of the resources for learning, self-directed activity, self-pacing of learning, and provisions for opportunities to share with others new learnings have all been outgrowths of basic assumptions about learning, characterizing open education, that have been incorporated into learning centers.

Another important facet of learning centers is their focus upon the uniqueness of each individual learner with respect to his or her style, rate, and patterns of learning, as well as differences in interests and aptitudes. To accommodate these individual differences, learning centers employ a process approach to individualization of instruction which includes systems for assessing, diagnosing, prescribing for, monitoring, evaluating, and reassessing individual learner needs and achievement. Such a system implies the need for differentiated staffing patterns and such system supports as computers, teacher aides, and technicians.

In summary, learning centers represent a high level of sophistication in the integration of human and situational resources, through systems design, to make possible the accommodation of individual student needs in relation to the development of the life-relevant process skills.

Notes

1.   Ben Wallace. *Survival Is the Name of the Game*. Mineola, New York: Mineola Public Schools, 1970, pp. 236-37.
2.   John Dewey and Arthur Bentley. *Knowing and the Known*. Boston: Beacon, 1949, pp. 123-297.
3.   E. Brooks Smith, Kenneth S. Goodman, and Robert Meredith. *Language and Thinking in the Elementary School*. New York: Holt, Rinehart, and Winston, Inc., 1970, pp. 122-23.
4.   Jerome Bruner. "Some Theories on Instruction Illustrated with Reference to Mathematics." *Theories of Learning and Instruction*, NSSE Yearbook, 1964. Chicago: University of Chicago Press, 1964, p. 310.

4.
The Process:
Individualization of Instruction

Individualization: Problems with
Current Definitions

Individualization of instruction has been defined in numerous ways. Most definitions encompass the concepts of self-pacing, self-scheduling of work periods, beginning instruction in a given subject at a point appropriate to the learner's past achievement, remediation of identifiable skills impeding learning, and self-selection of instructional resources.

Even though these concepts do indeed characterize individualization, they remain incomplete and somewhat amorphous, since they fail to provide the educator with a clear understanding of the tasks at hand, how these relate to one another, the professional competencies required to accomplish them, and the corresponding professional roles and situational supports required. An operational definition of individualization of instruction is required if it is to be meaningful and useful to educators. It must focus not merely upon pupil activities in an individualized approach but upon teacher behaviors as well.

A Systematic Process Approach
to Individualization of Instruction

Individualization of instruction is a dynamic process. Like

any such process, it is characterized by continuous interaction and change. The pupil interacts with his or her environment, which includes people and situational resources. As a result of this interaction, both pupil and environment are modified, and the need for new types of interaction is precipitated. The changes on the part of the pupil may be in the form of new learnings or modifications in previous behaviors or attitudes; they may also take the form of new or changed interests or aspirations. On the other hand, changes in the environment will take the form of new demands made upon the pupil, requiring still other learnings, and behavioral or attitudinal changes or modifications. This process is continuous. It is also complex.

Because individualization of instruction is a complex process, a systematic approach to it is essential. Systems design or a systems approach is an organized means of carrying out a process when the means are complicated and comprise many interrelated elements. For example, as stated in the preceding chapter, individualization is comprised of six interrelated aspects:

(1) assessment of learner needs;
(2) diagnosis;
(3) prescriptive strategies;
(4) interaction process;
(5) evaluation; and
(6) reassessment, follow-up, and recycling.

Each of these elements has its own specific content, tasks, jobs, personnel requirements, procedures, instruments, and techniques. These six subsystems are interrelated; when combined, they provide an organized means of individualizing instruction—they constitute a system. See Figure 1.

Subsystem 1: Assessment of
Learner Needs

Traditionally, the approach of public educational institutions to assessment and diagnosis of learner needs has left much to be desired. If the processes of assessment and diagnosis of needs are

Figure 1

Individualization
(The Teaching-Learning Process)

ASSESSMENT
(Collect Data on
Pupil Needs)

DIAGNOSIS
(Interpret Data)

PRESCRIPTION
(Select Curricular Strategies;
Design Curricula; Select
Instructional Materials;
Modify Learning Environment
to Meet Learning Needs)

INTERACTION
PROCESS
(Conference with Pupil;
Identify Impediments to
Progress; Make Changes or
Modifications in Prescription;
Counsel; Clarify; Praise; Encourage)

EVALUATION
(Measure Degree to Which
Pupil Has Achieved Designated
Learning Objectives)

REASSESSMENT, RECYCLING,
FOLLOW-UP

47

to benefit students, they must be systematically and skillfully administered by trained specialists, accompanied by related changes in the total educational structure, including patterns of school organization, instructional methodologies, and teaching-learning environments as the need for such changes is indicated.

Assessment of individual needs involves the collection of information about each pupil, the purpose of which is to gain insights into his or her own needs as these determine and are affected by what is to be learned. Needs assessment data may be grouped into two broad categories:

1. Data related to the status of the individual's development of life-relevant skills, as described in Chapter 3 (i.e., instrumental skills of reading, writing, speaking, listening, visual literacy, mathematics; productive-thinking skills; social interactive skills; creative and expressive behaviors; and self-process skills).

2. Data related to the learning style of the individual. Learning style refers to the way an individual might best learn or develop a given behavior at a given stage in his or her development. Identifying the learning style of an individual requires assessment and interpretation of his or her needs in relation to the demands of the environment (designated learning objectives) at a given time. These needs, when interpreted, yield a tentative profile that will provide clues regarding ways in which the environment might best be manipulated to the advantage of the learner as he or she works toward developing designated new behaviors. (See Appendix A: Learning Style Needs Assessment Profile.) Learning style is a complex concept. There has been some empirical data supporting the concept, but there has been little research to support theoretical models. Research has, instead, been directed toward investigation of individual facets of learning that might be fused, leading to a theory of learning style. At the college level this has been done by Joseph Hill and his associates, as noted earlier in this book, but it remains to be applied—with or without modifications—to the elementary school level. Learning style does not appear to be fixed but interacts with, modifying and being

modified by, the learning objective at hand. (See Figure 2.) Factors of learning style themselves may interact with one another in a given situation, modifying the significance of one factor and increasing the importance of another—depending upon the learning objective at hand. For example, a ten-year-old boy who has failed to learn to read and who, from the first grade onward, has resented adults in positions of authority, may require an instrumentation and social context that excludes an adult authority figure in the teaching-learning process. On the other hand, if this same child requires opportunities to develop oral language, then peer group interaction, or use of the cassette player-recorder in conjunction with mediated experiences might offer an effective social context, media, and instrumentation for learning, without inclusion of the adult authority figure. However, if the boy cannot attend to a task for more than 15 minutes at a time, this factor would further modify the organization, structure, and sequencing and time factors related to units of learning. As additional variables are introduced, each serves as a delimiting factor, reducing the alternative environmental options and focusing more directly upon those that will serve to facilitate learning the designated skill or behavior.

Needs Assessment Techniques

Needs assessment data may be secured using a wide variety of techniques in combination. The techniques to be used will depend upon the types of information required and the age group of the pupils. Some of these techniques include the following:

    (1) interviews with pupils, parents, teachers;
    (2) surveys and questionnaires;
    (3) informal inventories;
    (4) observational techniques;
    (5) standardized tests;
    (6) criterion-referenced tests;
    (7) small-group discussions;
    (8) longitudinal study of learning patterns/developmental patterns; and

Figure 2

Bennie's Model of the Interplay Between
Learning Objective, Learner Characteristics,
and Learning Environment

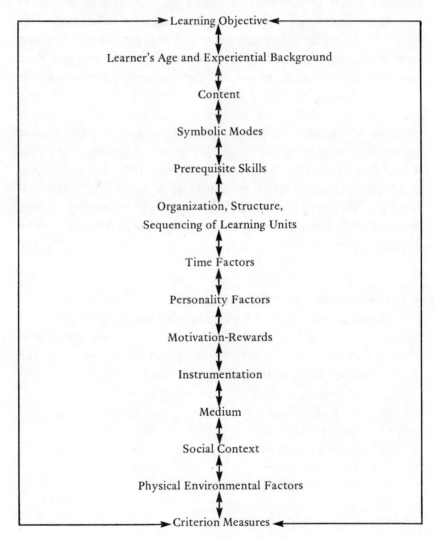

(9)   physical examinations.

Table 1 lists some specific examples of instruments and techniques that may be used to assess needs, with the principal focus on reading and language arts skills development and related areas. Appendix A contains samples of the various types of questionnaires and surveys that may be used at elementary through college levels to assess pupil needs.

Subsystem 2: Diagnosis of
Learner Needs

Data are not inherently diagnostic. Volumes of data may be collected about an individual, yet that data may say little to the untrained, unskilled practitioner. This fact is clearly evidenced currently by what seems to be a paucity of instruments for assessing individual learning styles. One might seriously question whether there is, indeed, a lack of significant available data about an individual's learning style or if, instead, there is a lack of expertise in selecting, organizing, and interpreting the pertinent data that are readily available, and in making the necessary skilled judgments based upon this data.

The diagnostic aspect of the individualized process that takes place in the learning center is critical. It is not a function performed by a technician, a lab assistant, an aide, or even an instructor. Diagnosis is done by a highly trained and skilled learning specialist. The training and abilities of the learning specialist will be discussed more fully in Chapter 6.

Diagnosis involves looking for patterns, discrepancies, inconsistencies, problems, strengths, causative factors of problems, and impediments to normal development and learning that may appear in all of the data that have been collected about an individual pupil. It involves analysis, interpretation, and the making of intuitive judgments based on experience.

Because the learning specialist is skilled in perceiving nuances and patterns that may provide important clues in rendering a diagnosis, certain key aspects of the assessment process should be

Table 1

Instruments of Assessment: Reading, Language,
and Related Areas of Development*

Instrument	Stand.	Non-Stand.	Group Admin.	Indiv. Admin.	Ages or Grades
Kindergarten Evaluation of Learning Potential		X		X	K-1
Bohm Test of Basic Concepts	X		X		K-1
Frostig Test of Visual Perception	X		X		K-3
Metropolitan Readiness Tests	X		X		K-1
Learning Method Test** (Modality Test for Teaching Word Recognition)	X			X	6-10 yrs.
Illinois Test of Psycholinguistic Ability	X			X	3-9 yrs.
Wechsler Intelligence Scale for Children	X			X	6-16 yrs.
Slingerland Test of Specific Language Disability	X			X	Gr. 1-4

(continued)

*See Oscar K. Buros (Ed.) *Reading Tests and Reviews: II* (Highland Park, New Jersey: The Gryphon Press, 1975) for descriptions of the instruments listed.

**The Mills School, 1512 E. Broward Blvd., Fort Lauderdale, Florida.

Table 1

(Continued)

Instrument	Stand.	Non-Stand.	Group Admin.	Indiv. Admin.	Ages or Grades
Rosewell-Chall Auditory Blending Test	X			X	Gr. 1-4
Botel Reading Inventory	X		X	X	Gr. 1-12
Durrell Analysis of Reading Difficulty	X			X	Gr. 1-6
Spache Diagnostic Reading Scales	X			X	Gr. 1-6 Retarded Readers Grades 7-12
Wepman Auditory Discrimination Test	X			X	6-8 yrs.
Stanford Achievement Tests: Reading Tests					Grades
Primary I	X		X		1.5-2.4
Primary II	X		X		2.5-3.4
Intermediate I	X		X		4.0-5.4
Intermediate II	X		X		5.5-6.9
Advanced	X		X		7.0-9.5
Stanford Achievement Test: High School Reading Test	X		X		Gr. 9-12
Stanford Diagnostic Reading Tests					
Level I	X		X		2.5-4.5
Level II	X		X		4.5-8.5

(continued)

Table 1

(Continued)

Instrument	Stand.	Non-Stand.	Group Admin.	Indiv. Admin.	Ages or Grades
SPIRE Individual Reading Evaluation					
Level I		X		X	Gr. 1-6
Level II		X		X	Gr. 4-10
Gillingham-Childs Phonics Proficiency Scales	X			X	Gr. 1-12
Diagnostic Reading Tests: Upper Level Survey Section	X		X		Gr. 7-13+
Iowa Silent Reading Test: Level 2	X		X		Gr. 9-13+
Iowa Silent Reading Test: Level 3	X		X		Gr. 9-13+
Gray Oral Reading Test	X			X	1.5-8.5
Goodman-Burke Reading Miscue Inventory		X		X	1.0-8.0
Keystone Visual Survey (Visual Screening)	X			X	K-Adult
Orthorater (Visual Screening)	X			X	K-Adult
Spache Binocular Reading Test (Visual Screening)	X			X	K-Adult

(continued)

Table 1

(Continued)

Instrument	Stand.	Non-Stand.	Group Admin.	Indiv. Admin.	Ages or Grades
Maico Audiometer Test (Auditory Screening)	X			X	K-Adult
Animal Crackers (Self-Perception)	X		X		K-3
Attitude Toward School†	X		X		K-12
Self-Concept Measures†	X		X		K-12
Attitudes, Emotional Maturity, Critical Thinking Measures†	X		X		K-12
Judgment: Deductive Logic and Assumption Recognition	X		X		K-12
Parent Interview Form††		X		X	
Pupil Interview Form††		X		X	
Interest Inventories††		X		X	

†Available from Instructional Objectives Exchange, Box 24095, Los Angeles, California 90024.

††See Appendices for sample forms.

carried out directly by him or her. Pupil and parent interviews and administration of certain individual diagnostic instruments would be examples of assessment techniques that may provide much more pertinent information to the skilled specialist than to the unskilled practitioner.

Diagnosis is a continuous process. As the student interacts with his or her environment and, as a result, changes through the development of new or modified knowledge, skills, or attitudes, his or her needs will change. These new needs must be reassessed and diagnosed so that appropriate changes may be made in the prescriptive strategies being employed.

Subsystem 3: Prescriptive
Strategies Design

Prescriptive programming involves translating diagnostic statements about a student into viable teaching-learning strategies. It is in this phase of the instructional process that the tailoring of the interaction setting (learning environment) and of the inter-action process (activities in which the pupil will engage) to meet individual needs occurs. In other words, the designing of prescriptive strategies is the phase of the individualized instructional process during which the teaching-learning environment is manipulated to meet individual needs. These needs are of two types; those relating to learning style, and those relating to status with respect to the life-relevant process skills described in Chapter 3. The purpose of manipulating the learning environment is to facilitate the student's achieving a designated set of learning objectives. These learning objectives were specified for the individual during the diagnostic aspect of the instructional process.

The design of prescriptive strategies involves much more than assigning a child to use particular instructional materials. For this reason, certain tasks must be accomplished beforehand, or this subsystem will break down. The following represents a list of the major tasks that must be concluded to develop a systematic approach to prescriptive programming. These tasks differ some-

Children learn in different ways and at varied rates. Accommodating these individual differences is a goal of learning centers.

what from the elementary and junior high school to the senior high school and university levels, and such variations have been specified where applicable. In schools where there is not a computer terminal available, certain facets of the system will be significantly less efficient.

Development of the Prescriptive Programming Subsystem

1. *Instructional objectives.* Specify instructional objectives for each of the life-relevant skills categories as described in Chapter 3.

2. *Instructional resources and techniques.* Identify instruc-

tional resources and techniques* that may be used to achieve the instructional objectives in each of the life-relevant skills categories. These resources and techniques should be classified according to the following:

a.   instructional objective/s which the resource/technique is geared to help the pupil achieve;

b.   content classifications (e.g., Africa-transportation; American literature-tales and legends);

c.   grade level designations for which the resource is appropriate;

d.   readability level of written material;

e.   media components;

f.   types of interaction to which the resource/technique lends itself (teacher-directed/pupil-directed, teacher-assisted, individual independent study, discussion groups, peer pairs for study, etc.);

g.   learning style factors (see Chapter 3 for a discussion of each of these factors).

At the senior high school and university levels far more instructor-prepared materials than commercially published resources will be used. One reason for this is that curriculum areas tend to be more specialized and diversified from school to school and from classroom to classroom at these levels. However, before high school and university instructors can incorporate audio-visual techniques for independent study into other instructional approaches, they will need to be trained in the potential uses and values of each type of media. At the university level, some learning centers have made excellent use of sound-slide equipment, videotape cassettes, and audiotape cassettes to prepare programs tailor-made to the needs of students in specific classes. Many universities have instructional development centers and other

---

*It is suggested that a professional library be developed containing a wide range of resources with pragmatic suggestions, instructional activities, and recommended techniques for developing the life-relevant skills.

types of media resource units with staffs that can provide instructors with assistance in the preparation of the various types of media lessons and programs designed to facilitate and enrich student learning. These instructor-made programs are then available to be used by students in the learning center. (Appendix C contains a list of suggested types of media programs that may be developed for learning centers at the senior high school and college levels to improve reading and language arts skills.)

3. *Cataloging*. All print and non-print media materials should be catalogued according to guidelines suggested by the American Library Association.

4. *Teaching-learning modules*. These learning units should be developed using the proper design and format.* Teaching-learning modules will be discussed more fully later in this chapter.

5. *Independent learning*. Organization for independent learning requires careful planning and preparation at the elementary and junior high school levels. Contracts, learning activity packages, and sequenced activity or prescription sheets are examples of techniques for organizing and managing independent study. (See Appendix B for sample contracts and sequenced independent activity sheets for reading and writing skills development.) Learning contracts will be discussed more fully later in this chapter.

6. *Pupil feedback and involvement in goal-setting and decision-making*. Care should be taken to develop procedures for involving pupils individually and in small groups in establishing their own goals and objectives for learning and strategies for

---

*Materials on the design of learning modules are available as follows: (1) *How to Build Modules and Learning Packets* (12 presentations on six audiotape cassettes developed by Ward Weldon, University of Illinois; Instructional Media Incorporated, 4235 South Memorial, Tulsa, Oklahoma 74145). (2) *Individualized Learning Using Instructional Modules* (six presentations on three audiotape cassettes developed by Richard W. Burns and Joe Lars Klingstedt; Educational Technology Publications, 140 Sylvan Avenue, Englewood Cliffs, New Jersey 07632).

achieving the designated learning objectives. Pupil feedback regarding the value and interest level of particular instructional resources and techniques is invaluable. It suggests to the pupil when such feedback is sought that his or her views and feelings are important. It also provides the educator with information that can be used to improve prescriptive programming efficiency. It is through pupil feedback, often during conferencing, that the learning specialist can substantiate the accuracy of the diagnosis, and the specialist in charge of designing the prescriptive strategies can identify the need for changes or modifications in the prescription.

7. *Criterion measures.* Ways of evaluating pupil success in achieving designated instructional objectives should be specified and designed. These may take various forms depending upon the nature of the learning objective they are designed to measure. Criterion performance measures may be written or oral in format. They might involve a teacher-pupil interview, presentation of a culminating project such as a media program developed by the student, or a report. An art project, invention, dramatization, or written essay or objective test may serve as criterion measures. Criterion-referenced tests might serve as overall assessment measures. Some of the newer basic reading programs have criterion-referenced testing and periodic and post-achievement tests built into them.

However, in the area of reading, caution should be exercised in the development and/or selection of criterion measures. Diagnostic techniques should not be confused with broader criterion measures. A pupil could conceivably demonstrate excellence in knowledge of grapheme/phoneme correspondences and even read with accuracy but not comprehend what is read. Criterion measures in reading and the language arts should focus upon evaluation of the over-all behavior to be developed.

8. *Flexibility.* Flexibility should be built into the prescriptive programming system and the evaluative strategies. Pupil responses to activities and resources should be continuously elicited and used to refine the system. Where appropriate resources

to accommodate a given learning style and/or to facilitate achievement of a designated learning objective are lacking, these should be developed using in-house talent and expertise or secured commercially. Naturally, those involved with the preparation of instructional materials will need to be trained to do this and provided with the required released time from other duties.

Pupils with Special
Educational Needs

Pupils with special educational needs, such as the slow learner, the gifted and talented, the learning disabled, the culturally disadvantaged, the bilingual, the physically handicapped, and the emotionally disturbed, require no labels in the learning center, where the principal focus is upon *individual* learning needs and styles. The non-print media used in varying social contexts offer unequalled opportunities for these students to learn in their own ways and at their own rates.

Nonetheless, it should be recognized that often children with special educational needs manifest conflicting or competing needs. For example, the gifted student can benefit from much independent study and work in small groups with other talented students in the learning center; the gifted student, though, also needs to develop social interactive skills that will enable him or her to fare well in the society at large, which is comprised of people of all abilities. It is also important, so that the potential contributions of the gifted to society are not lost, that the average and less able individuals learn to accept and profit by the talents of the more able. The development of appropriate social interactive skills for all students is critical. Prescriptive strategies which are designed to develop one skill area extensively at the expense or omission of another will ultimately leave learners with an incomplete education.

The importance of insightful approaches to the design of prescriptive strategies for each student cannot be over-emphasized. Certainly, stigmatizing and labelling students can and should be avoided through the flexibility provided by the learning center. Acceptance of individual differences is, at heart, what the learning center is all about.

The Teaching-Learning Module

Development of teaching-learning modules is basic to individualized instruction. The teaching-learning module is comprised of the following:

1. Instructional objectives.

2. Teaching-learning strategies for achieving the objectives. These are appropriately sequenced and may include a wide variety of media. Provision is made for independent study, and large-group and small-group experiences. The teaching-learning strategies contained in the module constitute the interaction alternatives appropriate for achieving the designated behavior or learning.

3. Media to be used in conjunction with each teaching-learning strategy are specified. The activities and media to be used are properly sequenced, and appropriate questioning strategies are applied to develop the various cognitive levels.

4. Interaction settings in which the learning activities will take place are specified.

5. Criterion measures are given that may be used to evaluate learner achievement of the designated learning objectives.

6. Strategies for providing opportunities for integration, application, and transfer of learning are built into the module.

From the larger learning module, the prescriptive programming specialist selects those strategies and resources appropriate for the individual learner based upon the learner's traits (learning style) and input competence (status of development with respect to the life-relevant skills described in Chapter 3). Certainly, if a computer terminal is available, the modules might be computerized, and the individual pupil modules more easily and efficiently constructed by using learner variables to sort instructional objectives, resources, activities, and criterion measures.*

*See work on *Computer Based Curriculum Planning*, Center for Curriculum Planning, State University of New York at Buffalo.

Integration, application, and transfer of learning. Although any well developed learning module would make provision for application and transfer of learning, the integrative aspect of the educational experience in learning centers is so vital that it is being discussed separately here.

An example of an approach to reading instruction that fails to provide for application, transfer, and integration of learning is one in which pupils interact on a continuous basis solely with spirit master sheets and workbooks. Pupils are instructed in specific skills in isolation, but rarely if ever are provided the opportunity to interact with and apply these skills to reading in the content areas, reading of literature, or to expository writing.

In the area of reading, pupils must have relevant experiences in using reading as a source of pleasure, and subsequently in the fulfillment of subject matter reading. The student who is able to read and follow directions in order to construct a model airplane, to arrive at a destination, to repair a mechanical or electronic device, or to cook is transferring, applying, and integrating new learning with other skills that have previously been acquired. Similarly, the youngster who is interested in a particular subject and who researches that subject, reading widely about it, is using reading as a means of securing information and as a source of pleasure in a natural situation.

In the language arts, examples of experiences that provide for application, transfer, and integration of learning are listed below:

1. Conducting an interview and taking notes.
2. Writing a script for a dramatic production, puppet show, skit, or recorded presentation.
3. Participating in a dramatic production or puppet show.
4. Reading a letter received and/or writing a letter.
5. Keeping a travel log or diary.
6. Preparing a menu, itinerary, or invitation.
7. Giving or following verbal or written directions (recipe, map, model building, sewing, etc.).
8. Participating in a formal discussion.

9. Writing and producing a television production.
10. Taking movies or slides, sequencing them in the case of the latter, and then writing and recording a narration to accompany them.
11. Giving a demonstration or making a presentation to a group.
12. Conducting a telephone conversation.
13. Writing a poem or story.
14. Writing a report or essay.
15. Writing for a newspaper—feature articles, news articles, editorials, or other journalistic forms.
16. Designing and preparing a program for a show or production.
17. Making a speech or giving a lecture.
18. Describing an experience.
19. Participating in mime and creative dramatics.
20. Writing a research paper.

Pupils need to have these types of experiences in order to effectuate application, integration, and transfer of learning. In addition, many of these experiences serve the dual function of developing creative and expressive behaviors and self-actualization processes.*

Contracts

A contract is a technique for organizing and managing independent study. It is basically a carefully sequenced series of activities that have been prescribed in order to achieve a designated learning objective. The student and teacher agree on the terms of the contract, and both sign the contract sheet.

Contracts may vary in format according to the age of the children with which they are used. In the primary grades, they

*See Sidney B. Simon, Leland W. Howe, and Howard Kirschenbaum. *Values Clarification: A Handbook of Practical Strategies for Teachers and Students.* New York: Hart Publishing Company, 1972.

should be simple and pictorial in format, allowing the child to readily understand what is to be done and how to keep a record of the work he or she has completed. (Samples of primary contracts may be found in Appendix B.)

As one moves up through the grades to the college level, contracts will assume various formats (see Appendix B for samples). Certain characteristics are common to all contracts regardless of the level for which they are prepared. These characteristics include the following:

1. Specification of at least one learning objective that should be achieved as a result of completing the contract.

2. Choice of materials, media, or experiences that will be used to complete the contract.

3. Choice of activities. An instructional material is different from an activity, which constitutes how the resource will be used. A given resource may be used in a variety of different ways depending upon the age level, competence, and interests of the learner in relation to the designated learning objective.

4. Choice of reporting alternatives or criterion measures.

In addition, the contract always makes provision for the following:

    a. Self-pacing.

    b. Means for the learner to self-evaluate his or her own work.

    c. Individual teacher-pupil conferencing.

    d. A record-keeping system to monitor pupil progress toward completion of the contract.

5. Development and/or application of cognitive abilities at the six levels, including: knowledge, comprehension, application, analysis, synthesis, and evaluation.

The Computer

A computer terminal can provide an essential support system for sustaining individualized instruction in the learning center. In the prescriptive programming phase, it can provide lists of instructional objectives appropriate for an age group in a given skill category; it can also provide correlated lists of instructional resources and activities that may be appropriate for a given age group and sorted by learner variables for achieving a designated objective. In addition, it can direct the instructor to sources that would contain suggested activities for achieving each objective.

The computer terminal can provide the prescriptive programmer with an on-going record of the types of learning experiences and the specific instructional resources with which a given learner has interacted, and an account of the types of responses and degree of success he or she has had with each. This data would assist future prescriptive programming for a given learner as well as for those with similar learning styles and needs.

Establishing a Timeline
for Developing Subsystem 3

In a functioning school, the accomplishment of the tasks associated with the development of the prescriptive programming subsystem might take several years and phases. It would also require an appraisal of local talent and identification of types of staff development and training required.

At this point, some of the tasks discussed have already been accomplished by state education departments, individual school districts, universities, and publishing companies, and a school district might draw upon and adapt what has been done by others. However, it should be recognized that in implementing new approaches and retraining professional staffs, the *process* is the product. Staff members can learn much through doing, selecting, and evaluating. It would be a mistake to attempt to impose upon a staff complete banks of ready-made instructional objectives, learning modules, contracts, or procedures which they had no part in developing or selecting. On the other hand, if adequate training and guidance by persons with expertise in these areas are not made available to professional staffs, that too might undermine the success of this facet of the learning center project.

The time required to establish a fully functioning, well

equipped, well staffed, and properly used learning center will depend upon the level of readiness and skills of the professional staff, the funds available, the status of the district with respect to already available audio-visual equipment and media materials, and space availability. The understandings and degree of commitment of the administrative staff to the learning center concept will also have a significant bearing on the time requirements for the establishment of a center. Some of the questions that may be asked to guide the development of a time-line follow:

1. What are the present levels of readiness among the professional staff, community, school board, and administrative personnel? What must be done to develop readiness? How long will developing the necessary readiness take? How shall it be done and by whom?

2. To what degree does the professional staff possess understandings and skills in individualization of instruction, process education, in open education, and learning centers? What must be done to develop prerequisite understandings and skills in each of these areas? How long will it take?

3. What types and quantities of educational media and audio-visual equipment are already available in the school? To what extent are these used? What additional materials and equipment will be required? Have AV equipment standards been established for classrooms, the learning center, and special rooms such as speech, art, music, etc.?

4. Are the goals of education and a philosophy of education clearly defined for the district? Is the learning center concept compatible with the goals and philosophy? Will the learning center facilitate achieving the goals in ways that are consistent with the philosophy? Is there a commitment to individualized instruction? Has individualization of instruction been clearly defined and agreed upon by professional staff, school board, and administrative staff?

5. Is there adequate space available to develop a learning center complex? All facets of the complex? Certain facets of the

complex only? Is money available for needed remodeling? How long will it take to develop the physical facility? Will it be done in stages over a period of several years?

6. Are teachers experienced in organizing for independent learning? Are they experienced with small-group learning techniques? How long will it take to develop these skills?

7. Are teachers trained in the uses of the educational media and audio-visual equipment? How much time will be required for in-service education and such instruction through the learning center?

8. Has curriculum been designed? Have contracts and teaching-learning modules been developed? How long will it take to initiate, complete, evaluate, and revise these contracts and modules?

9. Has a learning center staff been selected and trained? How much basic training will be required? How much on-the-job training will be required, and how long will it take before necessary skills are developed so that the learning center may function optimally?

10. Have procedures been defined for implementing the various facets of a process approach to individualization of instruction?

The answers to these questions should help to provide some idea with respect to whether a fully functioning, optimally operated learning center will require two or ten years to achieve. Inasmuch as the learning center is or can be the vehicle for training staff in many of these areas, it is not expected that all of these tasks will be accomplished prior to the actual implementation of the learning center; many will be accomplished as a result of teacher involvement in the development of the center. Certainly, for some school districts that are not accustomed to long-range planning of this sort, the notion of implementing an innovation over a period of several years may seem foreign. One might only suggest that this type of long-range planning has been long overdue in the field of education, where innovations have been implemented one year and dropped the next because instant success had not been achieved. Patience and perseverance are required to launch and operate a successful learning center.

Practical Considerations in Programming
Students for the Learning Center

If every learning center had achieved the ideal with respect to physical design, size, furnishings, equipment, instructional resources and supplies, and staffing, this section could be omitted from the chapter. However, since this is not yet the case, certain practical considerations that must be taken into account when designing prescriptive strategies for pupils to carry out in the learning center are listed below. There is little point in designing prescriptive strategies that will not be feasible in their implementation because they do not take into account limitations of size, design, staffing, equipment, and training in relation to the learning center. These practical considerations include the following:

1. How many students can the learning center comfortably accommodate at any one time, taking size and staffing into consideration? What are the implications of this for scheduling?

2. Given a particular age group of students and the various types of activities in which they will be engaged at the center, how many teachers, specialists, teacher aides, or volunteers will be needed to assist them, and what must be the qualifications or special abilities of those who will be helping the students?

3. What restrictions do the furnishings and design of the learning center place upon the types of activities and numbers of pupils engaged in each (e.g., number of project tables, carrels, areas for games, etc.).

4. Are there any activities that could not occur simultaneously in the learning center because they would interfere with one another?

5. What is the equipment inventory? If 20 pupils required cassette players at the same time, would there be a sufficient supply? How many items would be kept on hand in the learning

center and how many could go out on loan to classrooms? Is there sufficient back-up equipment so that when pieces of equipment are in disrepair, it will not measurably affect the functioning of the center?

6. Have pupils and teachers been oriented to the learning center, the use of the equipment, the available instructional resources, and all basic procedures? What implications does the extent of their familiarity with the center have for scheduling, design of prescriptive strategies, approaches employed, and staffing requirements?

7. Does the learning center have a maintenance budget? Is it adequate for replacing commercially prepared activity sheets and response booklets if these are to be consumed? Is it adequate for replacing filmstrip-making materials, blank cassette tapes, 35mm film for slides, other types of supplies, and lost or damaged equipment? Does it make provision for ordering of new equipment and/or instructional materials?

Ideally, the design of prescriptive strategies should be based primarily, if not solely, upon pupil needs; however, in considering the various limitations of a given situation, it may become necessary to develop alternative strategies which will still focus upon pupil needs but will take into account, as well, delimiting factors found in the local school setting.

Subsystem 4: Interaction Process

The interaction process is that aspect of individualization during which the student carries out the learning prescription. It involves the student interacting with his or her environment, which includes people and resources in prescribed settings which have been designed to meet his or her individual learning needs and learning style.

During this phase of the individualization process, the student is engaged in activities which are geared to facilitate the achievement of the designated learning objectives. The student paces his or her own rate of learning and may have agreed in consultation with the instructor to complete certain tasks within specific time periods.

Anderson* has described five types of interaction that might occur in individualized instruction. These include (1) various types of independent study; (2) the pupil receiving counseling, tutorial service, or personalized help from a member of the school staff; (3) homogeneous small-group learning; (4) heterogeneous small-group learning; and (5) large-group or whole-class demonstration, lecture, presentation, or audio-visual lessons followed by subsequent activity that will vary within a range the teacher has in mind.

Each of these is a relevant type of interaction that may occur in the learning center. A discussion of each follows.

Independent Learning
Interaction with programmed materials. Programmed materials provide broad and varied opportunities for pupils to develop needed skills or understanding of concepts and processes independently and at their own rates of learning. Basically, programmed materials present a particular limited unit of information to the student, to which he or she may respond—receiving immediate feedback regarding the accuracy of the response. Minimal teacher-pupil interaction is required with programmed materials, thus freeing the teacher to work with individuals and small groups of students tutorially, in discussion groups, in conferencing, or in other ways that require the presence and expertise of the teacher.

There are many forms of programmed instruction employed in learning centers. Some of these include computer-based instruction, electronic teaching machines, multi-media teaching

*Robert H. Anderson. "Sustaining Individualized Instruction through Flexible Administration." *The Computer in American Education.* Don D. Bushnell and Dwight W. Allen (eds.) New York: John Wiley and Sons, 1967, p. 31.

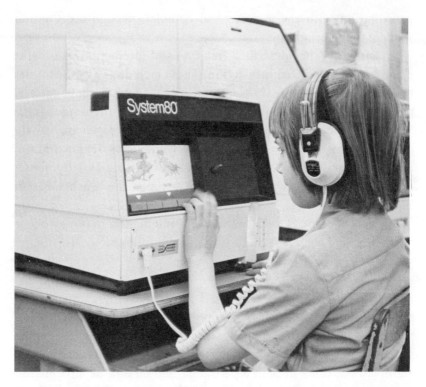

Teaching machines allow students to pace their own learning and to exercise some personal control over it. A form of programmed instruction, the System 80 device engages both auditory and visual modalities to help students develop basic reading and mathematics skills.

devices, manipulatives, multi-level skills kits, books, sound film-strips, and audio-card reader programs.

Programmed materials are used at all levels, kindergarten through college. At the primary grade levels, educators have found pupil response to audio-visual types of programmed instruction to be quite favorable. At the elementary levels, programmed materials will vary in lesson length from between a few to 30 minutes, depending upon the age group for which the material is intended and the type of material being presented. At the junior, senior high, and college levels, lessons may be somewhat longer, ranging from 40 to 60 minutes.

Programmed materials may be incorporated into contracts so that pupils spend a portion of their time in the learning center interacting with the programmed materials and another portion engaged in other types of activities.

Research. A student may use the learning center to research a topic. The student would spend time in the center locating and using the print and non-print media materials to secure information, take notes, and later organize these notes for the writing of a report, a script for recording, or for an oral presentation. Students may prepare slides and filmstrips in the center as presentational modes.

In one school, a group of students interested in rockets found some photographs of rockets in their learning center. Their appetites whetted, they asked the learning center director to assist them in locating other material on the subject. The director encouraged them to contact the public relations department of the local engineering-aircraft firm from which the photographs had come. The students not only received additional material in the mail, but also had a representative from the company visit the school to give a presentation on rockets and missiles. The visit was followed by a film on the subject sent to the learning center on loan. The interest of the children, combined with the alertness and skill of the learning center director, had led the students into activities that developed reading, listening, speaking, and writing skills as well as research skills.

Creative writing. Although creative writing should usually be preceded by lively group discussions which serve as a stimulus for thinking and subsequently for writing, there are available in learning centers resources that may be used independently by students to stimulate thought and creative writing responses. Some of these include open-ended stories on cassette recordings, filmloop composition starters, laminated pictorial cards that may be captioned or contain thought-provoking questions on the reverse side, and slides. (See Appendix C for a list of producers of commercial resources in this area.)

Production of media presentations. After writing original stories, story endings, narratives, or descriptions, the student may wish to record his or her work on an audiotape cassette, or prepare a filmstrip, sound-slide presentation, or even television programs (in centers equipped with TV equipment).

Listening activities. Students may use the learning center to listen to cassette recordings or discs for pleasure, for information, or to develop skills and appreciations. There are numerous multi-media kits which contain audiotape cassettes and sound filmstrip sets on cultures and countries, music, history, famous speeches, poetry, and literature.

At the college level, class lectures may be recorded on audiotape cassettes and made available to students if they should miss a lecture or if they wish to hear a lecture for a second time. This has been done in some college skills centers and used as a vehicle for teaching students note-taking, summarizing, and listening skills.

Cassette lessons may also be used to provide compensatory education for high school students with significant reading deficits. These audio lessons may present recordings of material contained in basic texts. They may also provide audio directions and guidance in completing required activities on lesson sheets or from books. When combined with slides and filmstrips, the options for providing compensatory education are enhanced even further.

Such lessons may also be used to assist the bilingual student who does not yet have sufficient mastery of the language to tackle the work in required texts. In addition, the non-English-speaking student may use audiotape cassettes in the learning center to develop English language skills. Dictation exercises and listening comprehension exercises may be made available to these students for independent study.

Individual Counseling, Tutorials,
Personalized Help from Learning Center Staff

Counseling. Counseling is a vital form of teacher-pupil interaction that takes place in the learning center or subsequent to learning center activities. It is usually in the form of the individual teacher-pupil conference. It is the function of the counseling process to help the student explore and clarify goals, attitudes, feelings, impediments to learning, problems, and aspirations, and to report progress made toward achieving designated learning objectives.

This is accomplished by focusing upon student perceptions and feelings, and by exploring alternative solutions to problems. During the process, the educator avoids didacticism, or imposing points of view, goals, values, or standards on the student. Values-clarification strategies may be employed during or as an outgrowth of the teacher-pupil conference. These methods are geared to encourage the student to consider alternative modes of thinking and acting by weighing the pros and cons and the ultimate consequences of each of the various alternatives open to him or her. The counselor strives to make apparent to the student all of the possible options.

During the individual teacher-pupil conference, it is the role of the teacher to provide encouragement and convey empathy and respect for the student. The conference should serve to enhance self-esteem. It is never the function of the conference to leave the student feeling a failure, incompetent, guilty, manipulated, dependent, or incapable of participating in decision-making affecting his or her own learning. The counseling function of the educator is one of the most important due to its personalized nature.

Tutorials and other personalized help. A tutorial is a situation in which a student individually receives instruction from a peer, an older student, a volunteer, a paraprofessional, a teacher, or a specialist. The tutorial instruction focuses upon some specific learning needs the pupil may have that can best be served through a one-to-one situation.

Teacher-pupil conferencing should take place frequently and at scheduled intervals as a means of monitoring the interaction and continuously assessing pupil needs.

Usually, the tutor keeps a record of sessions during which he or she has tutored a student. The date of the session, materials used, lessons completed, skills focused upon, and student achievement or learnings may be recorded on the tutorial form. (See Appendix D for sample tutorial forms.)

In addition to the formal tutorial, a student may receive individual assistance from an aide, a volunteer, a teacher, or a specialist in the learning center as the need for such assistance is requested by the student or appears to the staff member to be required. (See Appendix D for volunteer program forms.) The student may require assistance in operating audio-visual equipment, locating needed instructional materials or supplies, interpreting directions for completing a lesson, or in understanding certain learning center procedures. The student may also require an explanation of a concept presented in the materials being used, clarification of an incorrect response to some programmed material, or some brief on-the-spot instruction.

Small-Group Learning: Pupils with Similar Needs

Pupils having similar aptitudes and achievement history may engage collectively in a task or project in the learning center. Generally, the task or project is intended to provide the same educational benefit to each. For example, a group of pupils with similar aptitudes and types of reading skills deficiencies may be scheduled to visit the learning center at the same time to receive small-group instruction in reading directly from the reading specialist or from a volunteer working under the supervision of the specialist. In another instance, a group of gifted students about to embark upon an ecology project which involves photographing examples of environmental pollution in the community may be scheduled to visit the learning center for a series of lessons on photography and photographic compositions.

Small-group learning of these types is commonplace in learning centers and provides an efficient means of meeting individual needs when several pupils have similar needs.

Small-Group Learning: Benefits Through Heterogeneous Groupings

Small groups of pupils, presumably different from each other in aptitude, interests, experience, and other factors may engage collectively in an activity in the learning center when this activity promises to benefit each of them uniquely. Examples of such activities would include discussions, dramatizations, role-playing, puppet shows, creative dramatics, simulations, and self-directed photography. (See Appendix C for producers of commercial materials in these areas.)

One type of small-group learning that is common in learning centers involves an audio-visual lesson in which students are exposed to a common stimulus; however, responses expected of the students may vary within a particular range that the teacher has in mind.

Another type of small-group learning situation common in the learning center involves a presentation or audio-visual lesson in which students are exposed to a common stimulus; the responses expected of the students either at that moment or later will vary within a particular range that the teacher has in mind. For example, development of oral language, self-awareness, acceptance of feelings, and socializing skills are considered important learning objectives for pupils in the primary grades. Teachers in one particular school decided to have a station in the learning center that would allow them to focus upon development of these skills and understandings in small, heterogeneous groups. The interaction would be guided by the teacher. The station was dubbed "The Talking Table" because it was where the emphasis was to be upon verbal exchange. There were many media programs in the center containing sound filmstrips, large pictorial laminated study prints, silent filmloops, and slides that would be appropriate stimuli for discussions at "The Talking Table." Some included puppets. Many incorporated questioning strategies and appropriate follow-up activities. In using one such program, pupils watched a sound filmstrip in which boys and girls exhibited many different kinds of feelings, such as anger, fear, sadness, happiness, etc. The children subsequently discussed the situations they had observed in the filmstrip that had elicited each of the different feelings. The teacher barely had to encourage the children to tell about experiences they had had which aroused feelings in them similar to those experienced by the children in the filmstrip. Students gradually became more comfortable, as the session progressed, about discussing their own feelings. They talked about different ways people express various types of feelings and how these ways affect others. After a lively discussion, the boys and girls used crayons to draw faces on large paper plates, with each face depicting an expression of some feelings observed in the filmstrip. The plates were then hung in the learning center as mobiles, a reminder to the youngsters each time they visited the center of this pleasurable activity, the fact that everyone experiences many different kinds of feelings, and that their work is of value and worthy of being displayed prominently.

In a different situation, a group of eighth graders listened together to a cassette recording geared to stimulate divergent thinking, lively discussion, and then creative writing.

In another class, students examined and discussed a trunk of authentic African artifacts, making comparisons to objects having similar functions in their own culture, and attempting to analyze the reasons why each object was made as it was and of the

Instructional resources in learning centers tend to encourage and facilitate independent and small-group learning. Pictured are "talking books," programmed learning kits, and a cabinet which holds 360 different activity sheets, each in a separate compartment.

particular material selected by the craftsman for its construction. Subsequently, they viewed filmloops which showed many of the artifacts in actual use in African villages.

In still another situation, pupils discussed in a small group a field trip they had taken the week before; and then, some working individually and others in pairs, developed filmstrips to recoup the highlights of their field trip and to respond personally to the experience.

The opportunities for small-group learning, whether independent or teacher-guided, are limitless in the learning center, where the resources are varied and stimulating and the classroom teacher is freed to work intimately with a small group while the other students are employed and absorbed with pupil-directed resources and assisted by other members of the learning center staff.

Large-Group Instruction

Pupils may observe a demonstration, lecture, or audio-visual lesson in a large-group situation in an area in the learning center designed for this purpose. Subsequently, the students are to respond to the common stimulus by engaging in a prescribed or self-designed activity, depending upon the purpose of the experience.

Television, 16mm films, filmloops, and overhead transparencies are types of media that lend themselves to such lessons.

Monitoring the Interaction: The Teacher's Role

After prescriptive strategies have been designed for pupils in a given class, it becomes essential for the teacher to have some way of knowing how each pupil is progressing toward achievement of the prescribed objectives. The teacher will need to know, as well, lessons or activities that have been completed, the degree of success the pupils have been experiencing with the prescribed materials and activities, where there is a need for tutorials or other forms of personalized assistance, and where modifications or changes in the original prescription may be required.

Some of these tasks can be accomplished through pupil and teacher record-keeping. (See Appendix B for sample record-keeping forms.) Contracts are also helpful in monitoring the interaction. In some schools, the teacher receives a computer print-out at the end of each week which provides a summary of lessons completed and level of achievement in connection with programmed forms of instruction.

In addition to record-keeping systems that focus upon work

completed and achievement, it is essential that the teacher monitor the affective aspects of the interaction process. This is generally accomplished through conferencing with individuals or small groups who may be engaged in a project cooperatively. The teacher should keep a record of all conferences, indicating the date of each conference, salient points discussed, problems identified, recommendations made, and time stipulations mutually agreed upon for completing certain tasks. Conferencing need not necessarily take place in the learning center, but it should be accomplished frequently and at scheduled intervals.

The student brings to the conference his or her work folder. He or she makes a record of recommendations and time stipulations for completing tasks.

As a result of conferencing, the teacher should be able to provide feedback to the diagnostician and prescriptive programmer, either substantiating the diagnosis and the prescription, or making suggestions for modifications or changes in the diagnosis and/or prescription based upon new information and insights acquired.

Subsystem 5: Evaluation

Pupil evaluation involves collecting data regarding the pupil's degree of success in achieving designated learning objectives. The data may be collected through observations of performance or a completed project, such as a dramatization, media presentation, or construction of a model; it may be oral, such as through an interview or speech, or a discussion; it may be collected in written form, such as through the composition of a poem, an essay, an original story, a research paper, or a report; or it may be done through completion of an objective test.

These data are then organized, analyzed, and interpreted. Conclusions are drawn, and decisions rendered with respect to continuing, expanding, redesigning, modifying, or changing a prescribed teaching-learning strategy, learning environment, or the instructional objectives that had been designated. Evaluation implies value judgments on the part of the educator, and this suggests the importance of criterion measures being appropriate to the skill or behavior they are intended to assess.

The most common types of pupil evaluation that presently occur in schools are with respect to the instrumental skills of reading, certain facets of language, and in mathematics. Paper-and-pencil tests are the most common methods of assessment, in the form of standardized examinations and criterion-referenced tests.

Other than the instrumental skills, little attention has been paid in the past to systematic and periodic evaluation of pupil achievement with respect to life-relevant skills, namely the social interactive skills, analytic thinking skills, creative and expressive behaviors, self-processes, and visual literacy. Much more must be done to develop and utilize techniques for assessing these areas.*

Evaluation should be conducted by a skilled evaluation specialist.

Subsystem 6: Reassessment,
Follow-up, Recycling

Reassessment

Reassessment of student needs is done periodically during the course of the school year as the student completes units of study and activities intended to lead toward the achievement of prescribed learning objectives. Such reassessment is made with respect to socio-psychological growth and development in addition to cognitive development and attitudinal changes. The purpose of reassessment is to determine (1) the student's readiness to move on to the next stage of learning, and (2) the types of changes and modifications in the teaching-learning environment that might be

---

*See Anita Simon and E. Gil Boyer (Eds.), *Mirrors of Behavior: An Anthology of Classroom Observation Instruments*. Philadelphia, Pennsylvania: Research for Better Schools and The Center for the Study of Teaching, Temple University, 1967.

required as a result of changes in the student. The same types of techniques and instruments used for assessment are then employed in reassessment, for the process approach to individualization of instruction is a cyclical one and, accordingly, the procedures used for identifying learner needs are continuously repeated each time the process begins anew.

Recycling

If it is found that the student has not achieved the designated learning objectives after a prescribed course of study has been completed, alternative strategies must be identified that may be used to help the student in his/her work toward mastery. Naturally, when such recycling is required, it is incumbent upon the educator to attempt to identify impediments to learning and/or learning style characteristics that were not provided for appropriately in the original prescription.

Follow-up

As a result of reassessment, the educator might identify new student interests, skills, and/or weaknesses, or opportunities to provide either additional enrichment activities or reinforcement activities that would be an outgrowth of the prescribed unit of study just completed. Perceiving the need and/or opportunities for appropriate types of follow-up requires skill, alertness, and creativity on the part of the educator.

Individualized Instruction Process Model

The Individualized Instruction Process Model (see Figure 3) is descriptive of a system for identification of learner needs and concomitant manipulation of situational factors to accommodate those needs. The system is continuous.

Input competence refers to the identification of the learner's status with respect to development of the life-relevant skills. In

Figure 3

Process of Individualized Instruction

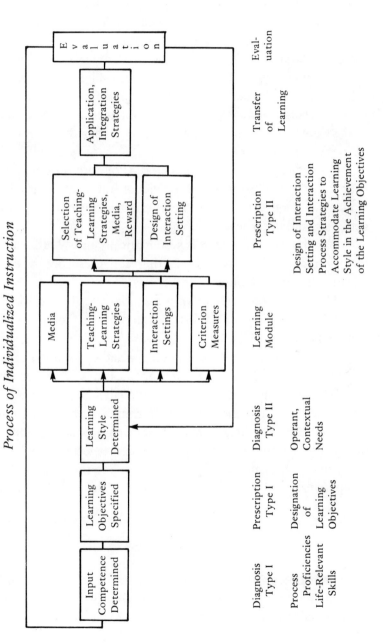

85

other words, it refers to the learner's readiness for the next stage of learning, taking into account prerequisite skills.

Learning objectives are then specified with respect to the life-relevant skills and in relation to the various content areas of the curriculum.

Learning style characteristics that will have a bearing on achievement of the designated learning objectives are identified.

Teaching-learning modules are contained in a bank and may be retrieved by learning objective/s and then by learning style characteristic variables.

Individualized learning modules (Prescription Type II) are then constructed based upon individual learner variables drawing from the larger bank of instructional objectives, resources, activities, and criterion measures.

Integration of learning is systematically provided for through inclusion of appropriate culminating activities contained in the teaching-learning modules.

Monitoring the interaction is essential after Prescription Type II has been designed. This does not appear on Figure 3, but it is assumed to be carried out.

Evaluation involves determining whether or not the learner has satisfied the designated criterion measures. If he or she has not, a reassessment of learning style and an appraisal of the difficulties or impediments to learning is made. Alternative teaching-learning strategies may then be engaged and modification of the interaction setting made. If the learner satisfies the criterion performance measure, a new diagnosis to determine the new input competence is made and a new entry into the system is initiated.

Chapter Summary

Individualization of instruction is defined as a complex process requiring a systems approach to carry out its six interrelated elements, which include: (1) assessment of learner needs; (2) diagnosis; (3) prescription; (4) interaction process; (5) evaluation; and (6) reassessment, follow-up, and recycling. Assessment is defined as the collection of data regarding the individual's learning needs and learning style. Diagnosis is defined as the interpretation of this data and the rendering of intuitive judgments based upon it. Prescription involves translating the diagnostic statements into viable teaching-learning strategies.

Before effective prescriptive programming occurs, certain tasks must be completed to prepare this subsystem. These tasks relate primarily to the resources, activities, approaches to integration and application of learning, and criterion measures. Organizing for independent study and the development of teaching-learning modules and contracts are critically important. The computer terminal is a desirable support system for sustaining individualized instruction—and the prescriptive programming facet, in particular.

The interaction process is defined as that aspect of individualization during which the prescription is carried out through student interaction with his or her environment. Five types of interaction relevant to the learning center have been cited and discussed. These include independent learning, counseling and various forms of personalized help, homogeneous small-group learning, heterogeneous small-group learning, and large-group demonstrations and presentations.

The teacher's and student's roles in monitoring the interaction are discussed, focusing upon record-keeping and conferencing as important techniques.

Pupil evaluation is defined as the rendering of judgments based upon available data regarding the learner's degree of success in achieving the designated objectives.

Finally, the reassessment, follow-up, and recycling subsystem is pointed to as necessary to extend learnings, reinforce or reteach certain objectives, and identify the learner's readiness for the next stage of learning.

The Individualized Instruction Process Model concludes the chapter, translating the entire individualized process into systems design graphically.

5.
Properties of
the Learning Center:
Physical Design, Resources
and Equipment

Criteria for the Design of the
Learning Center Complex

The design of the learning center should reflect certain beliefs about how children learn and the nature of knowledge as clearly and definitively as the lecture hall has traditionally reflected specific beliefs about learning and knowledge. The design should be consistent with the philosophy, objectives, and assumptions underlying the learning center concept (see Chapter 3). It should facilitate individualization of instruction and development of the life-relevant skills and behaviors in ways that reflect an understanding of how learning occurs at the stages of maturity of the students that the learning center will be servicing.

In addition, the design of the center should be conducive to independent, individual learning as well as small-group interaction. Students should be able to comfortably explore through various media topics of interest to them and be able to work toward developing the instrumental skills, at levels of increasing difficulty and sophistication, in contexts that are consistent with their styles of learning and levels of readiness. There should also be areas for large-group, audio-visual lessons and presentation, for conferencing, for diagnosis and prescriptive programming, for materials production, and for evaluation. The center should be attractively designed and must be appealing from an aesthetic point of view.

Coordinated color tones on walls, carpeting, furniture, and cabinets should harmonize and be neither too flashy nor somber. The overall effect should be one of balance and harmony.

A Model Learning Center Complex

A *basic* learning center complex would include the following types of areas:

1. Diagnostic and Evaluation Center.
2. Prescriptive Programming and Module and Materials Development Center.
3. Computer Terminal Area.
4. Small Conference Rooms.
5. Seminar Rooms.
6. Instrumental Skills Development Center (sectioned off into learning areas, each approximately ten square feet).
7. Library-Media Resource Center (also sectioned off into learning areas).
8. Graphic Arts Center (photography and television production).
9. Small Recording Rooms.
10. Large-Group Presentation and Demonstration Area.

The *extended* learning center complex would include all of the areas contained in the basic learning center and, in addition, the following:

11. Performing Arts Center (including a mini-theater).
12. Visual Arts Center.
13. Science and Invention Laboratory.

Each of these areas will vary in size according to function and the number of pupils to be accommodated at any one time. Areas in which incompatible activities will be occurring simultaneously would not be adjoining. For example, a high noise area such as the dramatics or music portions of the Performing Arts Center would not be situated next to areas requiring low noise, such as the Instrumental Skills Development Center, Recording Rooms, or

Diagnostic and Evaluation Center. In other words, the locations of the various areas should serve to enhance and complement the functions of one another rather than impede or conflict with their various functions. Areas that might satisfactorily adjoin one another are shown in clusters in Figures 4 and 5.

This chapter will focus upon the Basic Learning Center Complex, a design utilized by most schools, as opposed to the Extended Learning Center Complex, which only a relatively few institutions have implemented. It is in the Basic Complex that the focus is upon the utilization of audio-visual and automated forms of learning, programmed instruction, and independent learning with special attention paid to the concept of learning styles.

At the elementary levels and particularly in the primary grades, certain activities such as puppetry, creative dramatics, and mime would be used in the Basic Learning Center Complex regularly, even though they are forms of the performing arts. These techniques would be applied to and integrated with use of the media materials because they are essential types of learning experiences for younger children. Similarly, pupils at these levels would engage in drawing, construction of dioramas and other types of models, and development of their own illustrated books and poems.

Functions of Areas
in the Complex

Diagnostic and Evaluation Center. This is the area used by the learning specialist who meets individually with pupils, parents, and the professionals on the educational team to diagnose learner needs and evaluate pupil growth and development. A computer terminal is located in close proximity to this area to provide pupil profiles. Data are continuously added to, modified, or deleted from the bank as the child grows and develops and as needs change.

Prescriptive Programming, Module, and Materials Production Center. This area houses the persons charged with translating

Figure 4

The Basic Learning Center Complex

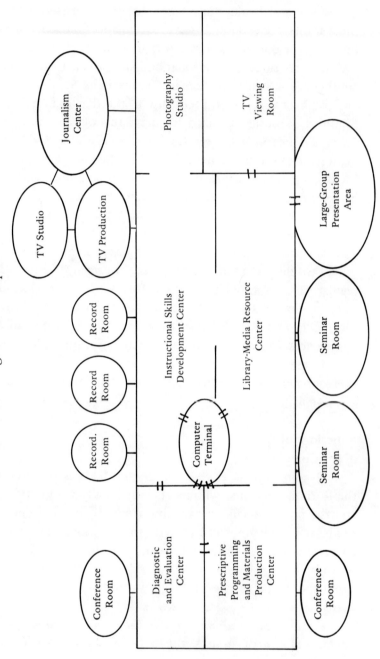

Figure 5

The Extended Learning Center Complex

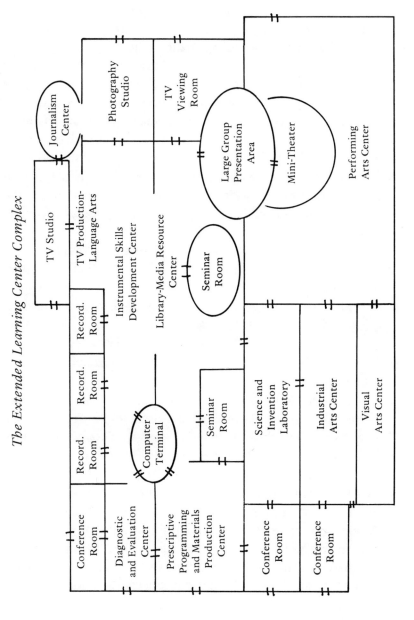

diagnostic statements about a child into viable teaching-learning strategies. Specialists who are knowledgeable in curriculum, the process skills, and instructional techniques, and who are talented and creative in designing and developing learning modules and instructional materials, work in this area as a team with a prescriptive programming specialist. The person responsible for prescriptive programming utilizes the computer terminal to monitor longitudinally the types of teaching-learning strategies used with each pupil, the instructional resources with which a pupil has interacted, and the experiences he or she has had. The curriculum designer-module builder, on the other hand, is assisted by a team of technicians and aides who follow directions in feeding new modules into the computer terminal and make changes and modifications in modules already in the computer. The aides and technicians also follow directions in the production and/or duplication of instructional materials.

Conference Rooms. These are used for conducting professional team meetings, case conferences, and individual teacher-pupil conferences.

Seminar Rooms. These are used for group instruction, role-playing, creative dramatics, discussions, demonstrations, informal and formal talks, and presentations. They should be of a size that will accommodate comfortably approximately 15 to 25 people.

Library-Media Resource Center. All print and non-print instructional resources are housed, used, and borrowed from this area, except for those materials expressly designed and intended for development of the instrumental skills. There would be some overlap between the two areas with respect to literature materials and teacher resources. The main thrust of the Library-Media Resource Center is the development of research and inquiry skills through the content areas, and providing fiction and non-fiction print material to be used by pupils to read for pleasure and for information. The learning activities in this area are coordinated by an Instructional Communications Specialist, under whose direction work one or more library-media aides. The computer terminal may be used by the Instructional Communications Specialist for information retrieval by topic, interest areas, and reading levels of any of the resources housed in the Library-Media Resource Center.

Recording Rooms. The Recording Rooms are small, soundproof chambers in which teachers or pupils may prepare cassette tape recordings, audio-card recordings, or sound-on-slide recordings.

TV Production-Language Arts Room. This room would be used by pupils to produce their own television shows. The purpose is to improve language arts skills through the many talents required to produce simple television programs. With appropriate guidance, even young children have been found to be capable of doing this work. Researching and scripting for the shows would be done in the Library-Media Resource Center, and the actual videotaping would be done in the TV Production Room. The room would be equipped with television monitors, stereo players, video recorders, and appropriate furniture.

TV Studio. This area would be used by teachers and pupils for the production of videotapes. It differs from the TV Production Room in that the latter would be limited to use of a process geared to improve reading and language arts skills. The productions in the TV Studio would be broader in scope and would allow teachers to produce videotaped lessons. A trained TV technician would be responsible for the two TV areas, with a teacher aide or paraprofessional always present in the TV Production Room.

TV Viewing Room. This would be an area at least the size of two standard classrooms. It would be looped for wireless viewing; several large monitors would be used for group viewing; and some small monitors would be available in carrels for individual or pupil team viewing. Pupils might use the computer terminal to call for a particular program when it is needed.

Photography Studio. This room would be equipped with cameras, dark room, and necessary realia for work with the

The Instrumental Skills Development Center is divided into learning areas each approximately ten feet square. It is carpeted, attractively decorated in coordinated color tones, and equipped with study carrels and low "cubbies" for instructional materials. Pupils work in small groups, individually, and in pairs, both independently and according to teacher guidance.

graphic arts. Slides, filmstrips, 8mm movies, and snapshots would be prepared here, in addition to special effects using photography techniques. Pupils would be taught visual literacy skills and how to use the graphic arts as an outlet for creative and expressive behaviors. Photography would be fused with the language arts as pupils researched, scripted, and prepared recordings to accompany filmstrips, slides, and films, and as they captioned scrapbooks of photographs. Kindergarten and primary pupils would be taught self-directed photography, and this would be used in conjunction with a language experience approach. A specialist in photography and the related graphic arts would be in charge of this area.

Mini-Theater. Although the mini-theater is actually part of the Performing Arts Center, it is important to the language arts program. Puppetry, dramatic poetry reading, creative dramatics, and mime are modes of expression that stimulate the imaginations of the young and are exciting vehicles for language development. Through mime, children may gain insight into a non-verbal communication mode that requires the ability to infer meanings. This type of activity adds another dimension to the study of language, and the skills developed in making inferences may then be applied to the spoken and written language modes of communication.

Puppetry is a delightful means of engaging elementary pupils in reading, writing, and speaking activities and in fusing the language arts with the visual and performing arts. Older pupils may read stories and then rewrite their own versions for a script, or they might write their own original scripts.

Instrumental Skills Development Center

Size and Location of
Physical Facility

The Instrumental Skills Development Center is the area devoted to the development of reading, writing, speaking, listening, visual literacy, and mathematics skills through mediated modes and programmed instruction. The language arts section of this area is at least 2,700-3,600 square feet in a school with a pupil population of 500 to 700 pupils.

Adjoining the Instrumental Skills Development Center are the Library-Media Resource Center, the Recording Rooms, the Diagnostic Center, the Prescriptive Programming Center, Conference Rooms, the TV Production Room, and the Photography Studio. In close proximity to the Skills Center are the Journalism Room, Seminar Rooms, TV Studio, and TV Viewing Rooms. The computer terminal is between the Instrumental Skills Development Center and the Diagnostic and Prescriptive areas.

Goals

In addition to the development of the instrumental skills, goals of the Skills Center include the fostering of initiative, responsibility, independence, positive self-concept, self-evaluative skills, and success in learning at every stage of development. Another important goal of the Center is that of providing opportunities for pupils to make choices and decisions with respect to their own learning. The accommodation of individual learning styles through the manipulation of environmental factors is more readily achieved in this area because of the nature of the instructional resources and staffing pattern.

Design and Arrangement of
Physical Facility

The Instrumental Skills Development Center, which is carpeted for functional as well as aesthetic reasons, is sectioned off with low three by five foot-high single or double faced room-divider shelves, each approximately four to six feet in length. These may have casters so that partitioned learning area sizes may be easily altered as the need arises. The carpeting serves an acoustical function as well as making it possible for pupils to work comfortably on the floor with games, puzzles, manipulatives, and other types of media. The room dividers help to assure privacy and reduce distractions as pupils engage in various types of activities simultaneously in varying social contexts.

Venetian blinds on the windows facilitate light control, which is important when using such visual equipment as viewers and projectors. Draperies on the windows enhance the appearance of the area and provide additional light control.

Bulletin boards of various sizes in different wall areas permit display of pupils' work, charts, decorative arrangements related to the language arts, time schedules, bulletins, and directions. Shelves of various sizes allow for display of artifacts, dioramas, books, and storage of media materials. The entire area is painted in an attractive color scheme consisting of three to four harmonizing colors, balanced and coordinated with the carpeting and draperies.

Electrical outlets are spaced on the base molding at five foot intervals around the entire room. The area is looped for wireless headset reception of closed circuit and broadcast television. Approximately 35 electrified carrels of varying sizes are attractively arranged in various areas of the Skills Center in addition to those in the Library-Media Resource Center. Project tables are also interspersed in the various sectioned learning areas, as are student desks which may be used as learning stations for individually used teaching machines and for other individual work projects. Stations where viewers and projectors will be used are situated so that natural window light will not create a glare or interfere with projection. Balance and harmony combined with functionalism should guide the design of the area.

Non-Instructional Equipment

This attractive area designed to accommodate learning in varying social contexts utilizing diverse instrumentations is equipped with furniture, cabinets, study carrels, and storage units that are utilitarian yet enhance the physical appearance of the area. Book and equipment carts, room dividers, and file cabinets also are required. Consideration is given again to functionalism, balance in scale, and color when selecting furniture and other types of non-instructional equipment.

Instructional Equipment

The Instrumental Skills Development Center is equipped with study carrels and a wide range of audio-visual equipment, teaching machines, multi-level kits, programmed learning devices, models, bulletin boards, multi-media materials and kits, realia, collections, dioramas, study prints, games, manipulatives and puzzles, artifacts, closed circuit television and videotapes housed in the center or elsewhere and called for by pupils as needed for viewing, and computer terminals.

All of the instructional equipment and resources in the Center are geared specifically toward the development of the instrumental skills. For the language arts, these should include equipment and resources appropriate for the development of receptive language communication modes (reading and listening skills) and for development of expressive language modes (writing and speaking). This equipment should be used in the recording rooms, small seminar and conference rooms, in the performing arts center, and in other areas in which it is required for language development activities in addition to being used in the Skills Center.

Table 2 shows the types of equipment found in the Instrumental Skills Center and the potential value of each for developing either receptive or expressive language in various social contexts. Where the equipment is geared toward transmission of receptive stimuli which can then be used as a point of departure for development of expressive language modes, this has been so indicated. A description of each type of audio-visual software used with the various types of equipment and the value of each in developing the language arts is provided in the following section.

Instructional Resources:
Guidelines for Selection*

Selection of non-print media materials, multi-level kits, and the various types of programmed instruction on the educational market today can be perplexing for the would-be buyer. In a highly competitive market, educational publishing houses have had

---

*See Appendix C for a selected list of producers of non-print media.

Table 2

*Educational Features of the Audio-Visual Equipment
in the Instrumental Skills Center*

Modality	Type Equipment	Receptive Mode	Expressive Mode	May Stimulate Expressive Lang. Dev. Through Follow-up	Social Context		
					Indiv.	Pairs	Small Group
Audio*	Cassette Players	X		X	X	X	X
	Cassette Player-Recorders	X	X	X	X	X	X
	Phonograph Player	X		X	X	X	X
	Headsets	X			X	X	X
	Wireless Directional Induction Loops	X					
Visual	Filmstrip Previewer	X		X	X	X	
	Slide Previewer	X		X	X	X	
	Slide Projector	X		X			X
	Filmloop Viewer	X		X	X	X	

*It is recommended that all audio equipment and headsets be standard ¼" jack type so that all headsets in the center can be used with any type of audio equipment.

Table 2

(*Continued*)

Modality	Type Equipment	Receptive Mode	Expressive Mode	May Stimulate Expressive Lang. Dev. Through Follow-up	Social Context		
					Indiv.	Pairs	Small Group
	Filmloop Projector	X		X			X
	8mm Movie Projector	X		X			X
	Controlled Reader	X			X	X	X
Audio-Visual	Sound-Slide Viewer	X	X	X	X	X	X
	Synchronized Sound Filmstrip Viewer	X		X	X	X	X
	Sound Filmstrip Viewer with Record Feature	X	X	X	X	X	X
	Sound-on-Slide Projector	X		X	X	X	X
	Sound-on-Slide Projector with Record Feature	X	X	X	X	X	X
	Sound Filmloop Viewer with Record Feature	X	X	X	X	X	
	16mm Movie Projector	X		X			X
	Audio-Card Reader	X	X		X	X	

Table 2

(Continued)

Modality	Type Equipment	Receptive Mode	Expressive Mode	May Stimulate Expressive Lang. Dev. Through Follow-up	Social Context		
					Indiv.	Pairs	Small Group
Audio-Visual	Television	X	X	X	X	X	X
Programmed Teaching Machines	Borg-Warner System 80	X			X		
	Hoffman Reader	X		X	X	X	X

to keep a close watch on trends in education and federal funding. Because the area of reading has been of major emphasis at local, state, and federal levels, dollars have been directed toward the improvement of reading programs over the past few years. Publishing companies have been particularly responsive to this trend as well as to the demand for better materials geared toward individualization of instruction. Daily, new materials arrive on the scene. However, the quality of these materials and their value in relation to cost has varied widely. (See Appendix C for criteria for selection of learning center resources in reading and language arts.)

In order to get the greatest value for the steadily shrinking dollar, the approach to equipping the Instrumental Skills Center with instructional materials must be scrupulously designed and systematically implemented. The following is a list of guidelines to assist those charged with this responsibility:

1. *Assess needs.* Identify the learning objectives in reading and the language arts. Ask teachers to specify types of learning problems and areas of instruction in which adequate resources are lacking or varied types are needed. Examine data on learner needs for clues to types of resources needed.

2. *Design criteria for selection of resources.* Criteria for selection of instructional resources should be consistent with assumptions and philosophy underlying the learning center concept and assumptions supporting the development of reading and language arts skills (see Appendix C for sample criteria).

3. *Survey instructional resources.* Visit materials exhibits and other learning centers; consult with learning center directors and reading specialists about resources that have been tried by them; invite local representatives from publishing companies and carriers of the media to visit your school to show their materials; and peruse instructional materials catalogs, marking off materials which might be of value and sending for these on a preview basis.

4. *Develop a system for ranking resources.* In selecting resources, it is important to get a sampling that reflects the range of learning objectives and learning style needs. At least one

resource that is tactile, one that is auditory, one that is visual, and one that is multi-sensory should be selected for each learning objective in reading. Resources should be ranked according to quality and effectiveness as compared with others of the same type.

5. *Learner verification.* Develop a system for trying resources being considered for purchase with the student population with which they will be used. Often, materials that are attractively packaged or that "look good" do not receive the expected response from pupils. Resources being considered for purchase should be used by teachers with a sampling of students. An evaluation of each resource should be carefully made using established criteria.

6. *Maintain purchase order copies.* When materials are finally ordered, a copy of the purchase order should be kept by the person charged with the responsibility for maintaining the Center. This will provide needed information if materials upon arrival or later are found to be defective, if damage occurs through normal use necessitating reordering of components, or if consumables require replacement on a yearly basis.

**Types of Instructional Resources
and Their Value to Reading
and Language Arts**

Instructional materials found in the Instrumental Skills Development Center differ from those traditionally used in classroom settings. Unlike the basal reader, the media materials, multi-level kits, programmed instruction with and without teaching machines, models, and realia tend to encourage independent and small-group work, requiring less teacher direction and more varied types of social interaction than might otherwise be possible. Pupils may interact with peers, older pupils, volunteers, teacher aides, the reading specialist, learning center director, and classroom teacher in the center as well as work individually. Opportunities for self-selection of resources, self-direction, self-pacing, and self-evaluation are made feasible through these media materials, and the individual pupil-teacher conference becomes an essential component of the interaction process. The media materials also make feasible the accommodation of learning style, whereas the basal-workbook approach used alone and primarily teacher-directed impedes meeting the range of diverse learning needs.

The following is a list of the various types of media and the potential value of each in developing the receptive and expressive language modes.

Cassette tapes. A cassette tape is a small cartridge containing a reel of tape and a "take-up" reel. It is used on a small cassette player or player-recorder and is an audio mode. There is much commercially prepared prerecorded cassette material available in reading and the language arts. These materials vary widely in format, organization, structure and sequencing of learning, motivational techniques employed (if any) with the cassette lessons, and in cost and technical quality.

Most cassette lessons range in actual recorded lesson time from eight to 20 minutes but average about 15 minutes. However, where there are reading and writing activities done in conjunction with the lesson, with the recorder off, an entire lesson may take 30 to 50 minutes to complete, depending upon the rate at which a given pupil works.

Cassette lessons may be accompanied by a variety of support materials or other types of media required for completion of each lesson. These may include study prints and/or puppets, laminated wipe-off cards, and activity booklets, sheets, and books; sometimes the activity book is in cartoon format. Some cassette programs contain activity books and multi-level, multi-interest area reading selections; others are accompanied by books of reading selections followed by comprehension and word study questions. Some cassette lessons are accompanied by lesson cards with answer key masks. In selecting any of these types of materials, pupil response to the material, or learner verification, should be the primary basis for purchase.

In addition to commercially prepared cassette material, blank cassette tapes allow pupils to record their own reading, speech, original stories, interviews, and oral presentations. The child who is shy and who may be reluctant to speak in a group situation may be quite at ease with a tape recorder. The recorder can help children develop confidence in their own verbal capacities. Pupils may delight in sharing taped original stories and language experiences. In teaching beginning reading, the taped story may then be typed and each child can compile a "book" or folder of his or her own stories.

Blank cassette tapes may also be used for the development of teacher-made lessons to meet individual pupil needs.

Cassette material allows the teacher to provide independent, self-directed work to meet the needs of each pupil while at the same time freeing the teacher to work with an individual pupil or with small groups requiring special remedial or enrichment work, or merely requiring clarification of a concept already introduced. The cassette lesson also frees the teacher to conduct individual teacher-pupil conferences which are essential to individualization and personalization of instruction.

Sound-on-Slide discs. The 3M Sound-on-Slide discs, which at the present time may only be used with the 3M Sound-on-Slide Projector or Projector-Recorder units, allow the student or teacher to organize and sequence a series of slides; each individual slide is then slipped in a sound disc onto which the pupil or teacher may record a narrative to accompany the slide on that disc. These Sound-on-Slide discs are then placed in a tray or carousel, and a synchronized sound-slide presentation is ready for showing. The sound discs, like cassette tapes, may be erased and recorded over and over again, thus reducing the cost per pupil use.

The Sound-on-Slide offers the advantage of requiring pupils to do research, categorize visual stimuli by attributes, organize and sequence these stimuli, write a narrative to accompany each slide, and then record the narrative. Pupils are thereby required to utilize a wide range of cognitive skills and expressive and receptive language modes. The projects offer opportunities for development of expressive and creative behavior as well as development of social interactive skills where pupils work in pairs or teams on these projects.

Audio-cards. Audio-cards vary in size and are simply cards on which visual-pictorial or visual-graphic stimuli are printed, pasted, or drawn; an accompanying sound track is then recorded on a magnetic tape at the bottom portion of the card. The audio-cards may be purchased prerecorded or blank for program development by the teacher or pupil. The cards require an audio-card reader for use.

Record discs. Most producers of media materials now offer the option of either record discs or audiotape cassettes in multi-media or sound filmstrip sets. Audiotape cassettes offer many more advantages than do record discs in terms of usability, durability, and accessibility.

Filmstrips. A filmstrip is a picture roll which may contain anywhere from ten to 50 or more individual pictures. The pictures on the role are sequenced and generally introduce and develop an individual concept or information on a single topic.

Filmstrips may be projected on a screen for group viewing, or they may be viewed by students individually or in pairs using a filmstrip viewer.

There has been a growing trend away from silent captioned filmstrips toward sound filmstrips which have their sound tracks on accompanying audiotape cassettes or record discs. Those with audiotape cassettes are more adaptable to both individual pupil use and group use.

Filmstrips can be prepared by teachers and pupils using a half-frame camera or blank filmstrip roles which may be drawn or written on using special colored pencils. Some companies manufacture kits which provide all of the necessary materials for making and showing write-on filmstrips. These may be used in both the primary and intermediate grades in the development of reading and language arts skills.

Slides. Colored slides, 2 x 2 inches, generally taken with a 35mm camera and placed on cardborad or plastic mounts, each present an individual picture. These pictures may be organized, sequenced, and shown on a large screen using a slide projector, or viewed individually by a pupil using a small electric or manual slide viewer. Cassette tapes or record discs may be recorded to present a narration to accompany slide sequences.

Multi-media kits. Multi-media packages and kits contain a variety of types of media on a given subject. For example, there are multi-media packages in reading that contain sound filmstrips, record discs, and books.

Some multi-media kits, particularly those intended for kindergarten and first grade, contain varied types of manipulatives.

Most multi-media packages are not self-directing. They require teacher planning, introduction, and guidance. Multi-media packages vary widely in quality and should be carefully evaluated.

Microforms. Microforms have information reduced to very small size. Currently there are two main types of "micro" material—microfiche and microfilm. Microfiche is rapidly becoming the most commonly used form in public elementary and middle schools. One microfiche, or card, of about 4 x 6 inches can hold nearly 100 book pages of print and photographs. These may be viewed and read by pupils individually or in small groups using a microfiche reader. Microfiche is less expensive and easier to store than books, and it is predicted that libraries will soon be using this material extensively. Microfilm rolls continue to be available and used, but the fiche format, with greater flexibility, is recommended.

Filmloops. Filmloops, often dubbed "mini-movies" by pupils, are short motion pictures on 8mm film which usually deal with a single concept in a very concise manner. These are usually in color and employ all of the techniques used in 16mm films, such as fade-outs and fade-ins, close-ups, time lapses, slow motion, and animation. Filmloops are encased in plastic containers, and these may be inserted into a filmloop projector and shown on a large screen, a table top screen, or in a carrel. Filmloop viewers with screens approximately 5 x 7 inches may also be used for individual and small-group viewing. The filmloop cartridge safeguards the film, is easy to handle, and eliminates the need for threading or rewinding film. There are now available filmloop viewers with record-and-playback features.

Films. Information and entertainment are provided by 16mm and 8mm motion pictures with sound tracks. Films circumvent reading handicaps of children and can be used successfully to stimulate and develop language at any level. The cognitive level of thinking and opportunities for language development will depend upon the skill of the teacher in using questioning strategies. In addition, sound 8mm filmloops have recently become available. The super 8mm filmloop replaced the standard 8mm filmloop several years ago and at present there are few, if any, producers of the older type film.

Television. Television has become an integral part of American life as a source of entertainment and information. During the 1950s and 1960s television monitors found their way into public school classrooms, and some districts established television production studios. Although both closed-circuit and broadcast television have much educational potential, this potential is yet to be realized in the public schools.

It would be difficult to overlook or deny the enormous impact that television has had upon children. Students in schools today have never known a world without television. As a result, they enter school with greater sophistication and awareness than any preceding generation, and they have become conditioned to receiving information and understandings in the creative, engaging, and entertaining ways available through television.

Television offers great promise for helping the professional educator to more effectively and efficiently provide for diverse student needs, thereby facilitating individualization of instruction.

There are today approximately 250 public television stations throughout the United States, many of which offer an instructional television school service. This resource can be utilized or adapted in any way that a teacher or learning center specialist sees fit. A program can be used as a complete lesson in and of itself or it may be used to supplement, reinforce, and extend previous lessons presented by the teacher. It can be used to stimulate discussions, writing experiences, research projects, or other activities.

In contrast to public broadcasting, closed-circuit television is received within a limited radius, through monitor-receivers which are connected to a special antenna designed to receive the signals. Many schools have the capability of receiving closed-circuit programming from a central studio within their school district, or from a central county or city school district studio. Many schools have their own libraries of videocassette tapes or may borrow such tapes from a central source. These schools use on-site videotape recording and playback equipment to schedule and play desired programs when and as these are needed by students or called for by teachers. In 1968, when this writer was coordinating a junior high school learning center, the videotape recording and playback equipment available used only reel-to-reel videotapes. These were difficult to handle by students and were easily damaged through use. Since that time, the videocassette has been developed, and both recording and playback methods have been greatly simplified. For example, the U-Matic Videocassette is a compact, self-contained, sealed unit that holds a reel of ¾-inch videotape and a take-up reel. The U-Matic cassette can provide up to 60 minutes of color or black and white programming. The videocassette player can be attached to any television set by a single wire to the antenna terminals. The player has proven to be extremely easy to operate and very reliable.

Videocassette technology has been viewed by some experts in the field as likely to become the *essential instrument* of open education rather than an ancillary aid. Videotape recording has been used as a means of developing cognitive and affective learnings through expressive modes. The use of videocassettes in

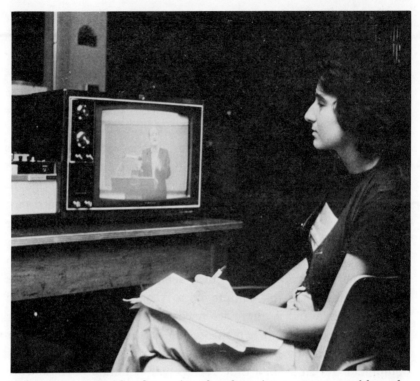

Videocassette technology in the learning center enables the educator at every level to better provide for individual student learning needs and differing rates of learning.

the learning center, with both small monitor-receivers in carrels and larger ones for group viewings, and recording equipment for production, will enable the educator at every level to better provide for individual student learning needs and differing rates of learning.

Teaching machines. Teaching machines may be hand-operated (Field Cyclo-Teacher), automated (Borg Warner System 80), or electronic (computerized programs). The instructional material used in teaching machines is called programmed instruction. This material is presented to the student one frame at a time, visually or audio-visually. The student indicates his response, pushes a lever or button, and then moves on to the answer. There are two patterns of programmed instruction, linear and branching. In the linear program, every pupil follows the same program on a given concept, body of information, or skill regardless of his responses. In a branching pattern, the student has the opportunity to review or receive opportunities for additional explanation or application of material not fully understood or assimilated.

Two examples of teaching machines which are being used increasingly in public schools for development of reading and language arts skills are the Borg Warner System 80 and the Hoffman Reader.

Multi-level kits. Multi-level kits provide material at a variety of reading levels with interest areas varied and/or focusing upon a single concept to accommodate the diversity of learner needs in a group or class. The materials are generally self-selected and the lessons self-directed, self-paced, and self-corrected by the pupil. As the pupils reveal a lack of understanding of a concept or inability to apply a skill, it is the teacher's role to provide instruction, assist pupils with their thinking, and perhaps direct them to other materials.

Study prints. Study prints are large laminated cards containing a picture or scene which may be an imaginative drawing or an actual photograph. The purpose of the study print is generally to stimulate oral and/or written language.

Games. Games are an excellent means of developing and reinforcing skills in an engaging and fun-filled manner. Pupils generally respond positively to games. Games may be commercially purchased or teacher-made. Books containing suggestions for teacher-made games are also available.

Computer assisted instruction (CAI). This is a supplementary tool that helps teachers provide the appropriate instruction and drill and practice necessary for development of specific skills, most generally in mathematics. CAI programs are also readily available in reading and language arts.

CAI combines three elements: (1) curriculum; (2) an instructional strategy or program; and (3) a computer system. The curriculum is generally developed in strands or topics, each focusing upon a specific skill area, such as equations, division, subject-verb agreement, punctuation, literal comprehension, etc. The computer system presents itself to the student and keeps records of each student's work, achievement, and error patterns. The diagnostic information which the teacher receives on a teletype printout pinpoints the specific concepts or processes with which the student is having difficulty.

The student receives CAI lessons through a terminal. The terminals can be either video or teletype terminals. During a CAI session, each student sits at a terminal, which need not be located near the computer itself. The computer recognizes the student by name and by identification number, retrieves from its memory bank the student's place in each area of curriculum, and then begins to present the appropriate new material to the student. When the computer presents a question to the student, the student answers by spelling out a word or choosing a numbered answer choice. Approximately 15 to 60 seconds is allowed for a student to respond before the correct answer is provided by the computer. The allowable response time may be preset by the teacher.

The exchange of information between the student and the computer is rapid and very concentrated, with a CAI session usually lasting no more than ten minutes. In addition to providing the student with a high degree of success, it provides immediate feedback of correct and incorrect responses.

In addition to CAI, computers may be used in the computer-managed instruction (CMI) mode, wherein the computer coordinates and prescribes learning activities but does not actually engage in the instructional dialogue itself. As a part of the CMI framework, the computer may be used to provide lists of learning resources and units for both teachers and students.

Realia. Realia are real objects such as artifacts, specimens, collections, models, mock-ups, and dioramas. These are particu-

Realia are real objects, such as artifacts, specimens, collections, mock-ups, and dioramas. These fourth-graders are intrigued by a trunk of authentic African artifacts in the learning center.

larly valuable in a language experience approach to stimulate language through direct sensory experiences. These materials are not intended to be self-directing. Questioning strategies are essential in verbal language interplay. Children might be asked to describe, list, identify, compare, name, classify, explain the uses of, label, analyze, organize by categorizing, relate, and interpret in relation to realia. These types of activities are no less valuable at the secondary and college levels. In addition, pupils may develop their own models, mock-ups, dioramas, specimens, and collections as culminating projects for units of study.

Chapter Summary

The learning center is a complex of areas the design for which emanates from certain underlying beliefs about how children learn and the nature of knowledge. The areas in the complex are designed so as to facilitate development of the life-relevant process and instrumental skills; and, in so doing, the center makes provision for the accommodation of diverse learning styles and the implementation of a process approach to individualization of instruction. The areas in the Basic Learning Center Complex include a diagnostic and evaluation center, a prescriptive programming and materials and module development center, an instrumental skills development center, small conference rooms, seminar rooms, a library-media resource center, a graphic arts center including photography and television studios, and a large-group presentation area. The Extended Learning Center Complex includes, in addition, a performing arts center, a visual arts center, and a science and invention laboratory. A wide range of audio-visual media materials, multi-media kits, games, manipulatives, and realia are available in the Basic Learning Center Complex.

6.
The Learning Center and the School or College Staff

The quality of the services provided by the learning center and the extent to which pupils and teachers take advantage of these services will depend in large measure on the understandings, skills, and abilities of both the learning center staff and the rest of the school's professional personnel. In addition, socio-political factors may enter the picture. These may be related to forms of competition for professional status, unfounded threats to job security that may be felt, coolness toward a colleague who has been elevated to a new position from the ranks, changes in titles, or simply resistance to administrative recommendations or plans for change. In some instances, power struggles that may be on-going and operating beneath the surface between cliques or special interest groups, or between the administration and a teacher union or teacher association, can have an effect upon the implementation of the learning center's services.

The functioning of a learning center requires not only differentiation of roles but also cooperative planning and teamwork—perhaps more than with any other permanent venture or innovative project that a school will undertake. All involved must feel a sense of commitment to the learning center concept as an approach for better meeting the needs of students.

The functioning of a learning center requires cooperative team-work and a sense of commitment to the concept as an approach for better meeting the individual needs of students.

Problems with Traditional
Patterns of Staffing

Public Schools

Traditionally, the self-contained classroom, the individual teacher, and a group of 20 to 35 pupils have been the units of organization for schools. The classroom teacher in this setting has been expected to be a specialist in a spectrum of educational areas, such as diagnosis of learner needs, curriculum design, instruction and instructional resources, classroom management, and evaluation. Simultaneously, he or she has been expected to deal equally well with the emotional, social, and academic problems and needs of each pupil.

This entire system for organizing schools and deploying human resources has been predicated on a fallacious egalitarianism which presumes that all teachers have the same talents, aptitudes, interests, abilities, intellects, and degrees of physical and emotional stamina, and that these are equally exhibited at every stage of each teacher's professional career. This false premise has effectively subverted many worthy educational innovations directed toward furthering the concept of individualization of instruction.

College Level

Similarly, at the college level, it has been presumed that knowledge may be compartmentalized into separate disciplines to facilitate learning, and that the most effective, if not the only, way of transmitting this knowledge to students is through a lecture which is delivered to an entire group at the same time—with the assumption that interest in and level of readiness for the material is the same for all students. The lecturer may not even know the names of the students to whom the lecture has been delivered. More probably, he or she will know nothing of the individual interests, aspirations, experiential backgrounds, motivations for taking the course, or other factors impinging upon the learning of individual students even after several months of weekly sessions with them.

Rarely do students even at this level influence the design of curriculum, course objectives, methods of achieving the objectives, or pupil evaluation procedures. Student evaluation is generally limited to a research paper or to written objective or essay-type tests.

Certainly, some colleges are making strides toward greater focus on individual student needs and greater involvement of students in the decision-making affecting their own learning. Colleges where open enrollment policies have been implemented have provided some forms of compensatory education, such as special courses and labs to improve basic reading, writing, and mathematics skills.

However, much more needs to be done to attempt to match teaching styles with learning styles, to personalize higher education; and to involve students in the formulation of course objectives, selection of strategies for achieving the course objectives, and development of more appropriate techniques for student evaluation.

Rationale for Differentiated
Plan of Staffing

Since the first attempt in the 1960s to implement differentiated staffing, at Temple City Unified School District in California, interest in the idea has grown tremendously. There have been many reasons for this growth. First, financial crises in the schools have given impetus to criticism of the traditional single salary schedule, which pays teachers equally, regardless of the difficulty of the task or scope of responsibility. There is also the growing recognition, previously discussed, that individual teachers simply cannot adequately perform all the necessary tasks demanded of them. Many new curricular and organizational reforms call for different teacher competencies as well as for upgraded skills and practices among the professional staff. Finally, the financial problems faced by all educational agencies today, both public and private, call for new ways of allocating resources. Differentiated staffing emphasizes that compensation for services should be tied to the level of difficulty of the task and expertise needed for the performance.

The Model Staffing Pattern

New patterns of organization of human resources are

inherent in the learning center concept. This chapter will suggest a model staffing pattern consistent with the learning center concept as it has been developed.

The model developed in this chapter should be viewed as just that, a model. Most schools and school districts developing learning centers will be working with established staffs and with budgetary limitations. It is suggested that movement toward an ideal staffing pattern be gradual. In smaller schools, it may be possible for one professional to fill dual roles. In larger institutions, it may be necessary for some of the designated specialists to be assisted and supported by aides, graduate assistants, and paraprofessionals.

As the professionals are trained and acquire expertise in performing their respective specialized roles, these roles will gradually be handled more efficiently and skillfully. As a result, the need may arise for greater differentiation or for some consolidation according to demonstrated talents and skills. Openness and flexibility will allow changes and modifications in staffing. This will facilitate movement toward a staffing pattern that will ultimately capitalize upon the talents, abilities, and skills of each member of the professional staff, so as to better meet the needs of the school's pupil population.

Rationale for the Model
Staffing Pattern

The learning center concept is based upon a process approach to individualization of instruction. Accordingly, the staffing pattern should reflect a logical, consistent, and functional correspondence between the process tasks (i.e., assessment, diagnosis, prescription, interaction, evaluation, reassessment/follow-up/ recycling) and the professional roles. Figure 6, *Model Staffing Pattern for the Learning Center*, suggests such a staffing pattern. This chart is followed by Table 3, *Task-Role Descriptors for the Learning Center*, which describes the tasks to be performed in conjunction with implementation of a process approach to

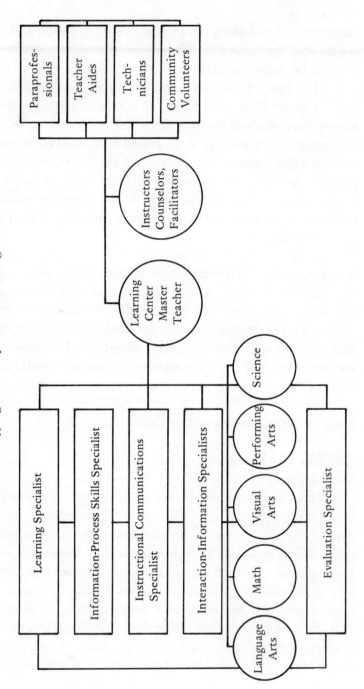

Figure 6

Model Staffing Pattern for the Learning Center

122

Table 3

*Task-Role Descriptors for the
Learning Center*

Professional Role	Function
Learning Specialist	Assessment-diagnosis of learner needs; consultant and counselor on the development of the self-processes, career education.
Information-Process Skills Specialist	Translates diagnostic statements about pupil into viable teaching-learning strategies; prescriptive programming; curriculum design; teaching-learning module construction; instructional materials selection and design in cooperation with the Instructional Communications Specialist; integration of curriculum areas, process skills, and career education.
Instructional Communications Specialist	Consultant and instructor in utilization of print and non-print media for the development of the process skills and for information retrieval; designs and develops non-print media for instructional uses, and instructs teachers and pupils in the development of non-print media in conjunction with learning-teaching activities and projects; coordinates the schedule and operation of the Library-Media Center working in close cooperation with the Instrumental Skills Development Specialists and the Learning Center Master Teacher.
Interaction-Information Specialists	Instruct and assist pupils with activities and projects involving the various areas in which each is a specialist; focus upon development of process skills through respective specialty areas following guidelines of the Information-Process Skills Specialist set forth in teaching-learning modules.

Table 3

(Continued)

Professional Role	Function
Evaluation Specialist	Conducts research and evaluation of specific teaching-learning strategies and of educational innovations; conducts systems analysis and process evaluations to identify weaknesses in the teaching-learning system and makes recommendations for change; conducts annual and longitudinal product evaluations to measure the overall success of the instructional program in satisfying the differentiated needs of the pupil population.
Master Teacher	Assists and trains teachers in techniques of individualization of instruction, and in implementation of the teaching-learning strategies included in the modules developed by the Information-Process Skills Specialist; assists in organization for independent study and scheduling of the Learning Center Complex; does demonstration teaching; trains teachers in organization and management techniques for individualization of instruction; encourages and supports teachers as they try new instructional techniques.
Instructors, Counselors, Learning Facilitators	Provide instruction to pupils; conduct individual pupil-teacher conferences; monitor the interaction process, identifying problems and keeping track of individual progress; counsel pupils; assist Information-Process Skills Specialist; provide encouragement and praise to pupils; assist pupils in development of social interactive skills; tutor pupils; responsible for development of the life-relevant process skills and instrumental skills through the humanities and the social sciences.

Table 3

(Continued)

Professional Role	Function
Paraprofessionals	Assist with instruction of pupils as they work in the various areas of the Learning Center Complex.
Teacher Aides	Assist Specialists with clerical tasks and other non-instructional tasks such as materials preparation; assist pupils with use of equipment and in locating materials in various areas of the Learning Center Complex.
Technicians	Maintain audio-visual equipment; assist in photography studio; duplicate audio- and video-tapes; instruct in use of video equipment.
Volunteers	Assist pupils in the Learning Center Complex under the direction and supervision of the specialist in charge of the area in which the volunteer is working.

individualization of instruction through the learning center. Guidelines are provided for identifying those aptitudes, personal qualities, and types of training required by each of the specialists described in Table 3. The types of training recommended have been designed to develop those skills that each of the respective specialists will require to successfully function in his or her job. It is recommended that schools develop their own performance goals, modifying and adapting those suggested here to meet their unique needs.

The Learning Specialist

The Learning Specialist is a discerning individual with highly developed organizational and analytic thinking skills. He or she is adept at analysis and interpretation of behavior. In an observational or interview situation, the Learning Specialist is alert to subtleties of gesture, facial expression, voice, verbal language, and body language. An ability to organize divergent types of data and to order these and perceive patterns and configurations is essential. The Learning Specialist is a flexible person, open to new data inputs and ready to modify or change previously made judgments as new information about the student becomes available. This is an empathic person with a desire to help each individual to gain increasing self-awareness and to develop self-actualizing behaviors.

Performance goals. The Learning Specialist will be able to do the following:

1. Organize and interpret data relating to the development and style of learning of the individual student.

2. Make intuitive judgments based upon the available data regarding the student's readiness for the next stage of learning, possible impediments to learning, and types of manipulation of the learning environment that might facilitate learning.

3. Conduct an interview effectively by establishing rapport with the student, parent, or teacher; conveying acceptance, empathy, and positive regard through words, tone, manner, and gesture; eliciting essential information both through verbal exchange and observations.

4. Administer and interpret diverse instruments of assessment, such as tests, surveys, formal observational techniques, anecdotal reports, and inventories.

5. Employ counseling techniques in working with students and parents.

6. Be familiar with instruments and techniques for assessing the status of the student with respect to the life-relevant process and instrumental skills.

7. Be familiar with instruments and techniques for assessing learning style.

8. Keep organized notes and records.

9. Write clear, concise, well-organized diagnostic reports with recommendations.

10. Use the computer terminal to store and retrieve data relating to student needs and developmental patterns.

11. Employ values clarification techniques effectively with students and teachers.

12. Conduct group counseling.

13. Work cooperatively as a member of a team comprised of other competent specialists.

14. Be flexible, seek alternative solutions to problems, and take risks associated with innovation and change.

15. Accept and value individual differences among students and teachers.

16. Continuously seek new and better ways of doing things.

General educational background. The Learning Specialist will possess the following general educational background:

1. Child growth and development (all stages).

2. Child psychology, preadolescent, and adolescent psychology.

3. Philosophy of open education.

4. Principles and practices of instruction with focus on a process approach to individualization of instruction.

5. Educational methods and practicum focusing on the instrumental and process skills.

6. Psychological foundations of learning, cognition, reading, and language development.

7. Systems design and systems engineering in education.

8. Computer technology for information retrieval in education.

Specialized training and educational background. The Learning Specialist will possess in-depth training and educational background in the following:

1. Test and measurement techniques.

2. Diagnosis and treatment of learning disabilities and learning disorders of all types, including but not limited to those in reading, language, mathematics, and speech.

3. Observational and interviewing techniques.

4. Identification of learning style.

5. Counseling techniques, both individual and group.

6. Group dynamics and sensitivity training.

7. Human relations and personnel management.

8. Early childhood education.

9. Career education and values clarification techniques.

10. Behavior modification techniques.

Information-Process
Skills Specialist

The Information-Process Skills Specialist is a highly creative individual with a keen sense of the types of activities and experiences that will stimulate student interest and facilitate learning at each stage of development. This is a person who recognizes and is responsive to the differences as well as the commonalities among pupils at a given stage of development. This is also a well organized, systematic, and inventive person who actively seeks out and discerns relationships and patterns in the separate instructional areas and seeks ways of integrating experiences to achieve multiple ends. He or she is a pragmatic yet imaginative individual with a deep interest and involvement in all of the broad aspects of curriculum and instruction and in the diverse ways of achieving specific learning objectives. He or she is flexible, welcomes change and new ways of doing things, and is innovative and willing to experiment.

Performance goals. The Information-Process Skills Specialist will be able to do the following:

1. Translate diagnostic statements about an individual pupil into viable teaching-learning strategies.

2. Design and develop teaching-learning modules that integrate curriculum areas and the process and instrumental skills, have a broad career education base, and are sufficiently flexible to accommodate various learning styles.

3. Design and develop a system, content, and structure for independent study.

4. Recommend specific instructional resources, activities, and experiences to meet individual and group needs in achieving a specified learning objective or set of learning objectives.

5. Design instructional print and non-print media materials to meet specific teaching-learning needs.

6. Preview and select instructional resources in cooperation with the Instructional Communications Specialist and the Master Teacher.

7. Work cooperatively with other members of a team of highly competent specialists.

8. Confer with pupils regarding their experiences with independent study designs and with particular instructional resources; elicit opinions and recommendations from pupils; and use pupils to assist in the design and/or production of instructional resources and teaching-learning modules.

9. Work in close cooperation with the Evaluation Specialist in the evaluation of innovations and specific teaching-learning strategics, and make change, modification, or expansion decisions based upon these evaluations.

General educational background. The general educational background of the Information-Process Skills Specialist is similar to that of the Learning Specialist.

Specialized training and educational background. The Information-Process Skills Specialist is specially trained and educated in the following areas:

1. Broad and specialized areas of curriculum, curriculum design, and instruction.

2. Design of teaching-learning modules; taxonomies of behavioral objectives; techniques for modifying the learning environment to accommodate individual learning styles.

3. Cognition; developing cognitive levels through appropriate questioning strategies.

4. Career education and values clarification techniques; development of the self-processes.

5. Treatment of learning disabilities and learning disorders of all types.

6. Techniques for developing the process skills at each stage of the student's development.

7. Curriculum and instruction for the gifted child.

8. Curriculum and instruction for the bilingual student.

9. Curriculum and instruction for the slow learner.

10. Curriculum and instruction for the educable mentally retarded.

11. Early childhood education; theories of learning at each of the respective developmental levels, including childhood, preadolescent, adolescent, and the young adult.

12. Organizing for independent learning; resources for independent learning at each stage of student development.

13. Organizing for small-group learning; techniques for small-group learning.

14. Instructional resources and equipment, print and non-print, and their educational application; audio-visual equipment and their educational applications.

15. Techniques for developing the instrumental skills at every stage of learner development.

16. Behavior modification techniques.

17. Operation of learning centers.

Instructional Communications Specialist

This is an open, flexible, accepting person who genuinely enjoys helping both pupils and teachers in making the fullest utilization of print and non-print media for teaching-learning purposes. This is a well-organized individual who understands systems design and how to implement it to achieve smooth operation of the Library-Media Center and its satellite areas. The Instructional Communications Specialist encourages inquiry and discovery through the use of print and non-print media. This is an individual with an appreciation and love of literature and a desire to share and stimulate similar feelings in children. Because the Instructional Communications Specialist works so closely and directly with other professionals and children, good human relations skills are essential. This is an adaptive person who is discerning with respect to selection of new instructional resources and who can do long-range planning and work cooperatively with the Learning Center Master Teacher and the Information-Process Skills Specialist.

Performance goals. The Instructional Communications Specialist is able to do the following:

1. Organize and maintain the Library-Media Center.

2. Train and supervise teacher aides and/or paraprofessionals to perform clerical tasks and to assist pupils in the Library-Media Center.

3. Use puppetry, creative dramatics, dramatic readings, and non-print media to stimulate pupil interest in and response to literature and poetry.

4. Counsel, assist, and guide pupils as they work in the Library-Media Center toward developing and applying inquiry skills, analytic thinking skills, social interactive skills, and language arts skills.

5. Provide instruction in information retrieval, both print and non-print, and research and inquiry skills.

6. Serve as a consultant to teachers in the uses of the print and non-print media for instruction, for techniques to develop

inquiry and analytic thinking skills, and for scheduling projects to be undertaken by pupils in the Library-Media Center.

7. Assist pupils with production of media materials in conjunction with projects.

8. Establish criteria for selection of media materials for the Library-Media Center.

9. Develop a circulation and loan system of print and non-print media materials and audio-visual equipment.

General educational background. The Instructional Communications Specialist has the same general training as the Learning Specialist.

Specialized training and educational background. The Instructional Communications Specialist is additionally trained and educated in the following:

1. Library science; types and uses of non-print and print media; instructional communications.

2. Reading and language arts instruction, literature.

3. Graphic arts including photography and television technology.

4. Questioning strategies for developing various levels of cognitive ability; teaching of inquiry skills, library research skills, and information retrieval skills.

5. Human relations, group dynamics, and small-group learning techniques.

6. Individual counseling techniques; conferencing.

Interaction-Information Specialists

The Interaction-Information Specialists are highly creative, flexible, and innovative individuals who are sensitive and responsive to the needs, problems, and interests of children and adolescents, and desirous of helping them to develop their innate potentialities through the various media in which each of these professionals is a specialist. The number of Interaction-Information Specialists will vary according to the size and budget of the school; however, there should be at least five such specialists, with each one of the five having a proficiency in a different one of the following special areas:

1.   Reading and language arts.
2.   Mathematics.
3.   Visual arts and visual literacy.
4.   Performing arts.
5.   Science and invention.

Where budget permits, there would be on staff several additional specialists as follows:

1.   Visual—Graphic Arts.
     a.   Painting, drawing, graphic processes of printing and commercial art
     b.   Photography and commercial art
     c.   Video graphics
2.   Visual—Plastic Arts.
     a.   Architecture, interior design, landscape, dress, costume and theater design, sculpture
     b.   Crafts—ceramics, jewelry, leatherwork, weaving, woodwork
3.   Performing Arts—Music.
     a.   Vocal music
     b.   Instrumental music
4.   Performing Arts—Drama and Theater: Dramatics, Puppetry, Mime, Dramatic Poetry Readings.
5.   Performing Arts—Dance.

The Interaction-Information Specialists in the Visual and Performing Arts and Sciences are aware of the ways in which the instrumental skills may be integrated with their respective specialties; they work in close cooperation and plan regularly with the Instrumental Skills Specialists to achieve this integration. Each of these specialists is keenly aware of the ways in which his/her specialty can be used by the child to interpret his or her experiences in highly personal terms and develop expressions which are uniquely his or her own. In addition, the Interaction-Information Specialists are familiar with the art forms as means of training perception and judgment.

Performance goals. Interaction-Information Specialists are able to do the following:

1. Serve as consultants on techniques for integrating their specialty areas with the other curriculum areas and with the instrumental and process skills.

2. Work with pupils toward the development of the process and instrumental skills through their respective specialty areas.

3. Serve as consultants in curriculum and module construction and design.

4. Foster in pupils positive attitudes toward themselves and toward the specialty areas.

5. Integrate the specialty area with career education objectives as designed in the teaching-learning modules.

6. The reading-language arts specialist should, in addition, be able to:

a. Design and guide the implementation of a school-wide remedial, corrective, and developmental reading and language arts program.

b. Organize and coordinate the instrumental skills development center's program and services.

c. Instruct teachers in the use of the print and non-print media for development of reading and language arts skills.

d. Instruct teachers, and organize and coordinate pupil projects in the use of audio-visual equipment and techniques for the development of expressive language skills.

e. Organize, develop, and serve as a consultant for the school-wide literature program.

f. Work in close cooperation with the Instructional Communications Specialist and Information-Process Skills Specialist in curriculum design, module construction, preparation of instructional resources, and selection of commercially prepared instructional resources.

g. Work in close cooperation with the Learning Specialist, who also is trained in reading and in identification of individual learner needs.

h. Work in close cooperation with the Learning Center Master Teacher in planning demonstration lessons and implementing teaching-learning modules.

i. Instruct pupils having serious reading deficits and develop special learning center programs for them in cooperation with the Learning Center Master Teacher and classroom teachers.

j. Serve as a consultant on the selection of appropriate reading-testing instruments.

General educational background. The general educational background of the Interaction-Information Specialists is similar to that of the Learning Specialist.

Specialized training and educational background. In addition, the Interaction-Information Specialists have specialized training as follows:

1. Intensive training in their respective specialty areas.

2. Techniques for developing reading, language arts, mathematics, and visual literacy skills through the visual and performing arts and sciences.

3. Techniques for working with children having various types of learning disabilities and special educational needs.

4. Techniques for developing the process skills through the visual and performing arts and the sciences.

5. Techniques for integrating the arts and humanities with the social sciences and toward development of the process and instrumental skills.

6. Group dynamics and group processes; sensitivity workshops; and individual counseling techniques.

7. Intensive training in individualization of instruction.

8. Instructional resources and equipment appropriate for instruction in the respective specialty areas.

Evaluation Specialist

The Evaluation Specialist is a well-organized individual skilled in systems design and research techniques and possessing well developed analytic thinking skills. He or she is proficient in dealing with mathematics and mathematical analysis and in representing statistical data graphically. This specialist has interpretive abilities and is skillful in quantifying diverse types of data for statistical analysis.

Performance goals. The Evaluation Specialist is able to do the following:

1. Organize and implement a school-wide testing program.
2. Develop designs for evaluation.
3. Serve as a consultant and expert on evaluation.
4. Review educational research and make recommendations for innovations and changes.
5. Conduct on-site educational research and make recommendations to modify, change, expand, or discontinue a practice or teaching-learning strategy.
6. Conduct systems analysis, and develop means to increase the efficiency of the educational system and the teaching-learning process.
7. Design computer programs to facilitate various aspects of the educative process and to serve as environmental support for the various Specialists in performing their functions.
8. Write evaluation reports and summary critiques of specific areas of educational literature researched.
9. Make recommendations to the Learning Specialist and to the Interaction-Information Specialist based upon evaluation and research.

General educational background. The Evaluation Specialist has the same basic training as the other Specialists with certain additional specialized training.

Specialized training and educational background. The Evaluation Specialist possesses specialized training in the following broad areas:

1. Testing and measurement.
2. Research and evaluation design principles, procedures, and techniques.

3. Critiquing of research designs and reports.

4. Statistics and statistical analysis techniques.

5. Systems design and systems engineering as applied to education.

6. Computer technology in education.

7. Report-writing techniques.

8. Educational philosophy, principles and practices; techniques for evaluation of individualized instruction and open education practices.

9. Implementing educational innovations.

10. Group processes, group dynamics.

11. Behavior modification techniques.

Master Teacher

The Learning Center Master Teacher is an expert in the implementation of the strategies included in the teaching-learning modules designed by the Information-Process Skills Specialist. A highly creative, flexible individual, the Master Teacher is able to spontaneously adapt strategies, techniques, and environment to facilitate learning for the individual pupil. The Master Teacher is an open, accepting person who reaches out to and encourages and supports teachers and pupils as they experiment with new teaching-learning techniques and behaviors. This is a person who is willing to take risks, to innovate, and to inspire confidence and trust in others as they try new and unproven instructional methods. The Master Teacher is a self-confident, independent person skilled in human relations and group processes. He or she is well-organized but not routinized. An adaptive person, the Master Teacher accepts and welcomes differences in teachers as well as in pupils and helps both to grow and develop skills in ways and at rates that are appropriate for them individually. The Master Teacher is expert in the utilization of all types of instructional resources and equipment to facilitate learning and is in constant and close touch with his or her environment and with local, national, and international developments in politics, society,

*The Learning Center Master Teacher is an expert in the imple-
mentation of the strategies included in teaching-learning modules.
He or she is skilled in adapting these strategies and the
environment to facilitate learning for the individual pupil.*

economics, and science. He or she has a good appreciation for the
visual and performing arts and their value for providing a vehicle
for creative and expressive behavior.

Performance goals. The Master Teacher is able to:

1. Implement the teaching-learning strategies included in
the teaching-learning modules, making on-the-spot modifications
and adaptations to accommodate immediate learner needs or
interests not previously taken into account and to integrate
current events and daily occurrences into learning activities.

2. Organize the environment for independent learning.

3. Help students move toward independence in learning.

4. Counsel, praise, encourage, challenge, and motivate students to learn.

5. Conduct demonstration teaching sessions.

6. Inspire and upgrade the teaching skills and techniques of instructors and classroom teachers.

7. Take risks associated with innovation and change, and encourage teachers and instructors to take similar risks.

8. Supervise and coordinate the schedule of the learning center complex.

9. Utilize diverse print and non-print media materials, equipment, and all facets of the environment to facilitate learning.

10. Assign and supervise the work of instructors, teacher aides, paraprofessionals, and volunteers who work in the learning center with students.

11. Be responsible for the decor and attractiveness of the learning center.

12. Employ effectively values clarification techniques and questioning strategies at the various cognitive levels and demonstrate these to teachers and instructors.

13. Establish positive rapport with students and teachers or instructors.

14. Empathize with students in the age groups using the learning center.

15. Accept and value individual differences among students and teachers.

16. Employ effectively small-group learning techniques and demonstrate these to teachers, instructors, and paraprofessionals.

17. Participate in all decision-making concerning the services, schedule, and functioning of the learning center.

18. Work cooperatively as a member of a team comprised of other competent and highly skilled specialists.

General educational background. The Master Teacher has the same general educational background as the Learning Specialist with the exception that the Master Teacher has, in addition, a broad foundation in the liberal arts, the natural sciences, and the visual and performing arts. The Master Teacher would not require the same type of training in systems design and systems engineering as would the Learning Specialist.

Specialized training and educational background. The Master Teacher has the following specialized training:

1. Techniques for developing the process and instrumental skills at each stage of student development.

2. Techniques, principles, and practices for instructing pupils with special educational needs. This would include the learning disabled, bilingual, reading disabled, students with language disorders and disorders in perception and/or cognitive processing of stimuli, the slow learner, the gifted and talented, and pupils with any other types of special educational needs or handicapping conditions.

3. Sociology and psychology.

4. Group processes, group counseling, personnel management, and human relations skills; techniques for small-group learning.

5. Questioning strategies and values clarification techniques.

6. Organization and development of teaching-learning modules; implementation of such modules.

7. Organizational techniques for independent learning; management of independent learning.

8. Instructional uses of the media and all facets of instructional communications.

9. Programmed learning; teaching machines; computer-assisted instruction.

10. Individual counseling and conferencing techniques.

11. Use of computer-based resource units and teaching-learning modules.

12. Techniques for implementing open education practices.

13. Techniques for teaching the process and instrumental skills and for integrating curriculum areas.

Making the Transition from Traditional
Staffing Patterns and Role Definitions

To initiate the new staffing pattern, it is suggested that those persons on the existing professional staff be identified who possess the aptitudes, talents, and interests required to assume one of the new roles. These individuals should then be trained for their new positions. Provision will need to be made for conducting team meetings of specialists so that their respective skills might be cooperatively brought to bear upon the implementation of the process approach to individualization of instruction.

The following section describes some common existing staff positions that might be used as points of departure for development of the new specialist roles.

The Reading Consultant

The well-trained reading consultant, who might possess additional foundations in counseling techniques and a broad background in both psychology and the language arts, most closely approximates today the role and training of the Learning Specialist. Trained in diagnostic-prescriptive techniques, learning disabilities, testing and measurement, consultative techniques, and in developmental patterns of learning, the reading consultant may be trained to assume the role and responsibilities of the Learning Specialist. (The reading consultant is distinguished here from the reading teacher, whose experience is primarily with small groups of remedial reading cases and whose training may be somewhat less extensive than that of the consultant.)

The Curriculum Specialist:
Language Arts

Curriculum specialists and directors of instruction with specialized training and experience in the communication skills of reading, writing, speaking, listening, and visual literacy can most readily be trained to become designers of prescriptive strategies or prescriptive programming specialists. It is through the communication skills that teaching and learning occur. For this reason, the curriculum specialist who will assume the new role should have extensive training and ability in this area.

The Library-Media Specialist

The trained and qualified Library-Media Specialist most closely approximates the role of Instructional Communications Specialist. There exist problems, though, with existing approaches and practices related to the role of Library-Media Specialist that might impede a smooth transition to the newer position. Some Library-Media Specialists are this in name only. Trained as librarians, some have had only a few courses in the media and many are, in fact, afraid of audio-visual equipment. Some lack the interest, talent, or background necessary for designing non-print media materials for instructional uses.

The traditional role of the librarian as a keeper of books changed when the new media arrived on the educational scene; however, in some instances, those holding these positions failed to change. Today, the demands of the role are changing further, becoming even more diversified and requiring greater creativity and talent. The librarian will require retraining and much exposure to some of the premises of open education and the learning center approach.

In addition, administrators will need to determine whether they are providing adequate clerical assistance for their library-media specialists, and whether or not the scheduling and use of library-media center facilities are the most advantageous ones available to students and teachers.

Special Teachers

Interaction-Information Specialists could be recruited and trained from among the most creative, talented, and effective special teachers of music, visual arts, graphic arts and sculpture, dramatics, dance, handicrafts, mathematics, science, and the humanities. These special teachers would work closely with the other specialists to coordinate and integrate the delivery of the activities and approaches included in the design of the teaching-learning modules to meet individual needs of pupils. They would rarely function in isolation of one another, and the focus of their instruction would be upon the development of the life-relevant process and instrumental skills and appreciations.

Classroom Teachers

From among the ranks of classroom teachers, or perhaps from among the special teachers, a Master Teacher or someone having the potential to become a Master Teacher may be found. Similarly, other remaining positions would be filled from the teacher ranks.

Many of the photographs contained in this book were taken by an elementary school music teacher who is a photographer as well. This teacher voluntarily conducts small-group sessions for intermediate students in the learning center, teaching them about the workings of various types of cameras available in the center and developing visual literacy and language arts skills through subsequent photography projects in which the students engage.

Multi-Disciplinary Teaching Teams
and the Learning Center
at the Secondary Levels

Learning centers may serve as the focal point for the functioning of multi-disciplinary teaching teams at the secondary levels and for training the members of these teams in the elements of individualization of instruction. Offering a broad range of print and non-print media materials, programmed instruction, and a staff of specialists (which during the transitional stages may include the Reading Consultant, the Library-Media Specialist, and the Learning Center Director/Master Teacher) as well as teacher aides and volunteers, broader options are afforded team members for identifying and providing for individual student needs.

In addition, through the guidance and assistance of the learning center specialists, team members can begin organizing the print and non-print media and programmed materials into integrated teaching-learning modules. The teams may also begin designing contracts that will enable them to provide forms of compensatory education for students with significant reading deficits and for bilingual students; offer remediation in basic skills; and provide challenging independent and small-group learning experiences for all students, capitalizing upon the availability of supportive learning center personnel and the vast array of stimulating materials and equipment.

These teams, which may be comprised of a science teacher, a mathematics teacher, a social studies teacher, and an English teacher, would meet daily for approximately 50 minutes. The learning center director and/or the reading consultant would be present at these meetings to offer suggestions and provide guidance and training in all facets of individualization of instruction and utilization of the learning center. The library-media specialist would assist in the development of the teaching-learning modules and contracts.

Each multi-disciplinary team would be responsible for the learning of approximately 125-150 pupils. In effect, the reading consultant would become the learning specialist for these pupils. The guidance counselor would participate in team meetings as required to assist with identification of student needs, and to provide inputs on values clarification techniques, career education, development of the self-process skills, and approaches to conferencing and counseling. It is presumed, of course, that the competent counselor is well versed in these areas as well as in group processes and, thus, can help team members to move toward functioning as a cohesive, cooperative unit. Where the reading consultant happens to be a trained counselor as well, the services of the guidance counselor would not have to be relied upon to the same extent.

Multi-disciplinary teaching teams are perhaps one of the most

The physical design of a learning center complex should make provision for accommodating various types of activities appropriate to the age groups of the students to be served. These fourth grade puppeteers delight first graders with their original rendition of the "Three Billy Goats Gruff."

effective approaches to breaking down the compartmentalization of subject matter at the secondary levels and shifting the focus from content to individual student needs in relation to the life-relevant process skills and in focusing upon diverse styles of learning. Learning centers serve a vital function in facilitating these shifts in emphasis.

Teacher-Pupil Ratios
in the Learning Center

The title of this section is, in fact, a misnomer; however, parents and educators have become so conditioned to think in these terms, that the title was used here to focus upon what is generally a real concern. In the learning center, students are provided with various types of assistance according to need and learning objectives by members of the center's staff who possess various types of training and expertise. If a student needs a type of assistance that requires merely the expertise and training of a teacher aide, such as in locating and using materials and equipment, then that assistance is provided by the aide. On the other hand, if a student requires the expertise of a professional educator, as is the case with small-group instruction and conferencing, then that instruction is provided by the professional educator. It is wasteful of time, money, and the expertise of professional educators to have them engaged in activities which can be carried out as effectively by a teacher aide, a volunteer, or even a student.

Ratios and Maturity
Levels of Students

The amount and types of assistance required by students in the learning center are generally functions of their maturity levels and the types of activities in which they are likely to be engaged. The amount of previous training and experience students have had with the various forms of independent study and small-group learning is also significant in determining the amount of assistance that they will require in the learning center.

Primary levels. At the primary levels (grades K-3), students will require much more assistance and guidance from learning center personnel than at any other level. At these levels, learning how to work cooperatively in a small group, listening to others, expressing one's own ideas, and learning to work independently

The ratio of learning center personnel to students will vary according to the numbers of students engaged in a particular type of activity at any one time. Pictured is a "sharing period" during which the teacher reads aloud pupil responses to a media experience aimed at stimulating creative writing.

are important objectives. Patience, praise, and encouragement on the part of learning center personnel are the key words.

Much of the learning at these levels will be exploratory, followed by discussion and sharing with adults in the center and with peers. Periods of independent individual learning will be of shorter duration than at the upper elementary and secondary levels. First- and second-graders will be less likely to be involved in formal research projects and more likely to be involved in exploration with manipulatives and games.

It is suggested that at the primary levels, the ratio of adults, including aides and volunteers, to children be approximately one adult for every six children. At least one of these adults should be a professional educator who is present in the center with 30 children. If the center is large enough to permit greater numbers of children to use it simultaneously, then this ratio would still be maintained.

Intermediate and middle grades. Students in grades four through eight are generally capable of working independently, individually, and in pairs and small groups for periods of longer duration than primary youngsters. There will, of course, be exceptions where emotional problems and/or maturational lags might interfere with a student's ability to focus on a task for any significant length of time or cause him or her to interfere with the learning of other students. In these cases, an aide may be assigned to closely monitor the independent learning of such a student, reducing the ratio of children to aides to better handle such problems. In addition, teacher-guided small-group learning may be more frequent for these children.

In any case, all pupils need to be prepared for independent learning and oriented to procedures and standards of behavior in the learning center. (This will be discussed further in the next section of this chapter.) When students are embarking upon a new project or activity that requires the use of resources or equipment with which they have had little or no prior experience, time should be scheduled for them to receive instruction or guidance from a member of the learning center staff so that they might then proceed with their work.

As a rule, the ratio of learning center personnel to students in the intermediate and middle grades will depend upon the numbers of students that will be engaged in a particular type of activity at any one time. Table 4 suggests guidelines for establishing such ratios according to the type of activity in which students might be engaged. These guidelines are apt to vary according to the size of the learning center, the special needs of pupils, previous experi-

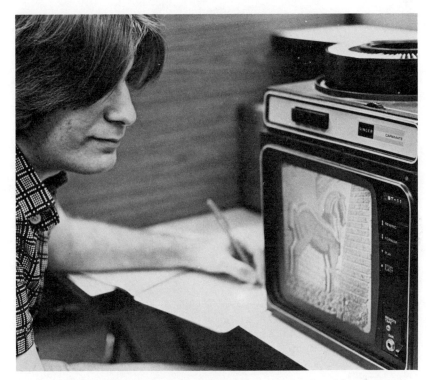

At the high school and college levels, students should require less direction in working independently in the learning center.

ence of the students with independent learning and with the learning center, the qualifications and training of the teacher aides, and the availablity of reliable and capable volunteers. In such centers, the options available to the professional educator for serving children are greatly increased.

High school level. At the high school level, students should require less direction in working independently in the learning center, but they still need the personalization of instruction that results from individual diagnosis of abilities and individual teacher-pupil conferencing. Whereas one professional educator was required in the learning center for every 60 pupils engaged in research or programmed learning at the intermediate and middle

Table 4

Learning Center Staff-Pupil Ratios:
Intermediate and Middle Grades

Type Activity	Ratio of Prof. Educ. to Pupils	Ratio of Paraprof. to Pupils*	Ratio of Trained Aides to Pupils*	Ratio of Students to Staff
Research and Programmed Learning	1:60		1:15	1:12
Large-Group Audio-Visual Lesson		1:60	1:60	1:30
Small-Group Follow-up	1:60	1:60	1:30	1:15
Guided Small-Group Instruction	1:30	1:15	1:60	1:8 to 1:10
Independent Small-Group Learning	1:60		1:20	1:15
Adjunct TV Programming		1:30		1:30
Video Lessons			1:30	1:30
(Follow-up will vary)				
Demonstration Teaching	1:30 (Large Group) 1:10 (Small Group)			1:30 1:10
TV Production		1:6		1:6
Tutorials	1:1	1:1	1:1	1:1
Assessment of Pupil Needs	1:1 to 1:6	1:1 to 1:90	1:90	Varies
Diagnosis	1:1			1:1
Conferencing	1:1 to 1:6	1:1 to 1:6		1:1 to 1:6

*Work of aides and paraprofessionals is assigned and supervised by professional educators.

grades, at the high school level this ratio may be increased to 1:100; and the ratio of trained teacher aides to pupils might be increased to 1:30. This, however, does not follow all the way down the line. Small-group learning remains small-group learning, and still requires the same kinds of staff-pupil ratios; tutorials remain tutorials with the same ratios, and so on. Again, these ratios will depend in large measure upon how much preparatory organizing for independent learning occurred, the types of resources and activities, the needs of the students, and their previous experiences with independent learning and the learning center itself.

At the ninth grade level, it might be found to be necessary to maintain the ratios set for the middle grades because of the turbulence and "acting out" types of behavior that often characterize students' growth and maturation at this level. These determinations will need to be made by the professional staff after careful assessment and consideration of all factors.

College level. At the college level, the learning center can enrich and widen the avenues normally available for independent learning. However, more staff will be required for production of videotape cassettes, sound-slide programs, programmed learning, computer-assisted instruction, and films to support the various courses of study. Ratios of students to staff are irrelevant in these areas.

With respect to the use of the learning center for independent study, staffing will have to depend upon the size of the center and the number of students that will be using it at any one time. Paraprofessionals or aides would handle the day-to-day operation of the center; however, a learning center director who would be a professional educator would be in charge of the overall operation. More technicians would be involved in the operation of the college center because of the emphasis upon production using television, film, and computers.

In the event that students upon entry to college are found to be deficient in basic reading, writing, study, or mathematics skills,

At the college level, the learning center can enrich and widen avenues normally available for independent learning.

they might make a self-referral to the Learning Specialist in the Instrumental Skills Development Center for a diagnostic work-up and a prescribed skills program. The Learning Specialist might be responsible for as many as 500 students. However, he or she would be assisted by a secretary, graduate assistants, and advanced students.

The graduate assistants, who would have specialized training in administering certain instruments of assessment, would make available to the Learning Specialist test data and other information on the student prior to the Learning Specialist's individual interview with the student. This data, along with the interview, would assist the Learning Specialist in rendering a diagnosis and designing a prescriptive program for the student to help strengthen needed skills. Subsequently, the Learning Specialist would confer with the student at intervals during the semester.

The Skills Center would be run by a graduate assistant and as many aides as might be required, depending upon the size of the center and number of students being served.

The Role of the Educator in Orienting and Training Students to Use the Learning Center

Training of students is required to ensure the proper utilization of the learning center. It is the responsibility of the professional staff to provide this training, establishing and conveying to students guidelines and procedures for using the center and conducting themselves while in it. Students may be involved in the actual establishment of these guidelines. Some of the areas that will require attention in establishing procedures and guidelines for student use of the center are listed as follows:

1. How will students learn about the resources and equipment available in the center?

2. How will students be able to find what they need?

3. How will students learn to operate the equipment?

4. What guidelines should be established to assure proper care of equipment and materials?

5. How will students borrow and return equipment and materials?

6. How will students seek assistance when it is required, and from whom should they seek this assistance?

7. How and where will students keep records of work completed in the center?

8. How will students know when they may visit the learning center? Will some type of pass or admittance form be used?

9. How will the student know when to seek a conference with the teacher?

10. What rules of behavior will be enforced in the learning center? What will be the consequences of violations of the rules of behavior?

11. Will the student be held responsible for equipment or materials damaged accidentally? Through improper use?

12. Will pupils be permitted to borrow to take home equipment and materials? What will be the procedure for this?

13. What will be the rules of conduct for moving through the hallways to and from the learning center?

A formal orientation to the learning center, including discussion of rules and procedures and instruction in the operation of the various types of equipment, would be desirable. This would also provide students with the opportunity to be formally introduced to the various members of the learning center staff and to learn about the respective roles of each. (See Appendix F for a Pupil Orientation format.)

Implementing the New Learning Center with Traditional Staffing Patterns: Helping Teachers to Get Started

In schools where more traditional types of staffing patterns exist than those described in this chapter, it will nonetheless be necessary for members of the staff to decide who will be responsible for carrying out each of the various major tasks (i.e., diagnosis, prescription, etc.) associated with individualization of instruction. The following suggestions are intended to focus upon some of the tasks and approaches that might help classroom teachers begin to make effective use of the learning center.

Materials Catalogs

Provide each teacher with a catalog of the resources in the learning center.

Audio-Visual Techniques Booklets

Provide teachers with booklets containing directions and suggested instructional uses of the various types of audio-visual equipment that may be used by pupils for production.

Initial Planning Sessions

The Learning Center Director should schedule a series of initial planning sessions with each teacher. Each session would be from about 40 to 60 minutes in length, and at least three such sessions would be required. The teacher would be requested to bring to these sessions any pertinent information that he or she might have that could help provide insights into the individual needs and styles of learning of the students in the class. The teacher might bring information acquired informally as a result of classroom observations and informal talks with a student. The teacher would also bring standardized test data, writing samples, and information secured through parent interviews and past performance by the student. The Learning Specialist (reading consultant) would be present during this initial series of planning sessions. A Needs Assessment Profile may be developed for each student (see Appendix A). After interpreting the available data, the team would develop tentative prescriptive strategies.

Developing Tentative
Prescriptive Strategies

Because the resources in the learning center initially will be new to teachers, and may even be new to the Learning Center Director, initially designed prescriptive strategies must be tentative and subject to learner verification. Even with materials preview sessions for teachers, the uses of the multitudinous resources in a learning center and the types of activities that may be applied to them or develop as an outgrowth of their use can only be ascertained as a result of very careful examination of the materials and observations of students using them.

For this reason, during the first two years of a teacher's

initiation into the learning center, it would be advisable for him or her to be physically present in the learning center with his or her class as an active participant in the activities. Similarly, it would be advisable to limit the number of resources to be used by students initially so that the teacher will not be overwhelmed by the task of trying to monitor pupil interaction with a diversity of resources with which he or she is unfamiliar. The teacher's presence in the learning center will also provide the opportunity to observe demonstration lessons conducted by the learning center teacher.

Grouping Students for Learning

In the primary grades, small-group learning will be more the norm than in the intermediate and middle or high school grades. Students may be grouped by reading skills achievement, by interests, or randomly. Pupils may on occasion wish to group themselves. The classroom teacher will need to be helped to examine the needs of the children in the class and to determine the social contexts that will facilitate the achievement of the desired learning objectives in the most expeditious and satisfying ways for the children. Unless contracts have already been developed, independent learning beyond the primary grades will be difficult to manage. Unless teaching-learning modules have been produced beyond the primary grades, integration of the development of the instrumental skills with the curriculum areas will be difficult. Small-group learning must be planned in advance, and should be an outgrowth of units of study in social studies, science, the arts, and the humanities. If teaching-learning modules have not been developed with small-group learning built into them, problems may arise in deriving the greatest benefits from the learning center at the upper elementary and secondary levels.

Introducing Contracts

Introduce the teacher to the concept of the contract. Show him/her sample contracts. Explain their use. Examine the format of the contract. Help the teacher to develop his/her first contracts. (See Appendix B for sample learning contracts.)

Developing Record-keeping Procedures

At some point the question will be raised regarding ways of keeping track of individual and group progress, achievement, resources used, and changes in groupings, resources, activities, etc. The system for record-keeping should be as easy to use as possible for the classroom teacher. It should require a minimum amount of time to maintain while providing the teacher with the information he or she needs at a glance. Any forms that the teacher will require for record-keeping should be typed and duplicated by the teacher aide in the center. Even if the record-keeping system that a teacher wishes to use initially is inadequate, and its shortcomings have been pointed out, it may be necessary for the teacher to begin using the center before he or she will feel ready to recognize its shortcomings and be ready to make the necessary changes (see Appendix B).

The record-keeping system used by teachers will vary according to the grade level, kinds of activities, and types of social contexts in which the students will be working. For example, in the primary grades, the teacher may assign the students to groups that will remain the same for perhaps a four to eight week cycle. The groups would rotate each week, moving to a different one of the established learning stations (see Figure 7). Each student would keep track of the lessons completed on primary contracts (see Appendix B). In addition, the Learning Center Master Teacher would keep a record of the stations, the groups scheduled to be at each station, and the rotational pattern. At the end of the year, the classroom teacher would transfer to a cumulative record the information regarding resources used by each pupil, levels, lessons completed, pupil attitudinal response to the experience/s, and/or success factor rating. Ideally, this cumulative data would be computerized.

In the intermediate and secondary grades, contracts would serve as the record-keeping form whereby both teacher and student would have a copy of the contract, and during conferen-

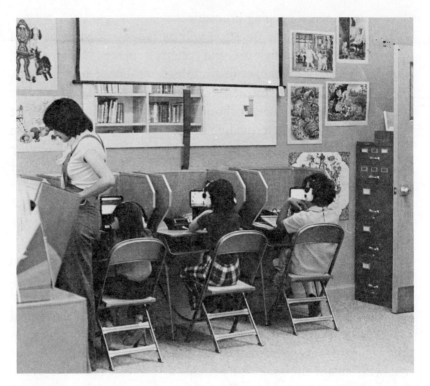

Students may work at learning stations individually, in pairs, or in small groups. The learning station contains the materials and equipment needed to complete activities that will help the student achieve a designated learning objective.

cing, the teacher would record on his or her copy the work completed to date or the number of the contract completed. A conferencing record form might also be used (see Appendix B, "Conferencing Teacher Record Form"). Again, where programmed instruction is used, the computer terminal can be invaluable not only for record-keeping, but also in identifying the error patterns of a student over several lessons and in printing-out a remedial prescription based upon the error pattern. At the end of each day or week, the teacher could call for a print-out of work completed by an individual student or by a group of students. The

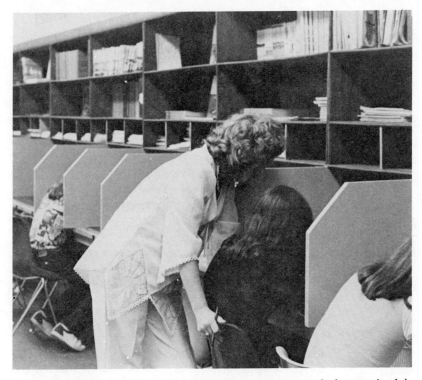

Teacher aides provide students with assistance as it is required in the learning center.

printout would include the level of pupil achievement for each lesson. This writer has had experience in using a computer terminal in this way, and although the initial programming of the computer was a time-consuming and tedious job, the efficiency of the operation that ultimately resulted made the initial investment of time worthwhile.

Developing Learning Stations

A learning station is actually a physical arrangement for completing a particular type of contract. The station contains the materials and equipment required to complete an activity designed to help the learner achieve certain specified instructional objec-

Figure 7

Sample Learning Station:
Primary Level

Station:	Sound-on-Slide
Objectives:	To develop visual literacy skills
	To develop social interactive skills
	To develop creative and expressive behaviors
	To develop writing, reading, speaking, and listening skills
	To develop sequencing skills
Resources:	Slides taken by teacher of a class project (e.g., incubation and hatching of eggs), a field trip (e.g., to zoo), or a performance (e.g., a puppet show, mime, dance, or dramatization).
	Sound-on-slide recording discs; story boards; pencils.
Activities:	Students select and sequence the slides to be used, write narratives to accompany each slide, and then record the narratives.
Student Participants:	(specify names)
Adult Assistant:	Learning Center Teacher
Date/s:	....

tives. Students may work at learning stations in small groups or individually. They often work in pairs, as well.

During the initial planning sessions with the teacher, learning stations may be established geared to help students to achieve certain needed skills. Figure 7 illustrates how the teacher might develop learning stations. The number and types of stations would obviously vary according to the needs of the students, the resources on hand, and the number of learning center staff members possessing the required skills to assist at various types of stations.

Other learning stations at the primary level might include the use of the audio-card reader, the Borg Warner System 80, games and manipulatives, filmloops, and various cassette programs appropriate for small-group learning.

At the intermediate levels, stations would be more pupil-directed, and students would require less adult assistance in completing activities.

Organizing a Whole Class Session

There will be times when the learning center is open to students on an unscheduled basis. At other times, the entire class may be in the center for a scheduled weekly visit. During a scheduled class visit, the session might begin with pupils sitting in a planning circle on the floor with their teacher and the learning center teacher. The teacher might describe each station briefly and remind students of what will be happening at each station and who will be assigned from the learning center staff to assist them. Rules of behavior might be briefly reviewed, focusing upon *courtesty, care* of material and equipment, and *control*. Students would be provided the opportunity to raise questions. Then the larger group would divide into smaller groups, with students moving to their respective stations, securing the materials they might need along the way.

Each pupil would have with him or her a work folder in which there would be a contract depicting each of the various stations established for the class for the month. Students may visit the learning center to work on their designated projects.

For some stations, a second contract might be required to keep track of specific lessons completed, such as with the Hoffman Reader or the System 80. (See Appendix B.)

At the end of a class session, the groups would return to the planning circle. Students might share with others what they accomplished. They might also talk about problems they encountered and how they solved them.

Students in the intermediate and middle grades would tend to work individually on reading skills contracts and in pairs or groups on curriculum-based research projects. In contrast to primary contracts, those for the upper elementary and middle grades would be written and not pictorial. It will be difficult for teachers of these grades to effectively utilize the learning center until teaching-learning modules and contracts have been developed.

Follow-up Planning and Evaluation Sessions

The learning center teacher should follow-up the initial planning sessions with periodically scheduled planning and evaluation sessions. These should be conducted about every other week on a scheduled basis where there is a new center being implemented. During these sessions, the teacher can give reactions to the class sessions that took place, raise questions, make requests, and make changes to improve services. These sessions should also be a learning experience for the classroom teacher. They offer the opportunity for the learning center teacher to introduce new materials, approaches, or techniques to the classroom teacher.

End-of-Year Evaluations

An end-of-year evaluation of the learning center should, after the first year, focus upon teacher and pupil attitudes and appraisal of the services that were offered and the types of curriculum projects and staff development needs that are still required. (See Appendix E.) The evaluation is an important means of involving staff and students in improving the services offered by the center.

Chapter Summary

The learning center requires new patterns of organization of human resources; it also requires the involvement of people at every stage of development and implementation. New staffing patterns should reflect a logical and functional correspondence between the process tasks of individualization of instruction and professional roles. Such a pattern suggests the need for seven professional roles: (1) Learning Specialist; (2) Information-Process Skills Specialist; (3) Instructional Communications Specialist; (4) Interaction-Information Specialists; (5) Evaluation Specialist; (6) Learning Center Master Teacher; and (7) Professional Instructors, Teachers, and Counselors. Paraprofessionals, teacher aides, technicians, and volunteers would support and assist the instructional process in various ways. Special aptitudes and differentiated training are required for each of the various professional roles. It is suggested that this model be adapted to the needs of individual schools and that a plan for making the transition to new patterns of staffing be gradual and take advantage of in-house talent and skills, particularly those of the reading consultant, the library-media specialist, and creative and effective teachers.

Multi-disciplinary teaching teams at the secondary levels may serve as effective vehicles for training staff, developing teaching-learning modules, beginning to focus upon individual student needs, and making full utilization of the learning center across disciplines to meet individual needs and to develop process and instrumental skills. The learning center at these levels is also an effective means of providing compensatory education for students who may require it.

Teacher-pupil ratios in the learning center will vary according to the age level of the students that the center is geared to serve and the amount of supportive help of teacher aides and paraprofessionals available in the center. Generally, as students become older, they are able to work independently with less teacher intervention for longer periods of time. However, the educator has a responsibility to orient and train students to use the learning center effectively and to greatest advantage. Similarly, where traditional staffing patterns exist, it will become the responsibility of the learning center staff, but more specifically the learning center teacher, to provide classroom teachers with the guidance and support that they will require to utilize the learning center in ways that will ultimately provide the greatest benefit for their pupils.

7.
Daily Operation of
a Learning Center

Introduction

Learning centers are busy places in which at any given time there may be a diversity of activities going on simultaneously. On a day-to-day basis, the students visiting the center will be engaging in prescribed activities for varying lengths of time. The number of visits that a student makes to the learning center in a given week and the length of each of these visits will vary according to his or her individual needs. In order to develop a sense of what actually goes on in a learning center complex during the span of a week, and on any given day, one must look not only at the activities in which pupils are engaging, but also at the weekly schedule of the center and of its various staff members.

This chapter will examine a sample learning center schedule, and the types of professional and student activities that are provided for in the schedule. It will also examine how this schedule is implemented on a given day, focusing upon both professional staff activities and student activities. Obviously, the activities of both the professional staff and the students are affected by the delimitations of the physical facility, equipment, instructional resources, and paraprofessional and teacher aide assistance that are available. These delimiting factors will be taken into consideration when examining the actual daily operation of the learning center.

A Model Schedule

To develop a flexible schedule for a learning center which will provide the greatest benefits to teachers and pupils requires much skill and has implications for the entire school schedule. The model schedule for an elementary school learning center, shown in Figure 8, reflects a concern for making the learning center central to all other school activities. This schedule offers the advantages that result when time modules are combined in blocks by grade level; it also provides the advantages that can be derived from coordination of the schedules of the various areas in the complex and of the professionals supervising these areas.

As an aid to the reader, a model elementary school Learning Center Complex (utilizing the model schedule described) is shown in Figure 9.

The time blocks on the schedule may be divided into ten-minute modules which can then be combined in various ways and for different durations, depending upon the nature of the activities and experiences of students being scheduled in each of the areas in the complex.

During planning sessions with the Learning Center Master Teacher, the classroom teacher may request time modules of varying lengths for whole-class visits to the center or for individual and small-group visits. The length of these visits, once requested by a teacher, need not be fixed for the entire year. The teacher has the option of requesting visits of varying lengths depending upon the needs of his or her students and the projects at hand.

It should be noted that, though it is not visible on the schedule, on days when the Instrumental Skills Development Center is scheduled for a whole-class visit, the adjoining Library-Media Center is unscheduled, and vice-versa. This enables the staff to accommodate individual and small-group visits by pupils in one part of the complex, even though a class may be scheduled to be using the other part. It also frees the Library-Media Specialist to assist with research projects as he or she is needed. Both the

Figure 8

A Sample Learning Center Schedule

#	Time	Monday	Tuesday	Wednesday	Thursday	Friday
1	8:40-9:20	Team Meetings	*PROFESSIONAL	*WORK	Advisory Council Meetings	*SESSIONS
2	9:30-10:10	All 5th grades available for entire block	All 4th grades available	All 3rd grades available	All 2nd grades available	All 1st grades available
3	10:15-10:55					
4	11:00-11:40					Kingergarten
5	11:45-12:25		PROFESSIONAL	WORK	SESSIONS	
6	12:25-1:05	L	U	N	C	H
7	1:10-1:40	Open Time	Open Time	Kindergarten	Open Time	Open Time
8	1:45-2:15					
9	2:20-2:50					
10	2:50-3:20					

*These time blocks used for diagnostic-evaluation sessions, prescriptive programming sessions, follow-up sessions, teacher workshops, materials previews, etc.

167

Figure 9

An Elementary School Learning Center Complex

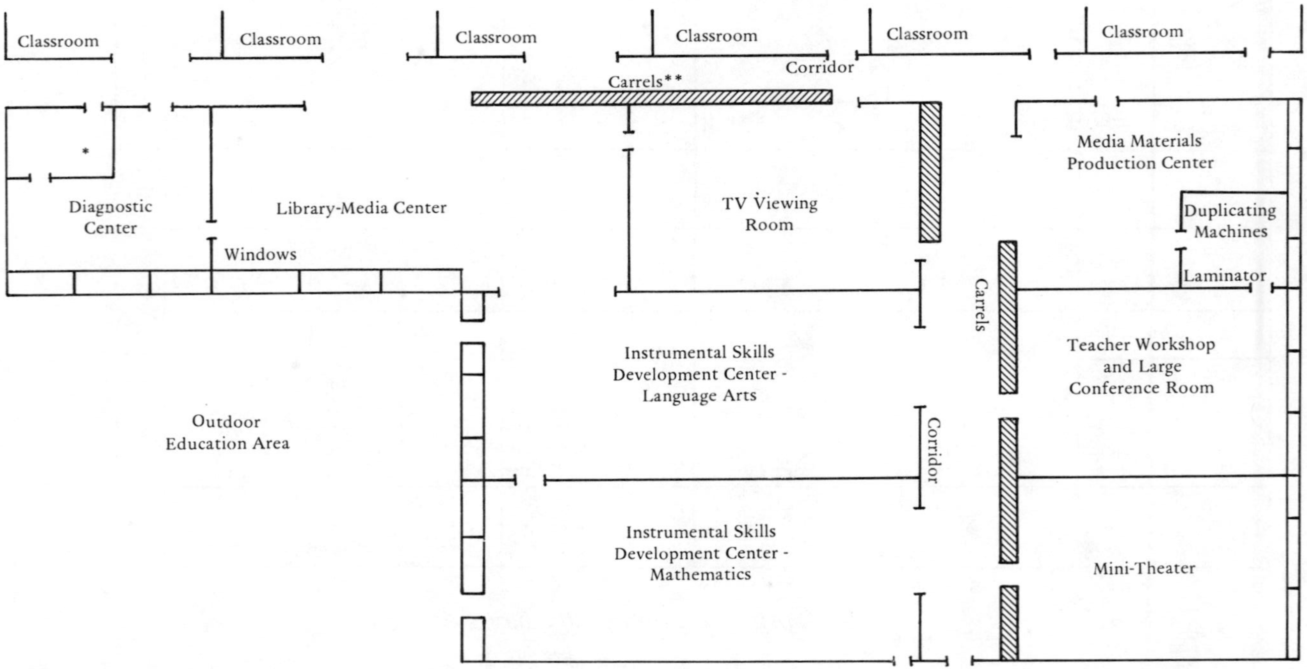

Classroom

Classroom

Classroom

Classroom

Classroom

Classroom

Classroom

Classroom

Corridor

Corridor

Corridor

Media Materials Production Center

Duplicating Machines

Laminator

Teacher Workshop and Large Conference Room

Mini-Theater

Carrels

Carrels**

TV Viewing Room

Instrumental Skills Development Center - Language Arts

Instrumental Skills Development Center - Mathematics

Library-Media Center

Windows

Diagnostic Center

*

Outdoor Education Area

*Conferencing-Recording Room.
**Carrels in corridors; carrels in other areas not shown.

168

Library-Media Specialist and the Reading-Learning Specialist work in the various areas of the complex and together with the Learning Center Master Teacher comprise the Learning Center's professional team. The building principal and district curriculum coordinators are consultants to this team.

It should be noted further that the flexible modular scheduling of classes by grade level groupings facilitates team teaching and coordination of curriculum and curriculum-related projects and activities, while not barring the possibility of peer tutoring in the center across grade levels or the use of the center simultaneously by many grade levels during the open flexible periods.

Types of Professional Work Sessions
and Demonstrations in the Learning Center

The learning center involves the professional staff on a daily basis in a variety of professional planning and work sessions, skills development efforts, demonstrations, and coordination meetings. The time slots during which these professional work sessions might take place are indicated on the schedule as such. These will include diagnostic evaluation sessions, prescriptive planning sessions, demonstration teaching lessons, materials previews, advisory council meetings, learning center team meetings, and evaluation follow-up sessions with teachers. Although not every one of these occurs every day, during the course of a week most will take place, and over a two-week time span virtually all will take place.

Diagnostic Evaluation
Sessions

At the beginning of each new school year, the Reading-Learning Specialist will meet individually with each classroom teacher to help the teacher interpret the information available on each student; this data will focus upon learner achievement and characteristics that will have a bearing on learning, growth, and development. In some instances, where a pupil has shown evidence of a learning disability, reading disability, or other problem that will impinge upon the teaching-learning process, the Reading-Learning Specialist will administer certain diagnostic tests and other individually administered measures to attempt to determine the nature of the problem. He or she will secure information that will provide the skilled examiner with clues for most effectively working with the student and facilitating learning (see Chapter 4). A cumulative diagnostic profile for each of these pupils will be prepared and maintained for as long as the pupil gives evidence of having special educational needs.

For those pupils, as well as all others, a Learning Style Needs Assessment Profile (see Appendix A) might be used in addition to provide clues with respect to how a student learns best. This information is then shared with and interpreted for the classroom teacher. Often, the teacher has additional inputs that prove to be valuable in diagnosing a pupil's needs. A child's relations to peers, frustration tolerance, self-concept, and other characteristics are usually most visible to the teacher who has daily contact with him or her, and who can observe the student in a wide variety of situations over a period of time. Although the teacher may not be skilled in interpreting behavior, he or she should be trained to make such observations. All of this information is shared during the diagnostic evaluation session.

Diagnosing reading problems. When diagnosing reading problems, the Reading-Learning Specialist will call attention to the following:

1. Is there a significant discrepancy between the pupil's achieved reading level and the expected level?

2. Is the pupil fluent with oral language; does he or she have an adequate spoken vocabulary to express ideas and feelings?

3. Has the pupil a rich and diversified experiential background?

4. Does he or she have an interest in books and in learning to read?

5. Are there discrepancies between the pupil's literal and interpretive comprehension, between total reading comprehension and word knowledge (vocabulary or understanding of word meanings)?

6. Does the pupil have an adequate sight vocabulary?

7. Does the student have adequate word knowledge (vocabulary)?

8. Does the student have and use word attack skills? Semantic cues? Linguistic cues? Phonetic analysis cues?

9. Is rate of reading adequate? Is there reading fluency? Does phrasing used by the pupil facilitate comprehension?

10. Does the student use punctuation cues to aid comprehension?

11. Is there evidence of perceptual difficulty, or visual or auditory impediments?

The Reading-Learning Specialist will make recommendations based upon an analysis of the answers to the above questions. These recommendations will serve as a guide to development of the prescriptive strategies to be engaged in when dealing with the reading problem.

Prescriptive Strategies
Planning Sessions

After the diagnostic evaluation sessions, perhaps two or three meetings are conducted between the teacher and the specialist responsible for developing or assisting in the design of the prescriptive strategies. Depending upon the staffing plan, this person might be the Information-Process Skills Specialist, the Instructional Communication Specialist, or the Learning Center Master Teacher. In smaller schools, the Reading-Learning Specialist may assume a dual role, thus being responsible both for diagnosis and design of prescriptive strategies.

In any case, it is during these sessions that the diagnosis for each student is translated into prescriptive strategies. It is decided during these sessions, based upon student needs, the social contexts in which pupils will work, the resources and activities that will be employed, and the time factors that will be applied to govern the frequency and duration of a given student's involvement with prescribed activities and experiences. Students may be grouped for certain activities where they have common needs. In addition, independent learning experiences would be specified, some involving the use of contracts which would be selected from a contract bank. Appropriate teaching-learning modules or teacher resource units would be retrieved from the computer terminal or from a file to be used by the teacher. Inherent in this approach would be provisions for individual student differences. Where necessary, new resource units, modules, and contracts would be developed to meet individual and group needs.

Follow-up and
Evaluation Sessions

After students have been working in the Learning Center for several weeks, and periodically thereafter, the classroom teacher and the Learning Center Master Teacher will meet to assess student progress, evaluate the quality of student experiences in the Center, troubleshoot, and make changes and modifications in prescriptive strategies originally developed. These sessions are continuous, spontaneous dialogues between the teacher and the Master Teacher. Changes in prescriptive strategies may result as new information is obtained through diagnostic teaching. They may result also when a student completes a unit of study successfully and his or her needs change, or when new and more effective techniques or resources become known or available. In addition, as a result of individual teacher-pupil conferencing, new information about student needs and interests may be secured, suggesting the need for certain changes or modifications in prescriptive strategies employed or confirming the soundness of those already used. For example, as John, a fifth grader, works with programmed materials to improve general reading comprehension, it is discovered that he very often misses the correct answers to questions when these questions test interpretive comprehension, such as the ability to recognize cause and effect, or make comparisons or inferences. Consequently, John is assigned to complete a series of contracts geared to develop interpretive comprehension (see Appendix B for a sample contract on Reading Comprehension). In another case, five seventh-graders are working together on a unit dealing with the "super hero/heroine." New materials arrive in the center (e.g., Spiderman Reading Motivation Multi-Media Kit; American Legendary Heroes Kit; or periodicals containing articles about the Bionic Man). So that students will gain the benefits of these new resources, alterations and additions are made to contracts or the teaching-learning module.

Demonstration Teaching
Sessions

An important function of the learning center is to serve as a vehicle for continuous professional staff development. One technique which may be employed by the Master Teacher to achieve this goal is that of demonstration teaching. The demonstration may involve a large group, a small group, or an individual student. For example, in one center, the Master Teacher divided a class into small groups and demonstrated the use of CEMREL's *Five Sense Store: Creating Dramatic Plots* module. The classroom teacher subsequently was able to use the techniques observed and apply them in the classroom. In another situation, the Master Teacher demonstrated in a small-group situation the use of the "cloze procedure" to encourage and train students to employ linguistic and semantic cues as decoding strategies in reading. In still another situation, the Master Teacher demonstrated in a one-to-one situation with a kindergartener how to utilize the Kindergarten Evaluation of Learning Potential (KELP) as both a diagnostic device and a teaching tool. The instructional materials and equipment in a learning center are so diversified (as are the techniques that may be applied to them to achieve different objectives) that demonstration teaching must necessarily be on-going in the center.

Materials Previews

Materials previews are sessions designed to introduce teachers to some new or previously unused instructional resource that may already be available in the center or that is being considered for purchase. Unlike the demonstration teaching lesson, a materials preview does not involve the actual use of the resource with students. Instead it focuses upon examination and accompanying explanation of the new material and its components for developing some skill area or for supporting some aspect of the curriculum. If it is a cassette program, perhaps one of the cassette lessons would be heard in part or in its totality. Similar types of examination and preview of filmstrips, slides, multi-level kits, and other media would occur. The explanation of the new material would generally include information about the segment of the student population for which the resource is intended, the skills which it may be used to develop and/or the content with which it deals, the social contexts in which it might be used by students, whether it is pupil-directed or teacher-directed, the media components and how they are related to one another, the organization and sequencing of units of learning, and related format features.

The materials preview presentation may be made by a sales representative or consultant from the publishing company marketing the resource, or it may be made by the Master Teacher, a district curriculum coordinator, or a teacher who may have already experimented with the resource with students. At the high school and college levels, it is conceivable that a student would do the presentation.

Materials previews should always be followed by learner verification of the new resource that is being considered for purchase. That is, the resource should actually be tried with students representative of the population for which it has been designed—and their reactions observed and elicited to assist in final decisions regarding the purchase of the resource.

Materials preview sessions may be scheduled at convenient times when teachers are brought together in appropriate groups (i.e., primary and intermediate divisions, subject areas, multi-disciplinary teams, etc.).

Learning Center
Team Meetings

The learning center team meeting is another type of session that is scheduled to take place in the center and that involves only members of the professional staff. The learning center team is comprised of those professionals who are responsible for coordinating and carrying out the operation and daily functioning of the center. Typically this would include the Reading-Learning Specialist, the Learning Center Master Teacher, and the Library-Media Specialist. Others might be included depending upon the type of staffing pattern that a school has adopted. The principal and district curriculum coordinators may serve as consultants to the team. If the "change agent" is someone other than a curriculum coordinator or principal, then this person would serve as a consultant to the team. Decision-making is shared and never the exclusive domain of the building principal.

During team meetings, policies and procedures of the learning center are discussed. Some of these may be brought to the Teacher Advisory Council for its consideration at a later time. The team meetings also serve as an on-going method for trouble-shooting, coordinating services and schedules of the center, and planning for future teacher workshops, demonstrations, and materials previews.

Initially, or as a new center is being developed, team meetings should be conducted at least once a week for about an hour. After a learning center has been functioning for a few years, the team meetings may be conducted every other week or once a month. However, monthly meetings may require more than an hour if the agendas are long. Keeping minutes of team meeting transactions and discussions provides a record of policy and procedural decisions made by the team for future reference. It further provides a record of problems that arise and how they are resolved, workshops and previews that are planned and later evaluated by the team, and any other pertinent business that may have to be recalled and referred to in the future.

**Teacher Advisory
Council Meetings**
The Teacher Advisory Council is a group that is representative of the various grade levels in the school. It is desirable to have representation from the teachers' association or union. The Advisory Council meets every other week initially for an hour session. During these sessions, policy and procedural alternatives are discussed and recommendations made to the learning center team. These policy and procedural items might involve any of the following concerns but are not limited to these:
1. Use of paid teacher aides and role definitions.
2. Use of community volunteers and role definitions.
3. Professional role definitions and responsibilities in connection with the learning center.
4. Selection and use of equipment and resources.
5. Scheduling.
6. Evaluation of learning center services and procedures.
7. Types of workshops to be held for teachers.
8. Demonstration lessons.
9. Materials previews, scheduling and format.
10. Improvement of design or operation of the center.
11. Problems or dissatisfactions of any type associated with the center and its services.

The Teacher Advisory Council is another example of the shared decision-making which is vital to the successful functioning of a learning center, particularly during the initial stages of implementation and development.

Workshops for Teachers
Workshops are sessions geared to help teachers "learn by doing." Such workshops generally require at least two-hour blocks of time, although some types of workshops may be conducted in

an hour. Workshops may focus upon training teachers in any of the areas listed below, although this list is not intended to be exhaustive.

1. Methods of assessing learner needs.
2. Organizing for independent learning.
3. Preparing contracts for independent learning.
4. Implementation of teaching-learning modules.
5. Record-keeping techniques.
6. Development of resource units and teaching-learning modules.
7. Conferencing techniques.
8. Techniques for developing the life-relevant process skills and the instrumental skills.
9. Multi-media techniques.
10. Developing and using programmed instruction.
11. Instructional television.
12. Computer-assisted instruction.
13. Questioning strategies.
14. Values clarification techniques.
15. Small-group learning techniques.
16. Managing individualized instruction.
17. Organizing and arranging the learning environment for individualized instruction and to accommodate diverse learning styles.

Workshops should be offered to teachers regularly during times of the day when they are most receptive both mentally and physically. After-school workshops are perhaps the least desirable, although the most convenient and economical to conduct. They are the least desirable because they are conducted at a time of the day when teachers are tired and able to give less of themselves to the workshop experience. In addition, after-school workshops do not usually reach the majority of teachers, because attendance is voluntary and many teachers have other after-school commitments. Wherever it is possible, morning and summer workshops should be conducted in lieu of after-school sessions. Another possibility would be Saturday workshops. Naturally, unless teachers are under a contractual obligation to attend a given number of workshops per year, it would be necessary to offer in-service credit toward salary increments, or some other incentive to assure wide participation.

Presentations

Presentations may focus upon the same sorts of topics as workshops; however, the presentation is designed to introduce the topic and present information and ideas. Usually teachers are not actively involved in "doing" something that will leave them with some type of finished product. Instead, they take away ideas, new insights, information, and understandings. Often, workshops are preceded by presentations which stimulate interest and the desire to learn more about the subject at hand.

A Day in an Elementary School Learning Center

Introduction

Although there are, in fact, no two days in a learning center that are exactly the same, this section will attempt to present what might conceivably occur on a given day in an elementary school learning center. The Sample Learning Center Schedule (Figure 8) along with the Sample Elementary School Learning Center Complex (Figure 9) will serve as the bases for the learning center activities described. In other words, as is necessarily the case in any learning center, the physical design and the schedule will serve as delimiting factors. An endeavor will be made, within these limitations, to present a representative sampling of the types of activities that might occur in the center, so that the reader will gain a sense of what actually takes place to provide for the needs of students. The Monday schedule will be used in describing a typical day.

The Team Meeting:
8:40 to 9:20 a.m.

The members of the learning center team meet at 8:40 a.m. each Monday in the Diagnostic Center. The principal and the district coordinator of language arts are present. On the agenda are several items, including: (1) an appraisal of the functioning of the center over the past month; (2) planning of a workshop by the local performing arts foundation, focusing upon use of the CEMREL *Five Sense Store* language arts modules; (3) a learning center presentation for Open School Night for parents; and (4) preparing for a series of materials previews over the next two months.

The team meeting ends at 9:20 a.m., and the team members go to their respective areas in the complex.

A Large-Group Lesson:
9:30 to 10:50 a.m.

A special lesson is scheduled for the morning. An educational consultant from one of the major publishers of encyclopedias will give a demonstration lesson to two fifth grade classes. The lesson will last part of the period. Then the larger group will be divided into smaller groups to complete the follow-up and application activities under the guidance of their two teachers, the Library-Media Specialist, the Learning Center Master Teacher, the consultant from the publishing company, and a teacher aide. The pupils sit on the carpeted floor for the first part of the lesson. The materials, which include a film and follow-up activity booklets, are provided by the company without charge. The lesson deals with how to do research. It integrates language arts skill development with research and inquiry skills. Students use both the Instrumental Skills Development Center and the Library-Media Center to complete the follow-up and application activities. Whatever is not completed during the session on this day will be finished during open time slots in the learning center.

Inside the Diagnostic Center:
9:30 a.m. to 1:55 p.m.

While the large-group lesson is going on inside the Instrumental Skills Development Center and the Library-Media Center, other activities are occurring in the Diagnostic Center. Here the Reading-Learning Specialist is using manipulatives with a group of three second-graders to assess their perceptual development and visual-motor coordination. The children were referred by the classroom teacher, who suspects a developmental lag in these areas which is impeding success in learning to read and to write. The children seem to be enjoying themselves as they work with patterned blocks and then with colored wooden beads. They chat among themselves and with the Reading-Learning Specialist as they follow his directions.

The Reading-Learning Specialist works with these youngsters for approximately a half hour. Then a third-grader arrives for assessment of a suspected learning disability. The Reading-Learning Specialist administers the Slingerland Test of Specific Language Disability, an informal reading inventory. This is the third session with this pupil, as other tests have been given earlier.

During the next time slot, the Reading-Learning Specialist analyzes and interprets the data collected during the preceding needs assessment sessions with the three second-graders and the third-grader. The third-grader appears to have a problem with auditory receptive language which has manifested itself through an inability to comprehend and follow spoken directions and through a reading deficit. The Reading-Learning Specialist recommends a program to develop auditory perception and processing of language. Cassette tapes and audio-card reader programs will be used along with other classroom techniques to develop abilities in the deficit area; meanwhile, the deficit will be circumvented through the use of compensatory teaching-learning techniques until the deficit is corrected. Two of the three second-graders appear to have difficulty with visual patterning, and the third with visual memory. Manipulatives and various forms of programmed instruction will be used in the learning center to help develop these skill areas.

ITV in the TV
Viewing Area

At 9:30 a.m., before the large-group lesson in the Instrumental Skills Development Center gets underway, 15 third-graders arrive at the TV Viewing Room, where a paraprofessional greets them. The children have been sent to the Viewing Room by their teacher to see a lesson entitled "Sam the Giant," one of 15 lessons from a cable television system. The entire series from which this lesson comes is entitled "How Can I Tell You?" The series is geared to elicit students' feelings and attitudes by the presentation of various stories and dramatic situations. The particular lesson being viewed on this day by these third-grade children is an open-ended story of a tropical giant who is left in the North Pole for one week. The classroom teacher, in advance, has provided the paraprofessional with the strategy for preparing the pupils for viewing, as well as post-viewing strategies. As a post-viewing strategy for today's lesson, the children will be asked to draw interpretations of what happened to Sam. While these children are in the Viewing Room, their teacher is providing instruction in mathematics to the remaining ten children in the class who share a common skill need. Later in the day, at 2:15 p.m., these ten youngsters will view the same TV lesson while the teacher works with the group that has already seen the TV lesson. At some point, either with the paraprofessional or the teacher, the children will be given the opportunity to tell about and show their illustrations of Sam the Giant. The viewing time for the TV lesson is 15 minutes; however, with the preparatory and follow-up activities, the entire lesson may take 35 minutes. The post-viewing activities might be done at tables in the Viewing Room, while other students are watching some other ITV broadcast. Because the room is equipped with a wireless induction loop, students may use wireless headsets to view a program without distracting non-viewers engaged in post-viewing or preparatory activities.

**Inside the Materials
Production Area**

In the Materials Production Area, at 9:50 a.m., there are several teachers and a teacher aide developing the following materials and programs: (1) audio-cassette lessons which teach skills geared to develop the ability to recognize main ideas of reading selections (the cassette series includes lessons on categorizing, outlining, telegraphic messages, topic sentences with supporting details, captioning pictures, and titling paragraphs); (2) audio-card reader lesson sequences including word picture programs and idioms for bilingual students; and (3) lamination of learning station activity cards to stimulate creative writing. Teachers work in the Materials Production Center during their professional work periods and before and after school as they so choose. The teacher aide is on hand to assist as well as to carry out work assignments of a non-professional nature at the direction of the professional educators. Such work assignments are channeled through the Library-Media Specialist or another Specialist in the complex designated to assume this responsibility, depending upon the staffing pattern in the center.

**Activities in the
Mini-Theater**

Inside the Mini-Theater, six fourth-grade students are independently rehearsing a play entitled *Columbus* from the Educational Progress Corporation's *Plays for Reading*. The children are donning costumes made with the assistance of parent volunteers. The play was selected by these youngsters to be performed as their Bicentennial project. When the group is ready, the troupe will give several performances for other grades in the school. In another part of the Mini-Theater, a paraprofessional is working with another small group of students with the CEMREL *Five Sense Store* module on *Creating Characterization*.

**Instrumental Skills
Development Center**

Open Time: Individual and Small-Group Visits. At 1:10 p.m. a group of seven second-grade pupils arrive at the Instrumental Skills Development Center after their teacher called the center to clear the pupils' visit with respect to space availability. The students carry with them their work folders, in which are contained their contracts and completed work. Three of the children go to the System 80 lesson boxes and take prescribed lessons designed to develop basic sight vocabulary. The four others, who are reading one year below grade level, work together on a Hoffman Reader lesson geared to develop decoding and comprehension skills as well as positive attitudes toward reading.

Shortly after the arrival of the second-graders, two fourth-graders arrive to complete a filmstrip-making project, which is a culminating activity for a study unit on homonyms, synonyms, and antonyms. Their visit was cleared that morning. These students will use the filmstrip that they make to teach what they learned to their peers. The students know where to secure the needed materials and how to proceed independently. They also know that if they do not adhere to the behavior and study rules for working in the center, they will be asked to leave and will then be unable to complete their project on this day.

Three more students arrive at the center bearing a group prescription form; these students have been sent by their teacher to complete two individualized cassette learning packages, one on the use of apostrophes and the other on capitalization. The prescription was made as a result of the pupils having demonstrated in their writing a lack of understanding of the proper use of these mechanics of writing skills.

Later, four kindergarteners arrive at the center; two will choose a "talking story book"; the other two, who were diagnosed as lacking understanding of certain basic concepts relating to size, quantity, relative positions (e.g., behind, above, next to, etc.), will do System 80 lessons from the Basic Concepts Series. As soon as they complete their lessons, they will return to their classrooms. Their visit lasts approximately 15 minutes. The teacher aide or the Learning Center Master Teacher will write pertinent comments on the prescription forms (see Appendix B for sample prescription forms) that the children brought to the center with them. These comments will indicate to the teacher whether the pupils completed their lesson successfully, types of difficulties that any one of the children might have experienced in attempting to complete the lesson, and each child's adherence to the behavioral code and procedures of the learning center. If a significant problem is detected, the Master Teacher will suggest on the prescription form that the classroom teacher confer with him/her regarding the child and the prescribed work assignments.

In managing student visits to the center, an effort is made to stagger the arrival of students so that many pupils requiring assistance in getting started do not arrive simultaneously. If students know just where to find needed materials and can proceed independently, then their arrival will not pose a problem in terms of logistics and management, and they may come and go almost at will. If community volunteers are available, then the number present on any given day will have a direct bearing on the number of students that may be served in the center at any time and the types of activities to be accommodated.

Later, during open time, ten fifth-grade pupils with reading deficits of various types arrive at the center. Some are working with vocabulary development contracts; others with interpretive comprehension contracts, or other types of reading skill development forms (see Appendix B for sample reading contracts.).

The Instrumental Skills Development Center and the Library-Media Center are used during several open periods by pupils in grades three through five, who work independently with an audio-cassette tape spelling-language arts program entitled *On My Own in Spelling*. Pupils who require greater teacher direction and instruction work in the classroom with the program, while the other pupils work independently in the center.

It should be noted that the Reading-Learning Specialist works part of each day in the Instrumental Skills Development Center with pupils having special educational needs. These pupils may be scheduled to visit the center on a regular basis individually or in small groups during open periods, or they may work when their class visits the center.

During open periods, pupils of all abilities and with a wide range of needs and learning styles come to the Instrumental Skills Development Center to work individually, in pairs, or in small groups on prescribed areas of skill development. They engage in a variety of projects and activities appropriate to their needs.

Scheduled Whole Class Visits. Classes are scheduled to visit the Instrumental Skills Development Center at least once a week. When there is not a special large-group presentation, such as the one described involving two fifth-grade classes, pupils work individually and in small groups to develop reading and language arts skills, abilities, and appreciations. In order to examine what occurs when a whole class visits the Center for its scheduled weekly visit, we will look at the Thursday morning schedule, when second-graders are scheduled for the Center.

On this morning, one second-grade class arrives at the Center at 9:30 a.m. with the classroom teacher, who will remain with the group. In addition, on hand to work with the class are the Master Teacher, the Reading-Learning Specialist, and a teacher aide. The learning stations were planned and developed by the classroom teacher and the Learning Center Master Teacher during prescriptive programming sessions. At that time, the class was also divided into four groups, with six pupils to a group. Reading achievement was in this instance the criteria for the grouping.

The Learning Center Master Teacher and the classroom teacher each has a copy of the Learning Center Class Plan Sheet, which indicates the four stations and the materials to be used at each station. The adult who will assist each group is indicated on the Class Plan Sheet; also listed is the date that each group will work at a particular station. The materials at each station vary according to the needs of the children in the different groups; however, the learning objectives will remain the same.

When the class arrives in the center, the children are asked by the Learning Center Master Teacher to sit on the floor in a "planning circle." The students already know in which group they will be working, but they do not know to which station they will be going on this particular day. The Learning Center Master Teacher tells the children a little about each of the stations, which group will be at each station, and which adult will be assisting the group. The children are then given the opportunity to ask questions. One group at a time is then sent to its station, accompanied by the adult who will be working with the group. If the activity at the station is teacher-directed, then the materials to be used are ready at the station, having been put out by the teacher aide prior to the class's arrival. If the materials are to be used individually by the children and are completely self-directing, as would be the case with the System 80 or with "talking books," then each student secures his or her own materials.

In the primary grades, where the development of oral language and the socializing skills is important, many stations are designed to have pupils working in small groups, and activities are generally preceded and followed by group discussion. However, because it is desirable to begin teaching children how to work independently and to make choices even at these early levels, there is always at least one station designed with self-direction in mind. Student groups rotate in working at the various stations from week to week, so that after a four-week period, assuming that there are four stations, each of the groups will have worked at every station. In the primary grades, many of the follow-up activities at the various stations involve drawing or some other art form, thus focusing upon fine motor coordination; manipulative skills; concepts of color, size, and shape; and development of creative and expressive behaviors.

The children work at their stations for approximately 30

minutes; then the groups return to the "planning circle" to share their experiences with peers. The entire session lasts between 35 and 45 minutes. However, when children and teachers are first learning to use the center, it would be advisable to allow nearly an hour for a visit. The children keep their work in their folders, in which they file a record of their progress and the stations at which they have already worked. At the end of the month they may take all completed learning contracts home.

Stations need not be fixed. They can be changed at the discretion of the classroom teacher, working in conjunction with the Learning Center Master Teacher and the Reading-Learning Specialist.

Class and Individual Vists
to the Library-Media Center

While the Instrumental Skills Development Center is scheduled for whole-class visits, the Library-Media Center is open for individual and small-group sessions. Thus, during the morning time periods, when the two fifth-grade classes were engaged in the large-group session, pupils visited the Library-Media Center to do research, and to check out books and other resource materials. A teacher aide assigned to the Library-Media Center was on hand along with the Library-Media Specialist to assist students.

When teachers advise the Library-Media Specialist of a unit of study that they will be doing with a group of students, and the Library-Media Specialist has this information several days in advance, she will gather those resources that will be needed and place them on a cart so that pupils will have easy access to them. At other times, the teacher may want pupils to locate and secure the needed resources themselves.

During the morning, several students visiting the Library-Media Center viewed filmloops on Eskimo foods and filmstrips on Eskimo legends. These students were working on completion of social studies learning contracts. Two other students used the Land Forms Models Kits; they were learning about the formation of the surface of the Earth, and would later on be making their own land form models. Several students came to use the reference section; some to use the Spelling Mini-Systems; and others to check out books. Another student listened to and viewed a teacher-made Caramate (sound-slide) lesson on ecology and environmental pollution. This student had been absent on the day that the group studied this subject.

During the afternoon, the Library-Media Specialist meets with whole classes to provide instruction in the use of the Library-Media Center, research skills, and inquiry skills. The Library-Media Specialist may also instruct a small group of students in specific types of information retrieval skills and research skills if they have the need for these skills. At these times, other pupils in the class would be involved with research and book selection. On this particular afternoon, the Library-Media Specialist is using the Flintstone Library Skills Multi-Media Kit, a sound filmstrip program, in instructing second graders. Often the period is divided so that the skills instruction occurs first, with book selection, research, and application activities occurring during the second half.

Recording Room

The Recording Room is used by pupils when making cassette tape or sound-slide recordings. During the course of the morning, two first-graders recorded their own talking story book; three fifth-graders prepared a tape on the Caramate to accompany a slide sequence on historical landmarks in their community; and a teacher prerecorded a series of cards for the audio-card reader.

The School Becomes
the Learning Center

The school of the future will have not a room, area, or complex of rooms as its learning center. *The school of the future will itself be a learning center.* The physical design of space will be such that students and teachers will have available to them all day, every day the appropriate areas necessary to accommodate diverse learning styles and needs of pupils. These areas will be suitable in size and staffing to make student movement possible without elaborate scheduling restrictions. These areas will be an integral part of the entire teaching-learning environment and will not be set off in another part of the building.

In such a school, television, CAI, and other instructional media will no longer be merely ancillary instructional aids; they will instead become significant instructional technologies which, when combined with the expertise of the professional educator, will provide numerous teaching-learning options. This in no way suggests that in such a school technology will replace the teacher. The well-trained, highly qualified, skilled teacher or specialist can never be replaced. However, in such a school, professional roles would be redefined in the ways suggested in Chapter 6, and the concept of the "class" would be radically altered, particularly at secondary school levels. Teachers would spend more time with individuals and small groups of students, providing direct instruction and guidance. In addition, the traditional ratio of 30 pupils to one teacher would assume new interpretations. Although the overall ratio might remain unchanged, the number of pupils in direct contact with a teacher at any one time would be lessened, since teachers would be assisted by paraprofessionals and teacher aides. The paraprofessional and teacher aide would always receive direction and supervision from the professional educator. However, in the school of the future, their training and roles would be more clearly defined and would be of greater significance than is the case today.

Creative Uses of Physical Space

The use of space in public schools has changed little over the past two hundred years. Physically, the 20-room schoolhouse differs from the one-room schoolhouse *only* in the number of rooms. These rooms remain self-contained, and still accommodate 25 to 30 pupils, the traditional "class." The increase in the number of rooms in schools naturally necessitated the inclusion of corridors or hallways, which allow students and teachers to move from one room (or "schoolhouse") to another. In addition, the increase in numbers of pupils in a single school building further necessitated the inclusion of a large gathering place, thus the auditorium or the all-purpose room was included along with a gymnasium for indoor physical education. Beyond these additions, the interiors of schools have persisted in remaining largely untouched by the versatility of modern architecture, perhaps one reason being that the general approach to education has not changed significantly in most schools.

The notion of constructing all rooms in a school building of uniform size and design makes little sense when an endeavor is being made to accommodate individual student needs and styles of learning. A student who is preparing a tape recording does not require a room which can accommodate 30 students. However, a quiet area is required. A teacher working with six pupils or conferencing with one pupil does not require the same sort of facility as does the teacher who is presenting an audio-visual lesson to 75 students.

Similarly, the arrangement of furniture, the lighting, the spacing of electrical outlets, and the organization of instructional resources and equipment in the teaching-learning environment should reflect approaches to education that are consistent with what educators know about how children at various stages of development learn best.

Certainly, it would not be realistic to suggest that educators tear down existing school structures and rebuild them. However, there are numerous school districts that have found that creative remodeling of older school structures can result in modern physical facilities that can and do facilitate individualization of instruction—and where the learning center does, in fact, become the "heart" of the school.*

*See Mineola Junior High School, Mineola, New York.

To achieve this, educators in these schools have overcome many of the old "traditions" relating to the use of space. Doorways have been replaced by wide-open archways; corridors have been transformed into integral parts of the learning environment, containing the additions of shelving, study carrels, and furniture; the standard-sized classroom has been replaced by areas of twice or three times the size, as well as by areas only a fraction of the size, to accommodate different types of learning activities. Carpeting and attractive decor and painting of walls have also tended to transform the sterile institutional look of schools into aesthetically appealing, comfortable centers for learning.

As the school is transformed into a huge learning center complex through these dramatic changes, it becomes apparent that the nucleus of the transformation must remain the Basic Learning Center Complex. This is the hub of all activity.

Student Groupings

The need for flexibility and imagination goes beyond changes in the use of physical space. For a school to become a learning center, new and flexible ways of continuously grouping and regrouping students must be found. Perhaps instead of using 25 or 30 pupils, a traditional class size, as the point of departure for forming smaller interest and achievement groupings, a number such as 125 to 150 should be used. The larger figures would tend to increase the opportunities for grouping pupils according to achievement, specific skill needs, learning style, ability, or any other type of need; or for pupils to group themselves by interest area, peer preferences, or other appropriate criteria. As the pupil population is increased, the greater become the chances of forming groups with common needs and interests. If in Class A there are two pupils with a common need, and in Class B there are two more with the same need, and in Class C there are four more, it would be economical at some point during the day to serve the eight pupils by having them engage in a project cooperatively or to receive direct instruction together. They would return to the larger group to participate in other types of groupings or in large-group activities. Many teachers have long recognized some of the advantages of such an approach. As a result, they have engaged in forms of team teaching, which in some respects is based upon a similar concept, although more limited.

Continuously changing groupings offer flexibility in the use of professional personnel. Such flexibility, when used to greatest advantage, can result in the more efficient use of professional time and talent.

Flexible Scheduling and Integration of Curricular Areas

Despite the convenience inherent in current scheduling practices in today's schools, these practices impose artificial restrictions that are in direct conflict with what we know about the styles of learning of individual children. A frequent cry of many teachers is that there is insufficient time to teach all that is in the school curriculum. In most instances where this sort of pressure is felt, curriculum is being fragmented and compartmentalized. Spelling is taught as a separate subject each day, as are reading, penmanship, writing skills, language usage, social studies, science, mathematics, and health, to say nothing of the special subjects of music and art, which are handled as completely separate entities. Often the performing arts other than music are completely omitted from the curriculum. The organization of curriculum and scheduling practices are integrally related. Curriculum, to be meaningful and effective, must be integrated; and such integration must necessarily be reflected in the use of time, personnel, and instructional resources and activities.

The fact that some learners are slow to "get into" tasks or projects at hand must be reflected in time allotments and scheduling practices. Other students learn most efficiently when they can work at a single project uninterrupted for a long period of time. Still others learn best when tasks are short and activities varied frequently during a day. Presently, many schools are operating on the premise that these differences either do not exist or that they do not really matter. There is sufficient research available to substantiate that such differences *do* matter. For a school to become a learning center, such practices in scheduling and use of time and the related approaches to curriculum design will need to be reexamined and changed.

The Key: Flexible, Well-Trained Professionals

There is no substitute in education for the flexible, conscientious, well-trained, competent professional. Anything that will be done in education for children must rest with these people. There can be no learning centers without such professionals. Whether the school itself ever does indeed become a learning center will depend chiefly upon teachers and administrators who are competent and committed. Regardless of obstacles that may stand in the way, if the professional educators want their schools to become learning centers, in the fullest sense of the term, it *will* be done.

8.
The Learning Center as
a Catalyst for Change

The development and implementation of the learning center concept involves people at all levels. There are many persons in education who are fearful of change; this fact will have a significant bearing on the implementation of a learning center. Based upon research on change, certain conclusions can be drawn concerning approaches that would tend to be more successful in effecting change in the schools. Voelz (1973) has summarized these approaches as follows:

1. Teachers must educate other teachers about change.

2. There must be positive reaction to teacher group requests and decisions.

3. The proceedings must be kept largely informal. (They should not be highly authoritarian or administrative.)

4. Innovative successes must be noted and praised.

The successful development and implementation of a learning center requires an administrative stance that endorses and deliberately plans a course which will include these approaches.

It is vital that administrative personnel, including superintendent, assistant superintendents, supervisors, coordinators, directors, and building principal, have a full understanding of the learning center concept and concur on the criteria that will ultimately be used to evaluate a center's effectiveness.

Without such understanding and agreement, the appropriate decisions required to facilitate the four approaches described

195

above for bringing about controlled change cannot be consciously and consistently made. A lack of clear understanding will result in a haphazard approach to support for the innovation. The innovation can even be totally undermined, although perhaps unintentionally.

To help educate all administrative levels to the innovation and to guide the change process, two major strategies may be engaged. One is the use of outside consultants to serve as catalysts for change. However, frequently a problem is so complex that to understand its manifestations requires more time than the consultant has available; and the consultant must, in order protect himself or herself professionally, limit himself or herself.

The second strategy is that of an inside change agent. The latter has many more advantages considering that change is a slow process and that successful innovation must necessarily reflect the socio-political complexity of the school.

There are a variety of forms that change-from-within may take. However, inasmuch as change as it relates to the learning center concept involves implementation of a specific innovation, it would make sense for the change agent to be a person with interest and expertise in that innovation. He or she should also possess characteristics of an innovator.

Johnson (1973) has reported on a series of investigations conducted at Utah State University that probed the human and organizational elements of the change process. These studies suggest the types of personality characteristics that the highly innovative person possesses. Findings revealed that innovators are generally warm, sociable, attentive people, adaptable, ready to cooperate, outgoing, and trustful. They tend to be less afraid of criticism, assertive rather than submissive, risktakers, adventuresome, and somewhat uninhibited. They have vigor and spontaneity and often do not see all of the danger signals. Johnson points out that this latter description is important if one considers how easy it is to stop change by simply anticipating all of the dangers of making change. Another characteristic of innovators is their ability to create unique solutions to often difficult problems; they are imaginative and creative. They tend to be planners, and this is essential to goal determination and achievement. Innovators also tend to be more well informed, and more inclined to experiment with problem solutions.

Even with such a person available, it is nonetheless necessary that the structure of the innovation reflect an accommodation to the fact that a systematic approach to school problems requires technical competence from widely disparate groups. It would be unrealistic to expect even the best of innovators or change agents to singlehandedly tackle and resolve the complex school problems that will have a bearing on and directly affect successful innovation and change.

Freeing Teachers to Learn About the Learning Center Concept

There are numerous ways of helping teachers to learn about change and, more specifically, the learning center concept. The following are a few with which this writer has had experience and has found to be effective:

1. Planned visitations to other schools outside the district that have learning centers, individualized programs, library media centers, and open classrooms. Representatives from each grade level, and the librarian, reading specialist, and principal may make the visitations. Prior to each visitation, the staff would do well to prepare a list of observational guidelines in the form of questions to be answered during the visitations. (See Appendix G for a sample Visitation Guide.) Visitations should be geared to stimulate thinking, and synthesis and evaluation of concepts and methodologies for implementing individualization of instruction. A follow-up session to each visitation will allow faculty members to share their perceptions, make comparisons, and voice their concerns.

If there are already learning centers within the district, these may be visited as well.

2. Provide literature on learning centers and time for discussions and reactions to the readings.

3. Provide time for teachers to be involved in informal presentations and discussions on the learning center concept and to respond to and discuss the concept. Slides may be taken during visitations and shared with other members of the staff not making that particular visitation.

4. Provide time for a Learning Center Advisory Council comprised of a faculty member representing each grade level, reading specialist, librarian, a teacher union representative, the principal, and the "change agent" to meet to establish policy, a written philosophy, a physical design, procedures, and criteria for evaluation, and to discuss on a continuous basis problems related to development of the learning center.

5. Provide time for teachers to preview instructional resources and equipment and to participate in materials and equipment demonstrations by local representatives of publishing companies and audio-visual producers; provide time for reading specialist, librarian, and other key personnel to attend materials exhibits.

6. Send teachers to professional conferences which have as one of their topics the learning center concept or related ideas, such as diagnosing learning problems, uses of educational media, individualization of instruction, open education, organizing for individualization of instruction, developing learning modules and contracts, etc.

7. Provide time for in-service workshops.

8. Provide time for organizing for individualization through curriculum projects. For example, time will be required to develop (a) a Prescriptive Programming Resource Guide in which all the new instructional resources are correlated with learning objectives; (b) learning modules; and (c) learning activity packages, contracts, or other organizational alternatives for independent study. Teachers will learn by doing.

Teachers Educating Teachers

There is a vast difference between a college professor, administrator, or supervisor lecturing, teaching, or explaining to teachers the advantages of a new technique, method, or approach to instruction and that of teachers educating other teachers about change. Teachers are "front-line" people. The problems they confront on a daily basis are immediate ones that require practical, workable solutions. If something new works for one teacher, there is a good chance other teachers will feel that it might work for them too, particularly if the teacher or teachers who are endorsing the change are ones who are respected and accepted by their colleagues. The following list suggests some ways that teachers can educate other teachers to change in conjunction with the development of a learning center. The list is not intended to be exhaustive.

1. When making visitations to learning centers, arrange to allow the visiting teachers to speak informally with teachers in the host school. Visiting reading specialist and librarian should speak with host school reading specialist and librarian, and visiting principal should speak with host principal to gain insights into their respective concerns, roles in the change, and problems that might be anticipated.

2. Formulate a Learning Center Teacher Advisory Council of teacher volunteers. The members of the Advisory Council, because of their intense involvement in the project, will become the staunchest supporters and ambassadors of change and of the specific innovation, and they will do more to further change in the informal setting of the teachers' room than any expert on the subject might accomplish from a platform.

3. Select well-respected and capable teachers to preview and use new materials with pupils. In one school where teachers were resistant to any type of teaching machine, the reading specialist tried with her pupils the Borg Warner System 80 and found the learning units to be beneficial for many remedial reading cases. She also found that pupils responded positively to

the approach. She then shared her initial reservations and subsequent experiences with the machine with colleagues, who became more willing to learn about the uses and potential values of teaching machines and programmed instruction. In another instance, teachers were caught up with a lock-step workbook approach to teaching spelling. Two respected and capable fifth grade teachers piloted, modified, and adapted an individualized cassette-based spelling-language program which was housed in the learning center; they then conducted workshop sessions for their colleagues in the use of the program. Another fifth grade teacher piloted an individualized reading approach, and then conducted workshops for colleagues in her own building and later for colleagues from other buildings within the district. The majority of these teachers had been using the district basal adoption to teach reading and were interested in individualized approaches.

4. Superintendent's Conference Days may be used by teachers to conduct in-house workshops on the learning center and individualization of instruction for their colleagues within the pilot building as well as for the teachers from other buildings within the district. Educational consultants, many of whom are former teachers, from some of the major publishing companies may also be used to introduce new programs and techniques related to the learning center and to further the concept of individualization in general.

5. Curriculum projects result in products developed by teachers and for teachers. The skills and insights gained by teachers participating in curriculum projects very often are assimilated by non-participating teachers through informal daily contacts with those who developed the projects.

6. The teacher association or union representative on the Advisory Council serves a vital function. He or she educates other teachers and union leadership to the nature of the change, its implications, and advantages for the teacher group. Problems, questions, or concerns of the union can be readily identified and dealt with so that the change will not be impeded because of

political reasons or fear of threat to job security or to terms and conditions of employment.

Positive Reaction to Teacher
Group Requests

It is important to keep open channels of communication between teacher groups and administration. It is equally important that the administration be responsive to the concerns and requests of teacher groups where these will facilitate and further desired changes. The Teacher Advisory Council is one effective vehicle for keeping open channels of communication between teachers and administration. There is much evidence to suggest that the administrative structure under which an innovative program operates cannot be autonomous from those who execute the program. Through the intimate involvement of teachers in the planning and decision-making process, the chances are enhanced for effective change through the learning center.

Keeping the Innovative
Proceedings Informal

Changing behavior, according to experts on the subject, requires, among other things, a system whereby new behavior can be experimented with, reinforced, and made the foundation for yet a new cycle of behavioral change. The learning center provides such a system for teachers to experiment with new behaviors. Unlike a single in-service course or a professional conference, the learning center is ever-present; its process is on-going, and staff involvement is continuous and of a varied nature. It provides skills and resources required to solve practical problems. It not only initiates behavioral change, but properly implemented, it also structures the environment and relationships in such a way as to make possible the *fixing of behavioral change*. Teachers are not evaluated in the learning center; they are assisted and encouraged.

Ironically, too often the very groups most desirous of initiating and effecting change in the schools become the greatest inhibitors of change. As pressures of various sorts are exerted from the top of the educational hierarchy on down and from the community and school board, the innovative proceedings may gradually lose the informality essential for teacher experimentation with new behaviors. The following is a list of conditions, demands, and situations that may individually or in combination inhibit successful innovation and subsequent change by creating pressures that adversely affect the innovative procedure:

1. Demands for "instant success" in the form of "hard data," usually standardized test results, to "prove" that the innovation is "worthwhile"; demands for evidence that pupils are "learning better" even when the focus should be initially upon the process of behavioral and environmental changes.

2. Ambiguity and varied agendas of different groups, such as faculty, principal, central office, school board, and community with respect to the underlying philosophy, goals, and methods for achieving individualization of instruction and for implementing the innovation and/or achieving change (often the type of change desired is undefined).

3. Community volunteers observing teachers as they experiment with new behaviors; community volunteers who become involved in assisting with innovative programs but who have hidden agendas or reasons other than assisting for volunteering; and improper or superficial screening of volunteers.

4. Undertaking too many major innovative projects at one time and overscheduling the "change agent," consultant, or person responsible for guiding the innovations.

5. Ambiguity with respect to lines of authority and channels of communication, power struggles, internal conflicts, and vested interests of individuals and/or groups.

6. A condition in which those responsible for given outcomes are not doing the decision-making which will effect those outcomes (for example, the purchasing agent orders audiovisual equipment items for the center that are functionally

different from those requested by the educators involved in the project; or a principal unilaterally selects instructional resources to be used by teachers without involving them in the decision-making process).

7. Cutbacks in budgetary requirements or spending necessary to support and perpetuate the innovation. This would include insufficient appropriations for curriculum projects, staff development, equipment and supplies, and personnel to sustain, develop, and improve the innovation.

Noting and Praising
Innovative Successes

Success tends to breed success. Praise is an effective means of giving status and encouragement to teachers as they experiment with new behaviors, so that their small successes will be regenerative and lead to greater ones. The administrator who reserves judgment and praise until perfection is achieved will be less likely to see real change occur than the administrator who praises even the small successes and accepts as natural the initial floundering, uncertainty, reservations, and anxiety that accompany innovation and change.

Praise may be private and direct in the form of a compliment paid by the learning center director to a teacher, the principal to the reading specialist, or the superintendent to the principal or the "change agent."

Praise may be formal as in the form of a letter of commendation to a teacher conducting a workshop session for colleagues.

Praise may also be public in the form of status. Having visitors from other buildings or other school districts come to the center and talk with teachers makes teachers feel that what they are doing is important and worthwhile; and, consequently, that they are important, and doing something special and of interest to others. Similarly, arranging to have pilot project teachers conduct workshop sessions for colleagues is a means of giving status and indirect praise to the teacher or specialist. Articles in local newspapers and district news bulletins about the learning center and the work of the professional staff involved is prestigious and another indirect form of praise as well as good public relations.

Model Transfer, Evaluation,
and the Principal

The building principal is probably the most important single person in either encouraging or blocking the successful implementation of an innovation—and consequently change—in his or her building. Implementing an innovation is without a doubt additional work for all involved, but this is particularly true for the principal. It means additional planning, meetings, scheduling problems, evaluation, budgetary involvement, public relations, and support and encouragement for teachers. It means long-range planning and added involvements with central office, which in some districts principals have found desirable and judicious to keep at a minimum.

Nonetheless, let us assume that a principal is eager and willing to effectuate change and to be involved in implementing an innovation; that the principal has previously set a positive tone in his or her building; that channels of communication between management and teachers are open; and that the principal is somewhat democratic in leadership role and is flexible, cooperative, capable, hardworking, and knowledgeable about the specific innovation. Then, the two most important skills he or she must possess to successfully implement the innovation are (1) the ability to effectuate model transfer, and (2) understanding of the evaluative processes.

There is evidence to suggest that many schools of educational administration generally omit from their curricula training in the techniques of model transfer and in the conduct of process and product evaluations. This may be one reason why conceptual models developed as a result of research findings remain in textbooks, and schools continue to operate years behind research.

Perhaps this is an oversimplification of a complex problem; nonetheless, it is a real and significant deficiency that has resulted in many schools embarking upon innovations without a conceptual framework or philosophy and without a model. These "innovations" are simply observed superficially in other school districts and adopted with all of the external trappings but without a conceptual guide to serve as a point of reference for sound decision-making.

It is beyond the scope of this book to develop a design for training principals and other administrators in model transfer or in the ability to concretize a conceptual model, though much of the material in this book suggests ways of achieving this in implementing a learning center. Similarly, it is beyond the scope of this work to design a program for training administrators in the methodologies of conducting context, input, process, and product evaluations. Even where a research and evaluation specialist is available in a school district, it will still be incumbent upon the building principal to assume some responsibility for evaluation.

In situations where there is no person on the staff of the school district skilled in the evaluative processes, and where there is no staff person capable of effectuating model transfer in implementing a learning center, then it would be advisable to hire a consultant for this purpose, or at least to train staff in these areas.

In conclusion, the point to be made is that a lack of expertise on the part of the building principal in either model transfer or the evaluative processes, or both, will impede and may even undermine the successful implementation of the learning center. With this knowledge, districts would do well to assess their needs and available local talent and plan accordingly.

Chapter Summary

Through appropriate structuring of relationships and environment, the learning center can serve as an effective change catalyst.

It provides teachers with a system and an environment for experimenting with and fixing new behaviors by providing the skills, resources, and supportive services required to solve practical problems. Research has indicated that change may be facilitated through certain basic approaches, which have been summarized by Voelz (1973) as follows:

1. Teachers must educate teachers about change.
2. There must be positive reaction to teacher group requests and decisions.
3. The proceeding must be kept largely informal.
4. Innovative successes must be noted and praised.

However, even where these approaches are used, there may arise pressures from within the educational system or from external sources such as community or school board that can act adversely upon the innovative proceeding and even abort it, though perhaps not intentionally. Some of these pressures include demands for "instant success" with the innovation, disparate views on project goals and objectives, imposition of elements that would tend to inhibit teacher experimentation with new behaviors, overscheduling of the "change agent," ambiguity with respect to lines of authority and channels of communication, and insufficient budgetary support to maintain the innovation.

Despite the importance of all of these factors, the most vital to the success of the innovation are the skills, abilities, and attitudes of the building principal. Two skills required of the building principal are the ability to effectuate transfer of a conceptual model for a learning center, and the ability to conduct and guide the evaluative processes. If the building principal lacks these skills, it may be necessary to seek out some other talent from within the district or even to go outside the district to fill the gap.

References

Chapter 1
References

Arnspiger, V. C. *Measuring the Effectiveness of Sound Pictures as Teaching Aids*. New York: Columbia University, 1933.

Allport, Floyd Henry. *Theories of Perception and the Concept of Structure*. New York: John Wiley & Sons, 1955.

Barth, Roland S. *Open Education and the American School*. New York: Agathon Press, 1972.

Brauner, Charles. *American Educational Theory*. New York: Prentice-Hall, Inc., 1964.

Broudy, Harry S. "Historic Exemplars of Teaching Methods," *Handbook of Research on Teaching*, N. L. Gage, ed. Chicago: Rand McNally & Company, 1963, pp. 29-32.

Cremin, Lawrence. *The Transformation of the School*. New York: Vintage Books, 1961.

Dietrich, Dorothy, and Virginia Mathews, eds. *Reading and Revolution*. Newark, Delaware: International Reading Association, 1970.

Durrell, Donald D. "Challenge and Experiment in Teaching Reading," *Challenge and Experiment in Reading*, J. Allen Figurel, ed., International Reading Association Conference Proceedings, Vol. 7. New York: Scholastic Magazines, 1962, pp. 20-22.

Eads, L. K. "Research Leading to the Production of Primary Grade Educational Sound Films," *Proceedings of the New York Society for the Study of Experimental Education*. New York, 1938, pp. 70-90.

Evans, Richard I. *Jean Piaget: The Man and His Ideas*. New York: E. P. Dutton & Co., Inc., 1973.

Gray, H. A. "Sound Films for Reading Programs," *School Executive*, LX (February, 1941), 24-25, 29.

Handlin, Oscar. *John Dewey's Challenge to Education*. New York: Harper & Row, 1959.

Heisler, Florence. "A Comparison Between Those Elementary School Children Who Attend Motion Pictures, Read Comic Books and Listen to Serial Radio Programs to Excess with Those Who Indulge in These Activities Seldom or Not at All," *Journal of Educational Research*, XLII (November, 1948), 182-90.

Hill, Joseph E. *Conference on the Educational Sciences: Proceedings and Manuscripts*, The Institute for the Educational Sciences. Oakland, Michigan: Oakland Community College Press, 1973.

Hill, Joseph E. *How Schools Can Apply Systems Analysis*. Bloomington, Indiana: The Phi Delta Kappa Educational Foundation, 1972.

Jardine, Alex. "The Experimental Use of Visual Aids in Teaching Beginning Reading," *Education Screen*, XVII (September, 1938), 220-22.

Kearns, Doris, "The Growth and Development of Title III, ESEA," *The Process of Innovation in Education*, No. 2, The Educational Technology Review Series. Englewood Cliffs, New Jersey: Educational Technology Publications, 1973, pp. 74-81.

Mahoney, A., and H. L. Harshman. "Sound Film Experiment with Handicapped and Retarded Pupils," *Education Screen*, XVIII (December, 1939), 359-60.

Maslow, A. H. *Motivation and Personality*. New York: Harper and Brothers, 1954.

McCracken, Glenn. "The New Castle Reading Experiment," *The Reading Teacher*, IX (April, 1956), 225, 241-45.

McLuhan, Marshall. *Understanding Media: The Extensions of Man*. New York: McGraw-Hill, 1964.

Skinner, B. F. "The Science of Learning and the Art of Teaching,"

Programmed Learning and Teaching Machines, Lucius Butler and William J. Wiley, eds. New York: Selected Academic Readings, 1970.

Smith, Donald E. P., "The Physiological and Psychological Bases of Individual Differences," *Individualizing Instruction in Reading*. A Report of the Twentieth Annual Conference and Course on Reading, Donald L. Cleland and Elaine C. Vilscek, eds. Pittsburgh: University of Pittsburgh, July, 1964, pp. 20-21.

"Television: History of Television Development," *Compton's Encyclopedia*, 1968 ed., XXII, 78-79.

Waples, Douglas. *Print, Radio, and Film in a Democracy*. Chicago: The University of Chicago Press, 1942.

Witty, Paul A., and James P. Fitzwater. "An Experiment with Films, Film Readers, and the Magnetic Sound Projector," *Elementary English*, XXX (April, 1953), 232-41.

Additional Sources of Information

Anderson, Irving H. "A Motion Picture Technique for the Improvement of Reading," *University of Michigan School of Education Bulletin*, XI (November, 1939), 27-30.

Allen, James E., U. S. Commissioner of Education. Address Before National Association of State School Boards. Washington, D. C., October, 1969.

Armsey, James W., and Norman C. Dahl. *An Inquiry into the Uses of Instructional Technology*, A Ford Foundation Report. New York: The Ford Foundation, 1973.

Austin, Mary C., and Coleman Morrison. *The First R: The Harvard Report on Reading in the Elementary Schools*. New York: Macmillan Company, 1963.

Bobbitt, Franklin. *How to Make a Curriculum*. Boston: Houghton Mifflin Company, 1924.

Bottomly, Forbes. "An Experiment with the Controlled Reader," *Journal of Educational Research*, LIV (March, 1961), 265-69.

Bradley, Beatrice E. "Reading with a Dash of Showmanship,"

Elementary School Journal, LXI (October, 1960), 28-31.

Bushnell, Donald D., and Dwight W. Allen. *The Computer in American Education*, Commissioned by the Association for Educational Data Systems. New York: John Wiley and Sons, Inc., 1967.

DeBoer, Dorothy L., ed. *Reading Diagnosis and Evaluation*. Proceedings of the Thirteenth Annual Convention, International Reading Association, Vol. 13, Part 4. Newark, Delaware: I.R.A., 1970.

Department of Superintendence, Commission on the Curriculum, *Third Yearbook*. Washington, D. C.: The Department, National Education Association, 1925.

Doll, Ronald C., ed. *Individualizing Instruction, The A. S. C. D. 1964 Yearbook*. Washington, D. C.: The Association for Supervision and Curriculum Development, 1964.

Eckstrom, Ruth B. *Experimental Studies of Homogeneous Grouping: A Review of the Literature*. Princeton, New Jersey: Educational Testing Service, 1959.

Figurel, J. Allen, ed. *Challenge and Experiment in Reading*, Conference Proceedings of the International Reading Association, Vol. 7. Newark, Delaware: I. R. A., 1962.

Figurel, J. Allen, ed. *Vistas in Reading*, Proceedings of the International Reading Association Conference. Newark, Delaware: I. R. A., 1966.

Fleischmann Commission Report. Summarized by Board of Cooperative Educational Services. New York: Nassau B.O.C.E.S., Research and Development Division, 1972.

Frazier, Alexander. *Open Schools for Children*. Washington, D. C.: Association for Supervision and Curriculum Development, 1972.

Frazier, Alexander. "Our Search for Better Answers," *Educational Leadership*, XX (April, 1963), 453-58.

French, Russell L. "Individualizing Classroom Communication," *Educational Leadership*, XXVIII (November, 1970), 193-96.

Gardiner, Joseph S. "A Study of the Effects of the Audio-Tutorial Reading Program on Student Achievement, Attitudes, and Classroom Behavior," Unpublished Doctoral dissertation, Syracuse University, 1971.

Gash, Eleanor A. "A History of the Development of Public Elementary School Reading Clinics in the United States and an Analysis of Their Functions." Unpublished Doctoral dissertation, Hofstra University, 1972.

Gold, Milton J. "Focusing on Teaching Needs," *Educational Leadership*, XX (April, 1963), 434-37.

Gray, H. A., "Vocabulary Teaching Possibilities of Sound Films," *Modern Language Forum*, Vol. 1 (December, 1940).

Gropper, George L. "Why Is a Picture Worth a Thousand Words?" *AV Communication Review*, 11:93 (July, 1963).

Guss, Carolyn. "Films, Filmstrips, and Reading," *The Reading Teacher*, XVII (March, 1964), 441-46.

Hill, Joseph E., and August Kerber. *Models, Methods, and Analytical Procedures in Education Research*. Detroit: Wayne State University Press, 1967.

Jones, Daisey Marmel. "An Experiment in Adaption to Individual Differences," *Journal of Educational Psychology*, XXXIX (May, 1948), 257-72.

Lombard, Marilyn Dean. "Perceptions of Teachers and Media Specialists Regarding the Use of Instructional Technology in Teaching Reading." Unpublished Doctoral dissertation, University of Southern California, 1969.

Matteoni, Louise. "TV Cartoons in Initial Reading Experiences with Culturally Deprived Children." Unpublished Doctoral dissertation, New York University, 1966.

Mayhew, Katherine, and Anna Edwards. *The Dewey School*. New York: Appleton-Century Co., 1936, pp. 6-7.

Minsel, Clara. "Audio-Visual Materials and Fifth Grade Reading Achievement," *Science Education*, XLV (February, 1961), 86-88.

Nason, Harold M. "The Use of Television in the Teaching of Reading," *Reading as an Intellectual Activity*, Conference Proceedings of International Reading Association. New York: Scholastic Magazines, 1963.

Olson, Willard C. *Child Development*. 2d ed. Boston: D. C. Heath and Co., 1959.

Project on the Instructional Program of Public Schools, National

Education Association, *The Principals Look at the Schools*. Washington, D. C.: The Association, 1962, p. 15.

Ramsey, Wallace Z., ed. *Organizing for Individual Differences*, Perspectives in Reading, No. 9. Newark, Delaware: International Reading Association, 1967.

Robinson, Marie. "Federal Funds: .Right to Read," *American Education*, November, 1974, p. 40.

Rogers, Vincent R., and Bud Church, eds. *Open Education: Critique and Assessment*. Washington, D. C.: Association for Supervision and Curriculum Development, 1975.

Rothrock, Dayton. "Heterogeneous, Homogeneous, or Individualized Approach to Reading?" *Elementary English*, XXXVIII (April, 1961), 233-35.

Rothrock, Dayton. "Teachers Surveyed: A Decade of Individualized Reading," *Elementary English*, XLV (1968), 754-57.

Rugg, Harold, and Ann Schumaker. *The Child-Centered School*. New York: World Book Co., 1928, reprinted by Arno Press, 1969.

Schick, Frank L. *The Paperbound Book in America*. New York: R. R. Bowker Company, 1958.

Schramm, Wilbur. "What We Know About Learning from Instructional Television," *Educational Television: The Next Ten Years*. The Institute for Communication Research. Stanford: Stanford University Press, 1962.

Sheldon, William D. "Television and Reading Instruction," *Education*, LXXX (May, 1960), 552-55.

Sleeman, Phillip J., Galen B. Kelley, and Robert A. Byrne. "A Comparison of the Relative Effectiveness of Overhead Projection, Teaching Programs, and Conventional Techniques for Teaching Dictionary Skills," *Science of Learning*, III (1967), 67-69.

Smith, Nila Banton. *American Reading Instruction*. Newark, Delaware: International Reading Association, 1965.

Sullivan, Lorraine M. "The Use of Films and Filmstrips in the Teaching of Reading." Paper presented at the 3rd International Reading Association World Congress. August, 1970, Sydney, Australia.

Townsend, Agatha. "What Research Says to the Reading Teacher— Ten Questions of Individualized Reading," *The Reading Teacher*, XVIII (November, 1964), 145-49.

Travers, Robert M. W. "Efficiency in Rote Learning Under Four Learning Conditions," *Journal of Educational Research*, LX (September, 1966), 10-12.

Trump, Lloyd J. *Images of the Future*. Washington, D.C.: National Association of Secondary School Principals, Supported by the Ford Foundation, 1959.

Vilscek, Elaine C., ed. *A Decade of Innovations: Approaches to Beginning Reading*. Vol. XII, Part 3. Newark, Delaware: International Reading Association, 1968.

Warner, Dolores. "A Beginning Reading Program with Audio-Visual Reinforcement: An Experimental Study," *Journal of Educational Research*, LXI (1969), 230-33.

Wiener, Roberta Behr. "An Investigation into Open Classroom Practices in Nassau and Suffolk Counties, Long Island, New York, and the Types of Reading Programs Implemented in the Open Classroom." Unpublished Doctoral dissertation, Hofstra University, 1973.

Wilhelms, Fred T. "A New Progressive Education," *National Elementary Principal*, XLVII, 1 (September, 1967), 33.

Wiseman, T. Jan, and Molly J. Wiseman. *Creative Communications: Teaching Mass Media*. University of Minnesota: National Scholastic Press Assoc., 1971.

Witty, Paul A., with Ann Coomer, and Robert Sizemore. "Individualized Reading: A Summary and Evaluation," *Elementary English*, XXXVI (October, 1959), 401-12, 450.

Wolfe, James Madison. "Utilization of the Single Concept Sound Film in the Graphic Arts to Assist Students Who Have Reading Comprehension Problems." Unpublished Doctoral dissertation, East Texas State University, 1970.

Chapter 2
References

American Association of School Libraries, and the Department of Audiovisual Instruction. *Standards for School Media Programs*. Chicago: American Library Association, and Washington, D. C.: National Education Association, 1969.

Dunn, Rita, and Kenneth Dunn. *The Educator's Self-Teaching Guide to Individualizing Instruction*. New York: Parker Publishers, 1975.

Hill, Joseph E. *Cognitive Style as an Educational Science*. Oakland Community College: Oakland Community College Press, 1973.

Hill, Joseph E. *The Educational Sciences*. Oakland Community College: Oakland Community College Press, 1973.

Wepman, Joseph M. Personal correspondence between Dr. Wepman, Professor of Psychology, University of Chicago, and the writer, June, 1975 to July, 1975.

Additional Sources of Information

Armsey, James W., and Norman C. Dahl. *An Inquiry into the Uses of Instructional Technology*, A Ford Foundation Report. New York: The Ford Foundation, 1973.

Bailey, Catherine, ed. *Communication and Educational Redesign*. Communications Convocation, New York State Educational Communication Association, New York, November, 1972.

Bennie, Frances. "The Development of Learning Centers and the Construction of a Model for Learning Centers at the Elementary and Middle School Levels." Unpublished Doctoral dissertation, Hofstra University, 1975.

Bennie, Frances. "Pupil Attitudes Toward Individually Prescribed Lab Programs," *Journal of Reading*, XVII (November, 1973), 208-112.

Bennie, Frances. *Schwarting Learning Center: First Evaluative Report*, Title II-III Unigrant Project. Bethpage, New York: Plainedge Public Schools, 1975.

Bushnell, Donald D., and Dwight W. Allen. *The Computer in American Education*, Commissioned by the Association for Educational Data Systems. New York: John Wiley and Sons, Inc., 1967.

Congreve, Willard J. "Learning Center ... Catalyst for Change?" *Educational Leadership*, XXI (January, 1974), 211-16.

Emmerling, Frank C. "Salt for Education," *Educational Leadership*, XXI (January, 1964), 231-33.

Gash, Eleanor A. "A History of the Development of Public Elementary School Reading Clinics in the United States and an Analysis of Their Functions." Unpublished Doctoral dissertation, Hofstra University, 1972.

Henley, John Patrick. *Computer-Based Library and Information Systems*. New York: American Elsevier Publishing Co., 1972.

Horton, Lowell, and Phyllis Horton. *The Learning Center: Heart of the School*. Minneapolis: T. S. Dennison and Company, 1973.

Hostrop, Richard W. *Education Inside the Library-Media Center*. Hamden, Connecticut: Linnet Books, 1973.

Krohn, Mildred L. "Learning and the Learning Center," *Educational Leadership*, XXI (January, 1964), 217-22.

Leeper, R., ed. *Centers for Learning: Educational Leadership*, XXI (January, 1964).

Licklider, J.C.R. *Libraries of the Future*. Cambridge, Massachusetts: The Massachusetts Institute of Technology Press, 1965.

Ofiesh, Gabriel D. *The Librarian and the Learning Resource Director: Future Roles, Problems, and Issues*, an audiotape cassette program. Englewood Cliffs, New Jersey: Educational Technology Publications, 1972.

Ofiesh, Gabriel D. *Toward the New Learning Centers*, an audiotape cassette program. Englewood Cliffs, New Jersey: Educational Technology Publications, 1972.

Preston, Ellinor G. "The Librarian Sees His Role in the Materials Center," *Educational Leadership*, XXI (January, 1964), 214-16.

"Program Descriptions of Learning Centers." Project Individualized Instruction, Arline Winnerman, Director. Reports Nos.

123, 156, 187, 209, 275, 285. Suffolk B.O.C.E.S. II, Title III Project. Reports made March, 1973 through December, 1974 (Xeroxed).

Rapport, Virginia, assoc. ed. *Learning Centers: Children on Their Own*. Washington, D. C.: Association for Childhood Education, 1970.

Russell, Robert H. "An Investigation of the Multi-Media Laboratory Approach to Improvement of Reading in a Middle School." Unpublished Doctoral dissertation, Southern Illinois University, 1972.

Shores, Louis. *Audiovisual Librarianship*. Littleton, Colorado: Libraries Unlimited, Inc., 1973.

Spitzer, Lillian. "Looking at Centers for Learning Through Research-Colored Glasses," *Educational Leadership*, XXI (January, 1964), 249-61.

Teachey, William G., and Joseph B. Carter. *Learning Laboratories: A Guide to Their Adoption and Use*. Englewood Cliffs, New Jersey: Educational Technology Publications, 1971.

Tozier, Virginia. "The Child and the Library Center," *Educational Leadership*, XXI (January, 1964), 223-26.

Chapter 3
References

Bruner, Jerome. "Some Theories on Instruction Illustrated with Reference to Mathematics," *Theories of Learning and Instruction, N.S.S.E. Yearbook, 1964*. Chicago: University of Chicago Press, 1964.

Cole, Henry P. *Process Education*. Englewood Cliffs, New Jersey: Educational Technology Publications, 1972.

Dewey, John and Arthur Bentley. *Knowing and the Known*. Boston: Beacon, 1949.

Maslow, A. H. *Motivation and Personality*. New York: Harper and Row, 1954.

McLuhan, Marshall. *Understanding Media: The Extensions of Man*. New York: McGraw-Hill Book Company, 1964.

Smith, Brooks E., Kenneth S. Goodman, and Robert Meredith. *Language and Thinking in the Elementary School*. New York: Holt, Rinehart, and Winston, Inc., 1970.

Wallace, Ben. *Survival Is the Name of the Game*. New York: Mineola Public Schools, 1970.

Additional Sources of Information

Barrett, Thomas C., and Dale D. Johnson, eds. *Views on Elementary Reading Instruction*. Newark, Delaware: International Reading Association, 1973.

Barth, Roland S. *Open Education and the American School*. New York: Agathon Press, 1972.

Bennie, Frances. "The Development of Learning Centers and the Construction of a Model for Learning Centers at the Elementary and Middle School Levels." Unpublished Doctoral dissertation, Hofstra University, 1975.

Bruner, Jerome. *Process of Education*. Cambridge, Massachusetts: Harvard University Press, 1965.

Byler, Ruth, Gertrude Lewis, and Ruth Tutman. *Teach Us What We Want to Know*. New York: Mental Health Materials Center, Inc., 1969.

DeBoer, Dorothy L., ed. *Reading Diagnosis and Evaluation*. Proceedings of the Thirteenth Annual Convention, International Reading Association, Vol. 13, Part 4. Newark, Delaware: I. R. A., 1970.

DeVault, M. Vere, and Others. *Descriptor for Individualized Instruction: Development Procedures and Results*. Wisconsin University, Center for the Analysis of Individualized Instruction; sponsored by National Institute of Education (DHEW), Washington, D. C., September, 1973.

Doll, Ronald C., ed. *Individualizing Instruction, The A.S.C.D. 1964 Yearbook*. Washington, D.C.: The Association for Supervision and Curriculum Development, 1964.

Farr, Roger, and Samuel Weintraub, eds. *Reading Research Quarterly*, VII (Fall, 1971).

Frazier, Alexander. *Open Schools for Children*. Washington, D. C.: Association for Supervision and Curriculum Development, 1972.

Harmin, Merrill, Howard Kirschenbaum, and Sidney B. Simon. *Clarifying Values Through Subject Matter*. Minneapolis: Winston Press, 1973.

Hill, Joseph E. *Cognitive Style as an Educational Science*. Oakland Community College: Oakland Community College Press, 1973.

Hill, Joseph E. *The Educational Sciences*. Oakland Community College: Oakland Community College Press, 1973.

Hofstein, Saul. *The Nature of Process: Its Implications for Social Work*. Reprinted from the *Journal of Social Work Process*, XVI, Virginia P. Robinson Fund. Philadelphia: University of Pennsylvania Press, 1964.

Horton, Lowell, and Phyllis Horton. *The Learning Center: Heart of the School*. Minneapolis: T. S. Dennison and Company, 1973.

Hostrop, Richard W. *Education Inside the Library-Media Center*. Hamden, Connecticut: Linnet Books, 1973.

Kaplan, Abraham. *The Conduct of Inquiry*. Pennsylvania: Chandler Publishing Co., 1964.

Kohler, W. *Gestalt Psychology*. New York: Liveright Publishing Corp., 1929.

Krohn, Mildred L. "Learning and the Learning Center," *Educational Leadership*, XXI (January, 1964), 217-22.

Mayhew, Katherine, and Anna Edwards. *The Dewey School*. New York: Appleton-Century Co., 1936, pp. 6-7.

Ofiesh, Gabriel D. *Toward the New Learning Centers*, an audio-tape cassette program. Englewood Cliffs, New Jersey: Educational Technology Publications, 1972.

Patterson, C. H. *Humanistic Education*. Englewood Cliffs, New Jersey: Prentice-Hall, 1973.

Rapport, Virginia, assoc. ed. *Learning Centers: Children on Their Own*. Washington, D. C.: Association for Childhood Education, 1970.

Rubin, L. J., ed. *Life Skills in School and Society*. Washington, D. C.: Association for Supervision and Curriculum Development, 1969.

Rugg, Harold, and Ann Schumaker. *The Child-Centered School*. New York: World Book Co., 1928, reprinted by Arno Press, 1969.

Shepherd, David L., ed. *Current Emphases in Reading*, Proceedings of Hofstra University Reading Conferences Six, Seven, and Eight. Hempstead, New York: Hofstra University, 1970.

Singer, Harry, and Robert B. Ruddell, eds. *Theoretical Models and Processes of Reading*. Delaware: International Reading Association, 1970.

Chapter 4
References

Anderson, Robert H. "Sustaining Individualized Instruction Through Flexible Administration," *The Computer in American Education*, eds. Don Bushnell and Dwight W. Allen. New York: John Wiley & Sons, 1967.

Burns, Richard, and Joe Lars Klingstedt. *Individualized Learning Using Instructional Modules*, Educational Technology Cassettes. Englewood Cliffs, New Jersey: Educational Technology Publications, 1974.

Buros, Oscar Krisen, ed. *Reading Tests and Reviews II*. Highland Park, New Jersey: The Gryphon Press, 1975.

Center for Curriculum. *Computer Based Curriculum Planning*. Amherst: State University of New York at Buffalo, 1976.

DeBoer, Dorothy L., ed. *Reading Diagnosis and Evaluation*. Proceedings of the Thirteenth Annual Convention, International Reading Association, Vol. 13, Part 4. Newark, Delaware: I. R. A., 1970.

Hill, Joseph E. *Conference on the Educational Sciences: Proceedings and Manuscripts*, The Institute for the Educational Sciences. Oakland, Michigan: Oakland Community College Press, 1973.

Searls, Evelyn F. *How to Use WISC Scores in Reading Diagnosis*. Newark, Delaware: International Reading Association, 1975.

Simon, Anita, and E. Gil Boyer, eds. *Mirrors of Behavior: An Anthology of Classroom Observation Instruments*. Philadelphia: Research for Better Schools and the Center for the Study of Teaching, Temple University, 1967.

Simon, Sidney B., and Leland W. Howe, and Howard Kirschenbaum. *Values Clarification: A Handbook of Practical Strategies for Teachers and Students*. New York: Hart Publishing Co., 1972.

Wallace, Ben. *Survival Is the Name of the Game*. Mineola, New York: Mineola Public Schools, 1970.

Weldon, Ward. *How to Build Modules and Learning Packets*, audiotape cassettes. Tulsa, Oklahoma: Instructional Media Inc., 1975.

Additional Sources of Information

Baker, Gail L., and Isadore Goldberg. "The Individualized Learning System," *Educational Leadership*, XXVII (May, 1970), 775-80.

Banathy, Bela H. *Instructional Systems*. Palo Alto, California: Fearon Publishers, 1968.

Blitz, Barbara. *The Open Classroom: Making It Work*. Rockleigh, New Jersey: Allyn and Bacon, 1973.

Bloom, Benjamin, ed. *Taxonomy of Educational Objectives, Handbook I: Cognitive Domain*. New York: David McKay, 1964.

Bushnell, Donald D., and Dwight Allen. *The Computer in American Education*, Commissioned by the Association for Educational Data Systems. New York: John Wiley and Sons, Inc., 1967.

Chaney, Clara M., and Newell C. Kephart. *Motoric Aids to Perceptual Training*. Columbus, Ohio: Charles E. Merrill Publishing, Co., 1968.

Cleland, Donald L., and Elaine C. Vilscek, eds. *Individualizing Instruction in Reading*, A Report of the Twentieth Annual Conference and Course on Reading. Pittsburgh: University of Pittsburgh, July, 1964.

The Computer and Education, The Educational Technology Review Series, Number Nine. Englewood Cliffs, New Jersey: Educational Technology Publications, 1973.

Corrigan, Robert E., and Roger A. Kaufman. *Why System Engineering*. Palo Alto, California: Fearon Publishers, 1965.

David, Floyd W. *The PRIMIR (Primary Individualized Reading) Program*. Unpublished research conducted in the Seattle School District, 1973.

DeVault, M. Vere, and Others. *Descriptor for Individualized Instruction: Development Procedures and Results*. Wisconsin University, Center for the Analysis of Individualized Instruction; sponsored by the National Institute of Education (DHEW), Washington, D. C., September, 1973.

Diamond, Robert M. *Instructional Development for Individualized Learning in Higher Education*. Englewood Cliffs, New Jersey: Educational Technology Publications, 1975.

Doll, Ronald C., ed. *Individualizing Instruction, The A. S. C. D 1964 Yearbook*. Washington, D. C.: The Association for Supervision and Curriculum Development, 1964.

Drumheller, Sidney J. *Handbook of Curriculum Design for Individualized Instruction*. Englewood Cliffs, New Jersey: Educational Technology Publications, 1971.

Duane, James E. *Individualized Instruction—Programs and Materials*. Englewood Cliffs, New Jersey: Educational Technology Publications, 1973.

Duker, Sam. *Individualized Reading*. Metuchan, New Jersey: Scarecrow Press, 1968.

Dunn, Rita, and Kenneth Dunn. *The Educator's Self-Teaching Guide to Individualizing Instruction*. New York: Parker Publishers, 1975.

Eisele, James E. *et al. Computer Assisted Planning of Curriculum and Instruction: How to Use Computer Based Resource Units to Individualize Instruction*. Englewood Cliffs, New Jersey: Educational Technology Publications, 1971.

Fisk, Lori, and Henry Clas Lindgren. *Learning Centers*. Glen Ridge, New Jersey: Exceptional Press, 1974.

Frazier, Alexander. *Open Schools for Children*. Washington, D. C.: Association for Supervision and Curriculum Development, 1972.

French, Russell L. "Individualizing Classroom Communication," *Educational Leadership*, XXVIII (November, 1970), 193-96.

Gagne, Robert M. *Psychological Principles in System Development*. New York: Holt, Rinehart, and Winston, 1966.

Gainer, William L., ed. *Santa Clara Inventory of Developmental Tasks: Observation Guide and Instructional Activities Manual*. Santa Clara, California: R. L. Zweig Associates, 1974.

Gorth, William P., Robert P. O'Reilly, and Paul D. Pinsky. *Comprehensive Achievement Monitoring: A Criterion Referenced Evaluation System*. Englewood Cliffs, New Jersey: Educational Technology Publications, 1975.

Gropper, George L. *Instructional Strategies.* Englewood Cliffs, New Jersey: Educational Technology Publications, 1974.

Hall, Calvin S., and Gardner Lindzey. *Theories of Personality.* New York: John Wiley and Sons, 1957.

Hammill, Donald D., and Nettie R. Bartel. *Teaching Children with Learning and Behavior Problems.* Boston: Allyn and Bacon, 1975.

Harmin, Merrill, Howard Kirschenbaum, and Sidney B. Simon. *Clarifying Values Through Subject Matter.* Minneapolis: Winston Press, 1973.

Hill, Joseph E. *Cognitive Style as an Educational Science.* Oakland Community College: Oakland Community College Press, 1973.

Hofstein, Saul. *The Nature of Process: Its Implications for Social Work.* Reprinted from the *Journal of Social Work Process,* XIV, Virginia P. Robinson Fund. Philadelpha: University of Pennsylvania Press, 1964.

Huckins, Wesley C. *Humanism in the Classroom: An Eclectic Approach for Improving Teaching and Learning.* Rockleigh, New Jersey: Allyn and Bacon, 1974.

Hunkins, Francis P. *Involving Students in Questioning.* Rockleigh, New Jersey: Allyn and Bacon, 1975.

Hunkins, Francis P. *Questioning Strategies and Techniques.* Boston: Allyn and Bacon, 1972.

Individualizing Instruction, Educational Technology Review Series, Vol. 5. Englewood Cliffs, New Jersey: Educational Technology Publications, 1973.

Instructional Systems, Educational Technology Review Series: Number Eight. Englewood Cliffs, New Jersey: Educational Technology Publications, 1973.

Introduction to Individualized Instruction, Ten Multi-media Modules with Presenters' Manuals. Englewood Cliffs, New Jersey: Educational Technology Publications, 1973.

Introduction to the Systems Approach, Educational Technology Review Series, Vol. 3. Englewood Cliffs, New Jersey: Educational Technology Publications, 1973.

Kapfer, Philip G., and Miriam B. Kapfer *et al. Learning Packages in American Education*. Englewood Cliffs, New Jersey: Educational Technology Publications, 1973.

Kaplan, Abraham. *The Conduct of Inquiry*. Pennsylvania: Chandler Publishing Co., 1964.

Kaplan, Sandra N. *Providing Programs for the Gifted and Talented: A Handbook*. An Instructional Syllabus for the National Summer Leadership Training Institute on the Education of the Gifted and the Talented. Ventura, California: Office of the Ventura County Superintendent of Schools, 1974.

Kephart, Newell C. *The Slow Learner in the Classroom*. Columbus, Ohio: Charles E. Merrill Publishing Co., 1971.

Kibler, Robert J., and Larry L. Barker. *Objectives for Instruction and Evaluation*. Rockleigh, New Jersey: Allyn and Bacon, 1974.

Labuda, Michael, ed. *Creative Reading for Gifted Learners: A Design for Excellence*. Newark, Delaware: International Reading Association, 1974.

Mager, Robert F. *Preparing Instructional Objectives*. Palo Alto, California: Fearon Publishers, 1962.

Mann, Philip H., and Patricia Suiter. *Handbook on Diagnostic Teaching: A Learning Disabilities Approach*. Boston: Allyn and Bacon, 1974.

Martinson, Ruth A. *The Identification of the Gifted and Talented*. Ventura, California: Office of the Ventura County Superintendent of Schools in Cooperation with the Council for Exceptional Children and the National Institute of Education (HEW), 1974.

McHugh, Walter J. "Team Learning in Skills Subjects in Intermediate Grades," *Journal of Education*, XCLII (December, 1959), 22-51.

Miles, Ralph F., Jr. *Systems Concepts: Lectures on Contemporary Approaches to Systems*. New York: John Wiley and Sons, 1973.

Musgrave, G. Ray. *Individualized Instruction: Teaching Strategies Focusing on the Learner*. Rockleigh, New Jersey: Allyn and Bacon, 1975.

New York State Reading Association. *Media as a Means*. Albany, New York: New York State Reading Association, 1974.

Nielsen, Duane M., and Howard F. Hjelm, eds. *Reading and Career Education*, Perspectives in Reading No. 19. Newark, Delaware: International Reading Association, 1975.

Patterson, C. H. *Humanistic Education*. Englewood Cliffs, New Jersey: Prentice-Hall, 1973.

Ramsey, Wallace A., ed. *Organizing for Individual Differences*, Perspectives in Reading, No. 9. Newark, Delaware: International Reading Association, 1967.

Reissman, Frank. "Students' Learning Styles: How to Determine, Strengthen, and Capitalize on Them," *Today's Education*, National Education Association, September-October 1976, pp. 94-98.

Viox, Ruth G. *Evaluating Reading and Study Skills in the Secondary Classroom*. Newark, Delaware: International Reading Association, 1968.

Chapter 5
References

Computer-Assisted Instruction Workshop and Presentation, Instructional Systems, Inc., in cooperation with Nassau County
Board of Cooperative Educational Services. Nassau Educational Resource Center, September 27, 1976.

Hunkins, Francis P. *Questioning Strategies and Techniques.*
Boston: Allyn and Bacon, 1972.

Licklider, J.C.R. *Libraries of the Future.* Cambridge, Massachusetts: Massachusetts Institute of Technology Press, 1965.

Additional Sources of Information

American Association of School Libraries, and the Department
of Audiovisual Instruction. *Standards for School Media Programs.* Chicago: American Library Association, and Washington, D. C.: National Education Association, 1969.

Anderson, Irving H. "A Motion Picture Technique for the Improvement of Reading," *University of Michigan School of
Education Bulletin*, XI (November, 1939), 27-30.

Arnspiger, V. C. *Measuring the Effectiveness of Sound Pictures as
Teaching Aids*, Bureau of Publications, Teachers College.
New York: Columbia University, 1933.

Audio-Visual Technology and Learning, Educational Technology
Review Series, Vol. 6. Englewood Cliffs, New Jersey: Educational Technology Publications, 1973.

Bell, Martha J., and Pearl Ketover Tropp. *WLIW ITV Teachers'
Manual.* Garden City, New York: Long Island Educational
Television Council, Inc., 1976.

Bottomly, Forbes. "An Experiment with the Controlled Reader,"
Journal of Educational Research, LIV (March, 1961), 265-
69.

Boucher, Brian, Merrill Gottlieb, and Martin L. Morganlander.
Handbook and Catalog for Instructional Media Selection.

Englewood Cliffs, New Jersey: Educational Technology Publications, 1973.

Bradley, Beatrice E. "Reading with a Dash of Showmanship," *Elementary School Journal*, LXI (October, 1960), 28-31.

Bushnell, Donald D., and Dwight W. Allen. *The Computer in American Education*, Commissioned by the Association for Educational Data Systems. New York: John Wiley and Sons, 1967.

The Computer and Education, Educational Technology Review Series, Number Nine. Englewood Cliffs, New Jersey: Educational Technology Publications, 1973.

Dorsett, Loyd G. *Audio-Visual Teaching Machines*. Englewood Cliffs, New Jersey: Educational Technology Publications, 1971.

Dyer, Charles A. *Preparing for Computer-Assisted Instruction*. Englewood Cliffs, New Jersey: Educational Technology Publications, 1972.

Eads, L. K. "Research Leading to the Production of Primary Grade Educational Sound Films," *Proceedings of the New York Society for the Study of Experimental Education*. New York, 1938, 70-90.

"Educational Implications of Technological Change," *The Report of the Commission*. Washington, D. C.: U. S. Government Printing Office, 1966.

Feldman, Shirley C., Kathleen Keely, and Walter H. MacGinitie. "An Effective Aid for Teaching Reading," *The Reading Teacher*, XIII (February, 1960), 208-211.

Frazier, Alexander. "Our Search for Better Answers," *Educational Leadership*, XX (April, 1963), 453-58.

Fulton, W. R., and Kenneth L. King. *An Instrument for Self-Evaluating an Educational Media Program in School Systems*. Department of Audiovisual Instruction, National Education Association, 1969.

Gardiner, Joseph S. "A Study of the Effects of the Audio-Tutorial Reading Program on Student Achievement, Attitudes, and Classroom Behavior." Unpublished Doctoral dissertation, Syracuse University, 1971.

Gordon, George N., and Irving A. Falk. *Videocassette Technology in American Education*. Englewood Cliffs, New Jersey: Educational Technology Publications, 1972.

Gray, H. A. "Sound Films for Reading Programs," *School Executive*, LX (February, 1941), 24-25, 29.

Gray, H A. "Vocabulary Teaching Possibilities of Sound Films," *Modern Language Forum*, Vol. 1 (December, 1940).

Gropper, George L. "Why Is a Picture Worth a Thousand Words?" *AV Communication Review*, 11:93 (July, 1963).

Gross, Ronald, and Judith Murphy. *Educational Change and Architectural Consequences*. A Ford Foundation Report. New York: Educational Facilities Laboratories, 1968.

Guss, Carolyn, "Films, Filmstrips and Reading," *The Reading Teacher*, XVII (March, 1964), 441-46.

Haygood, Danielle H. "Audio-Visual Concept Formation," *Journal of Educational Psychology*, LVI (June, 1965).

Hedges, Robert Eugene. "An Investigation into the Effects of Self-Directed Photography Experiences Upon Self-Concept and Reading Readiness Achievement of Kindergarten Children." Unpublished Doctoral dissertation, Syracuse University, 1971.

Heisler, Florence. "A Comparison Between Those Elementary School Children Who Attend Motion Pictures, Read Comic Books and Listen to Serial Radio Programs to Excess with Those Who Indulge in These Activities Seldom or Not at All," *Journal of Educational Research*, XLII (November, 1948), 182-90.

Hostrop, Richard W. *Education Inside the Library-Media Center*. Hamden, Connecticut: Linnet Books, 1973.

Klinge, Peter L., *et al. American Education in the Electric Age: New Perspectives on Media and Learning*. Englewood Cliffs, New Jersey: Educational Technology Publications, 1969.

Komoski, Kenneth. "The Continuing Confusion About Education and Technology," *Educational Technology*, November, 1969.

Komoski, P. Kenneth. "'Technology' and the Classroom," *Educational Leadership*, XXV (May, 1968), 735-40.

Lance, Wayne D. *Instructional Media and the Handicapped.* Stanford University, California. ERIC Clearing House on Educational Media and Technology; sponsored by National Institute of Education (DHEW), Washington, D. C., December, 1973.

Lombard, Marilyn Dean. "Perceptions of Teachers and Media Specialists Regarding the Use of Instructional Technology in Teaching Reading." Unpublished Doctoral dissertation, University of Southern California, 1969.

Matteoni, Louise. "TV Cartoons in Initial Reading Experiences with Culturally Deprived Children." Unpublished Doctoral dissertation, New York University, 1966.

McCracken, Glenn. "The New Castle Reading Experiment," *The Reading Teacher*, IX (April, 1956), 225, 241-45.

McLuhan, Marshall. *Understanding Media: The Extensions of Man.* New York: McGraw-Hill, 1964.

Minsel, Clara. "Audio-Visual Materials and Fifth Grade Reading Achievement," *Science Education*, XLV (February, 1961), 86-88.

Nason, Harold M. "The Use of Television in the Teaching of Reading," *Reading as an Intellectual Activity*, Conference Proceedings of International Reading Association. New York: Scholastic Magazines, 1963.

New York State Reading Association. *Media as a Means.* Albany, New York: New York State Reading Assoc., 1974.

O'Reilly, Robert P., Robert J. Ambrosino, and Robert J. Noval *et al. The Place of Doors: The Facilitation of Student Achievement through Televised and Adjunct Programming.* New York: Bureau of Educational Communications, and the Bureau of School and Cultural Research, New York State Education Department, 1974.

Razik, Taher A., and Delgra M. Ramroth. *Bibliography of Research in Instructional Media.* Englewood Cliffs, New Jersey: Educational Technology Publications, 1974.

Schramm, Wilbur. "What We Know About Learning from Instructional Television," *Educational Television: The Next Ten Years*. The Institute for Communication Research. Stanford: Stanford University Press, 1962.

Schuon, Marshall. "Readin', Writin', and Television." *Newsday* (Long Island, New York), March 30, 1975.

Sheldon, William D. "Television and Reading Instruction," *Education*, LXXX (May, 1960), 552-55.

Skinner, B.F. "The Science of Learning and the Art of Teaching," *Programmed Learning and Teaching Machines*, Lucius Butler and William J. Wiley, eds. New York: Selected Academic Readings, 1970.

Sleeman, Phillip J., Galen B. Kelley, and Robert A. Byrne, "A Comparison of the Relative Effectivess of Overhead Projection, Teaching Programs, and Conventional Techniques for Teaching Dictionary Skills," *Science of Learning*, III (1967), 67-69.

Smith, Lewis B., and Glen D. Morgan. *Cassette Tape Recording as a Primary Method in the Development of Early Reading Material*, ED 083 544, 1973.

Sullivan, Lorraine M. "The Use of Films and Filmstrips in the Teaching of Reading." Paper presented at Third International Reading Association World Congress. August, 1970, Sydney, Australia.

Trow, William Clark, and Eugene E. Haddan, eds. *Psychological Foundations of Educational Technology*. Englewood Cliffs, New Jersey: Educational Technology Publications, 1976.

Using Programmed Instruction, Educational Technology Review Series, Vol. 10. Englewood Cliffs, New Jersey: Educational Technology Publications, 1973.

Wallace, Ben. *Survival Is the Name of the Game*. Mineola, New York: Mineola Public Schools, 1970.

Warner, Dolores. "A Beginning Reading Program with Audio-Visual Reinforcement: An Experimental Study," *Journal of Educational Research*, LXI (1969), 230-33.

Wiseman, T. Jan, and Molly J. Wiseman. *Creative Communications: Teaching Mass Media*. University of Minnesota: National Scholastic Press Assoc., 1971.

Witty, Paul, and James P. Fitzwater. "An Experiment with Films, Film Readers, and the Magnetic Sound Projector," *Elementary English*, XXX (April, 1953), 232-41.

Chapter 6
References

Hill, Joseph E. *Cognitive Style as an Educational Science*. Oakland Community College: Oakland Community College Press, 1973.

Other Sources of Information

Allen, Dwight and Robert A. Mackin. "Toward '76: A Revolution in Teacher Education," *Phi Delta Kappan*, May, 1970.

Fenwick, English. "Et Tu Educator, Differentiated Staffing?" Washington, D. C.: National Commission on Teacher Education and Professional Standards, N. E. A., 1969.

Hite, Herbert. "A Model for Performance Certification," Robert C. Burkhart, ed. *The Assessment Revolution*. Albany: New York State Education Department, 1966.

Krumbein, Gerald. "How To Tell Exactly What Differentiated Staffing Will Cost Your District," *The American School Board Journal*, May 1970.

Lee, Gordon C. "The Changing Role of the Teacher," John I. Goodlad, ed., *The Changing American School*. Chicago: National Society for the Study of Education, 1966.

Lipson, Joseph I. "Job Description for a Teacher in a New School," *Educational Technology*, February, 1970.

Ofiesh, Gabriel D. *The Librarian and the Learning Resource Director: Future Roles, Problems and Issues*, audiotape cassette. Englewood Cliffs, New Jersey: Educational Technology Publications, 1972.

Scobey, Mary-Margaret, and A. John Fiorino, eds. *Differentiated Staffing*. Washington, D. C.: Association for Supervision and Curriculum Development, 1973.

Teacher Education and Educational Technology, Educational Technology Review Series, Vol. 4. Englewood Cliffs, New Jersey: Educational Technology Publications, 1973.

Chapter 7
References

Ellsworth, Keil C. "A Structure for Innovation in Education," *The Process of Innovation in Education*, Educational Technology Review Series, No. Two. Englewood Cliffs, New Jersey: Educational Technology Publications, 1973.

Johnson, Homer M. "Modes for Adaptation—People and Processes," *The Process of Innovation in Education*, Educational Technology Review Series, No. Two. Englewood Cliffs, New Jersey: Educational Technology Publications, 1973.

Kurland, Norman D. "Educational Innovation and Basic Needs," *The Process of Innovation in Education*, The Educational Technology Review Series, No. Two. Englewood Cliffs, New Jersey: Educational Technology Publications, 1973.

Voelz, Stephen J. "Changing Teachers' Attitude Toward Change," *The Process of Innovation in Education*, The Educational Technology Review Series, No. Two. Englewood Cliffs, New Jersey: Educational Technology Publications, 1973.

Additional Sources of Information

Congreve, Willard J. "Learning Center ... Catalyst for Change?" *Educational Leadership*, XXI (January, 1964), 211-16.

Culkins, The Reverend John M. "Changing Resistance to Change," Special Report of the National Laboratory for Advancement of Education, *Individualized Learning for the Inner City* Washington, D. C., 1968.

Design for Evaluation of Instructional Programs and Innovations, Professional Policies Committee on Evaluation, Chairperson, Frances Bennie. Mineola, New York: Mineola Public Schools, 1972.

ERIE Staff Members. *How to Get New Programs into Elementary Schools*. Englewood Cliffs, New Jersey: Educational Technology Publications, 1972.

Fabien, Don. *Dynamics of Change*. Englewood Cliffs, New Jersey: Prentice-Hall, 1967.

Frymier, Jack R. "Authoritarianism and the Phenomenon of Rebellion," Robert R. Leeper, ed., *Curriculum Decisions and Social Realities*. Washington, D.C.: Association for Supervision and Curriculum Development, 1968.

Havelock, Ronald G. *Change Agent's Guide to Innovation in Education*. Englewood Cliffs, New Jersey: Educational Technology Publications, 1973.

Kimpston, Richard D., and Leslie C. Sonnabend. "Organizational Health: A Requisite for Innovation?" *Educational Leadership*, XXX (March, 1973), 543-47.

Mitzel, Harold E. "The Impending Instruction Revolution," *Phi Delta Kappan*, April, 1970.

The Process of Innovation in Education, The Educational Technology Review Series, No. Two. Englewood Cliffs, New Jersey: Educational Technology Publications, 1973.

Roberts, Arthur D. *Educational Innovation: Alternatives in Curriculum and Instruction*. Rockleigh, New Jersey: Allyn and Bacon, 1975.

Rubin, Louis, ed. *The Future of Education: Perspectives on Tomorrow's Schooling*, Research for Better Schools, Inc. Rockleigh, New Jersey: Allyn and Bacon, 1975.

Saylor, J. Galen, ed. *The School of the Future Now*. Washington, D. C.: Association for Supervision and Curriculum Development, 1972.

Chapter 8
Sources of Information

Chaney, Clara M., and Newell C. Kephart. *Motoric Aids to Perceptual Training*. Columbus, Ohio: Charles E. Merrill Publishing Co., 1968.

Gainer, William L., ed. *Santa Clara Inventory of Developmental Tasks: Observation Guide and Instructional Activities Manual*. Santa Clara, California: R. L. Zweig Associates, 1974.

Gross, Ronald, and Judith Murphy. *Educational Change and Architectural Consequences*. A Ford Foundation Report. New York: Educational Facilities Laboratories, 1968.

Hammill, Donald., and Nettie R. Bartel. *Teaching Children with Learning and Behavior Problems*. Boston: Allyn and Bacon, 1975.

Kephart, Newall C. *The Slow Learner in the Classroom*. Columbus, Ohio: Charles E. Merrill Publishing Co., 1971.

Labuda, Michael, ed. *Creative Reading for Gifted Learners: A Design for Excellence*. Newark, Delaware: International Reading Association, 1974.

Mann, Philip H., and Patricia Suiter. *Handbook in Diagnostic Teaching: A Learning Disabilities Approach*. Boston: Allyn and Bacon, 1974.

New York State Reading Association. *Media as a Means*. Albany, New York: New York State Reading Association, 1974.

Saylor, J. Galen, ed. *The School of the Future Now*. Washington, D. C.: Association for Supervision and Curriculum Development, 1972.

Appendix A

Needs Assessment Forms

LEARNING CENTER
PUPIL NEEDS ASSESSMENT PROFILE

Learning Style

Teacher: ....

Pupil: .... Grade: .... Date: ....

Directions: Check the items that best describe this pupil's learning style. Comment on needs where necessary.

I.   Modality: ☐ Visual   ☐ Auditory   ☐ Kinesthetic   ☐ Multi-Sensory

II. Medium: ....

III. Instrumentation: ☐ Cassette   ☐ Sound Filmstrip ☐ Filmloop
     ☐ 16mm Movie ☐ Audio Card Reader ☐ Controlled Reader
     ☐ Sound-on-Slide   ☐ Slide Viewer ☐ Filmstrip ☐ Television
     ☐ Study Prints   ☐ Hoffman Reader
     ☐ Programmed Instruction ....
     ☐ Print Forms ....
     ☐ Situational ....

IV. Social Context: ☐ Independent   ☐ Teacher Directed
     ☐ Teacher Assisted ☐ Individually   ☐ Peer Pairs
     ☐ Small Group ☐ Large Group
     ☐ Tutor: ...... Teacher ...... Peer ...... Volunteer
              ...... Specialist ...... Aide

V.   Physical Environment: ☐ Functions with Peripheral Noise Present
                              ☐ Functions with Peripheral Activities in Environment
                              ☐ Requires Physical Movement in Open Environment
                              ☐ Requires Absence of Environmental Distractors of Most Types

VI.   Organization, Structure, and Pacing of Units of Learning
       ☐ Able to Follow Written Directions
       ☐ Able to Follow Oral Directions
       ☐ Requires Frequent Repetitions of New Concept in Similar Forms
       ☐ Requires Many Opportunities for Application and Transfer of New Learning
       ☐ Makes Transfer of Learning to New Situations Easily
       ☐ Completes Tasks Relatively: ...... Quickly and Efficiently;
                                      ...... Slowly; ...... Average Rate

VII.   Reward System
       Motivated primarily by: ☐ Teacher/Adult Praise   ☐ Peer Praise
                                 ☐ Tangible/Material Rewards, Such as Privileges, Prizes, Good Grades
                                 ☐ Particular Activities Related to Learning Process

       Comments: ....

VIII. Interests, Hobbies, Talents, Reading Preferences with Respect to Content

IX.   Personality Factors   Comments

          Frustration Tolerance   ....
          Attends to Task at Hand   ....
          Attention Span   ....
          Self-Confidence   ....
          Peer Relations   ....
          Relationships with Adults   ....
          Independence   ....
          Acceptance of Constructive Criticism ....
          Acceptance of Teacher Direction   ....

X.   Reading (Specify grade equivalent:)
      ☐ Multi-Sensory Readiness ....
      ☐ Decoding...
      ☐ Vocabulary Development ....
      ☐ Comprehension: ...... Literal ...... Interpretive
                                ...... Critical and Creative
      ☐ Location and Study Skills ....
      ☐ Content Area Reading ....

XI.   Writing
      ☐ Spelling ....
      ☐ Handwriting ....
      ☐ Mechanics of Writing: ...... Capitalization ...... Punctuation
                                 ...... Sentence Structure
      ☐ Organization: Unity, Coherence ....

XII.   ☐ Listening ....

XIII.   ☐ Speaking ....

XIV.   ☐ Visual Literacy ....

XV.   ☐ Analytic Thinking Skills ....

(Use reverse side if necessary.)

INSTRUMENTAL SKILLS CENTER

Parent Interview Form

Interviewer: ....
Date of Interview: ....

Student: .... Birthdate: .... Age: ....
School: .... Grade: ....
Address: .... Telephone: ....
Father's Name: .... Mother's Name: ....
Father's Occupation: .... Mother's Occupation: ....
Father's Education: .... Mother's Education: ....
Siblings: Name   Grade   Age
....
....
....
....

Physical Condition: Height .... Weight ....
                        Date of Last Physical Exam: ....

Result of Last Physical Exam: ....
Is present general condition of health good? Yes ...... No ......
Much absence from school due to illness? Yes ...... No ......
Auditory Defects? Yes ...... No ...... Comments: ....
Visual Defects? Yes ...... No ...... Comments: ....
Does student complain of headaches? Yes ...... No ......
Speech Defects? Yes ...... No ...... Which ....

241

Problems with coordination? ...... Running ...... Skipping ...... Hopping
...... Throwing a ball ...... Writing/Printing ...... Drawing/Coloring
Has student suffered from any serious illnesses or been hospitalized?

Illness	Date	Result
....	....	....
....	....	....
....	....	....

School Life
Was child anxious to attend school? Yes ...... No ......
What schools has child attended, starting with nursery school?

School	Date	Grade
....	....	....
....	....	....
....	....	....
....	....	....

Is child happy in school? Yes ...... No ...... Uncertain ......
Is he or she cooperative in school? Yes ...... No ......
Comments: ....
....
In what areas is the student's achievement satisfactory?
....
In what areas is his/her school achievement unsatisfactory?
....
At what level did the reading difficulty appear? ....
Describe the difficulty with reading. ....
....

Home Conditions
Is any foreign language spoken at home? Yes ...... No ......
            Specify if "Yes" ....
Do parents live together? Yes ...... No ......
Cultural Level: High ...... Average ...... Low ......
               Books ...... Magazines ...... Music ...... Theater ......
               Ballet ...... Puppet Shows ...... Trips ......
To what places has the student travelled? ....
....
....

Economic Level? High ...... High middle ...... Middle ......
Low Middle ...... Low ......
Does child share in home responsibilities? Yes ...... No ......
Specify: ....
Does child get along well with siblings? ....
Do both parents spend adequate amount of time with child? Yes ......
...... No
Is child "troublesome" at home? Yes ...... No ......
Is child frequently punished? Yes ...... No ......

Social and Emotional Adjustments
Does child have many friends? Yes ...... No ......
Do his/her friends call for him/her? Yes ...... No ......
Will the child share his/her belongings? Yes ...... No ......
Does the child play well with others? Yes ...... No ......
Is the child argumentative? Yes ...... No ......
Is the child: ...... Shy? ...... Timid? ...... Passive? ...... Aggressive?
...... Dependent? ...... Resistant to rules or having limits set?
...... Resistant to adult authority? ...... Resistant to constructive
criticism? ...... Afraid to risk making a mistake? ...... Manipulative?
...... Low in self-esteem? ...... Feeling superior?
Does the child become upset easily? Yes ...... No ......
Does the child cry easily? Yes ...... No ......
Does he/she worry? Yes ...... No ......
Are there any ticks or other nervous mannerisms? Yes ...... No ......

Interests
In what activities does the student engage after school and on weekends? ....
Does he/she own any books? Yes ...... No ...... Kind? ....
....
Does he/she like to read? Yes ...... No ...... What? ....
....
Does he/she like to have stories read to him/her? Yes ...... No ......
Does he/she like to write? Yes ...... No ...... Types of writing experiences
he/she engages in of own initiative? ....
....
Has he/she shown or expressed a desire to improve his/her reading ability?
Yes ...... No ......

INSTRUMENTAL SKILLS CENTER

Pupil Interview Form

Interviewer: ....

Date of Interview: ....

Student: .... Age: .... Grade: ....

School: ....

1. What are your favorite subjects in school? ....

....

2. Which subjects do you enjoy least? ....

Why? ....

3. Do you like school? Yes ...... No ...... Most of the Time ......

4. How do you spend your time after school and on weekends? ....

....

5. Do you have any hobbies or special interests? What are they? ....

....

6. Do you take any type of lessons? ...... Music ...... Dance ...... Tennis ......

Golf ...... Gymnastics ...... Swimming ...... Painting/Drawing ...... Sculpting

...... Weaving ...... Sewing ...... Karate/Self-Defense

Others ....

7. Do you belong to any clubs or organizations? Which ones?

....

8. Do you have any best friends? Names? ....

....

9. What are your favorite television shows? ....

....

10. About how much time do you spend each day watching TV? ....

11. Do you like to read? Yes ...... No ......
12. What kinds of books do you enjoy? ....
....
13. Do you receive any magazines at home regularly? Which ones?
....
14. Have you taken any trips in the past that you have particularly enjoyed?
    Yes ...... No ...... Where? ....
....
15. Do you have any trouble reading your school books? Yes ...... No ......
16. How do you feel about your reading? ....
17. What do you think you might like to be when you are through with
    school? (Occupation) ....
18. If you had three wishes, what would you wish for?
    a. ....
    b. ....
    c. ....
19. Who do you live with at home (give relationships)?
....
....
20. Mothers occupation? ....
    Father's occupation? ....

Comments

INDEPENDENT STUDY
LEARNER SKILLS AND WORK HABITS
EVALUATION

Pupil .... Grade .... Date ....
Evaluator .... Position ....

	Skill	Rating +	-
1.	Pupil exercises his/her options with respect to materials and activities to be used in achieving an objective.	5 4 3 2 1	
2.	Pupil works independently.	5 4 3 2 1	
3.	Pupil allows others to work.	5 4 3 2 1	
4.	Pupil completes his/her work within reasonable and mutually agreed upon time limits.	5 4 3 2 1	
5.	Pupil contributes to a project or activity working in a small group.	5 4 3 2 1	
6.	Pupil self-initiates contacts and conferences with the teacher when required.	5 4 3 2 1	
7.	Pupil is able to identify and secure needed equipment and resources.	5 4 3 2 1	
8.	Pupil begins working promptly.	5 4 3 2 1	
9.	Pupil returns equipment and instructional resources to the proper place.	5 4 3 2 1	

10. Pupil takes proper care of resources.   5 4 3 2 1

11. Pupil self-evaluates his/her own work.   5 4 3 2 1

12. Pupil actively participates in individual teacher-pupil conferencing raising and responding to questions, describing problems, requesting changes, exercising options, expressing attitudes and feelings, and responding to teacher suggestions.   5 4 3 2 1

13. Pupil keeps accurate, up-to-date records of his/her own achievement and progress.   5 4 3 2 1

14. Pupil seeks assistance from peers or teacher aides when required.   5 4 3 2 1

15. Pupil attends to a task until it is completed.   5 4 3 2 1

16. Pupil accepts and uses constructive criticism to advantage.   5 4 3 2 1

17. Pupil accepts teacher direction and/or assistance when it is required and offered.   5 4 3 2 1

18. Pupil has a system for organizing and keeping his completed work and his unfinished projects.   5 4 3 2 1

COLLEGE READING AND
STUDY SKILLS QUESTIONNAIRE*

Name .... Section ....

Address .... Telephone ....

Class Standing.................. Today's Date .... Birthdate ....

Student Number ....

I. Educational Background: Graduation Date
A. Elementary School ....
B. High School ....
C. Other ....
D. Previous Reading Improvement Courses. When? Where? ....
    ....

II. Current Education:
A. Courses in present program:
    Subject   Course #   Title
    1. .... 4. ....
    2. .... 5. ....
    3. .... 6. ....

III. Goals:
A. What do you hope to gain from this course? ....
    ....
    ....
B. Have you decided on a future goal? Please specify. ....
    ....

*Courtesy of Queens College, New York

IV.   Interests:
A.   What kind of books do you like to read? ....
B.   What was the name of the last book you read? ....
C.   What magazines do you read? ....
D.   What newspaper(s) do you read? ....
E.   What was the last movie you saw? ....
F.   What do you watch on television? ....
      ....
      ....
G.   What hobbies do you have? ....
H.   What do you like to do in your leisure time? ....
      ....
I.   Do you belong to any clubs or organizations? ....
      ....
J.   Do you help with any service projects? ....
      ....

V.   What jobs have you held?
      ....
      ....
      ....

VI.   Do you wish to share any additional information with us that might be
      helpful in understanding your needs?

LANGUAGE ARTS
PRIMARY PUPIL PLACEMENT PROFILE

Pupil .... Teacher ....

Grade .... Date ....

	Almost Never	Some- times	Most of the Time
Conceptual Development	**0**	**1**	**2**
1. Identifies positional words (first/last, top/ middle/bottom, etc.)			
2. Tells how two items are alike.			
Language Development			
3. Describes an experience, picture or object.			
4. Recognizes the names and sounds of all letters.			
5. Understands what he/she reads.			
Auditory Memory			
6. Follows oral directions (sequence of 3).			
7. Recalls story facts in sequence.			
Auditory Perception			
8. Matches rhyming sounds.			

	Almost Never	Some-times	Most of the Time
Visual Memory			
9. Recalls word forms (i.e., is making progress toward the development of sight vocabulary).			
Visual Perception			
10. Matches words.			
Visual Motor Performance			
11. Copies a sentence.			
12. Follows written directions.			
Social and Emotional Development			
13. Works independently.			
14. Gets along with peers.			
15. Can focus on and attend to a given task.			

Appendix B

Organizing Independent Learning:
Sample Contracts and
Record-Keeping Forms

LEARNING CENTER
PRIMARY CONTRACT

1	2	3	4	5
6	7	8	9	10
11	12	13	14	15
16	17	18	19	20
21	22	23	24	25

_____
Program Title

_____   _____
Name   Date

                    _____
                    Date Completed

255

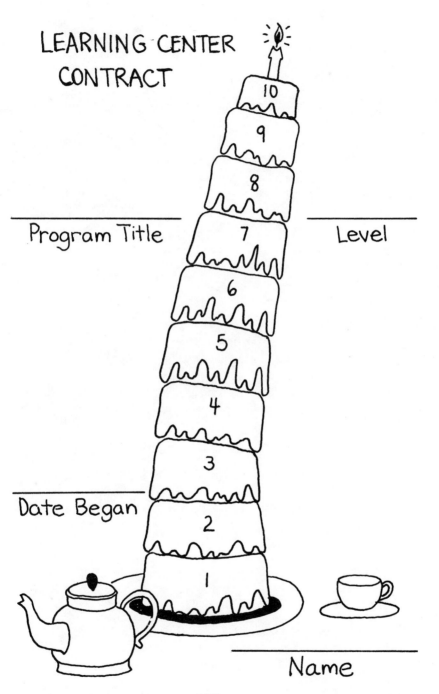

LEARNING CENTER
CONTRACT

10
9
8
7
6
5
4
3
2
1

_____
Program Title

_____
Level

_____
Date Began

_____
Name

257

LEARNING CENTER CONTRACT

Color in the ball
that has the same
number as the lesson
that you just completed.

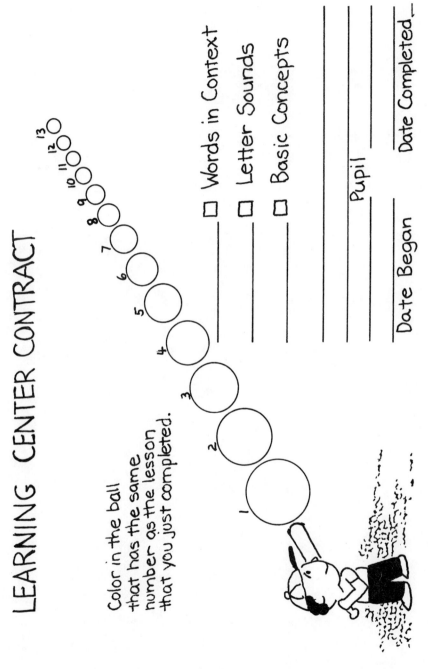

☐ Words in Context

☐ Letter Sounds

☐ Basic Concepts

_____   _____
Pupil

_____   _____
Date Began   Date Completed_

Talking
Table

Reader
Machine

Color in
the balloons
as you work
at each
station.

Games

Talking
Books

Learning Center
Grade_____
_____
Teacher
_____
Date   Name

261

Write in each balloon, the title of a book read.

Pupil

Grade   Date Completed

L.C. Tchr
Initials Upon
Completion

263

Certificate of Merit

Be it known that

_____

having completed with distinction

is hereby awarded this Certificate of Merit

this _____ *day of* _____ *197* ___ *at* _____ *School.*

_____
Principal

_____
Teacher

The
Talking Table

Listening
Lab

System
80

Hoffman
Reader

Games

Puzzles

_____
Name

_____ _____
Grade   Date Begun

_____
Teacher

LEARNING CENTER READING PRESCRIPTION

Pupil .... Teacher ....
Grade .... Date ....

Intermediate Grades

Directions: Your teacher will check the programs listed on this sheet that will help you to improve your reading. Use only those levels of the program that are indicated.

Material	Level
...... Reader's Digest Audio Lessons	
...... E.P.C. Audio Reading Program	
...... Imperial Intermediate Reading Program	
...... Checkered Flag Series	
...... Clues to Reading	
...... Hoffman Reader	
...... SRA	
...... Dimensions in Reading: An American Album	
...... Acoustifone RAP Reading Program	
...... Sports Close-Ups	
...... Girl Stuff	
...... Spiderman Reading Motivation Kit	
...... Aikido and Kung Fu: The Ancient Arts	
...... Bowmar: Dogs	

INTERMEDIATE READING CONTRACT

Interpretive Comprehension

No. 1 Understanding Relationships: Comparisons

Pupil .... Teacher ....
Grade .... Date ....

Objective: Given two objects, you will be able to state in writing how they are alike and how they are different.

Comparisons
Directions: Write the date on the line at the left as you complete each activity.

...... Benefic Thinking Skills Development Program: "Comparing" Sound Filmstrip

...... Pupil Activity Reference Book, pp. 9-10

...... Self-Help Cards: Comparing Pupil Activity Reference Book, pp. 34-38 (Model Answers)

...... Skill Development Cards (Content Areas) (Do any 3 skill cards on comparing)

...... EDL Listen and Think Level C, Lesson 5

...... EDL Listen and Think Level D, Lesson 5

...... EDL Listen and Read Level D, Lesson 5

...... Reader's Digest Reading Skill Practice Pad, pp. 14-16, 21, 27, 66, 67, 69, 79, 80

...... Califone, Language Concept Development Audio Cards (analogies)

Evaluation: Select a skill card on comparing from the Thinking Skills Development Box. (Do not select one that you have already completed.) Do the activity on the card. Have your teacher check your work. Read your comparison to a group of classmates; ask them to suggest other ways that the two objects are alike and different that you might not have thought of.

LANGUAGE ARTS CONTRACT:
Intermediate Grades

Language Arts Contract for ....

Date Started .... I will finish by: ....

Objective: Learner will write an imaginative or original story, story ending,
or response stimulated by a non print media form. Plan with
your teacher the activities you will complete.

VIEW
...... Disney Filmloops
...... An Early Learning Experiences Slide Set of Your Choice
...... An SVE Slide Set of Your Choice
...... Writing Corner Story Starters (Captioned Study Prints)

LISTEN
...... Open-Ended Stories Cassettes
...... Imagination Unlimited Cassettes

DO
...... Write and tape a factual narrative to accompany the slide set or
filmloop that you viewed.
...... Write an imaginative story about what you viewed or heard using the
third person ("he," "she," "it") to tell the story.
...... Write an original ending to the story you heard on the cassette.
...... Pretend you are the person or animal on the filmloop, study print, or
cassette story and write about what you see, hear, smell, think, and
feel.

JUNIOR HIGH SCHOOL
INDIVIDUALIZED READING PROGRAM
VOCABULARY DEVELOPMENT—BASIC & ADVANCED*

Name ....

Teacher ....

FIGURATIVE LANGUAGE

Objectives: 1. Learner will be able to identify examples of figurative language.
2. Learner will be able to differentiate between various types of figurative language.
3. Learner will be able to use figurative language in his own writing.

*Date
Completed*   *Circle each lesson number as it is completed.*

....   1. Listen and Read—D: Tape Lesson 11—"Figurative Language"

....   2. Skill Pacers—Olive—Orange—Tan—"Figurative Language"

....   3. Inference Tape Lessons (Mineola Summer Project) Lessons 1, 2, 3

....   *4. Skills Box I—Figures of Speech

....   *5. Listen and Read—GHI-2
                       Tape Lesson 3—Words and Your Senses
                       Tape Lesson 4—Meeting New Words

....   6. Word Pacer—Idioms

....   *7.   Tactics in Reading Kit II—Figurative Language (Card Nos. 25, 26, 27, 28) Lessons 1, 2, 3, 4, 5, 6, 7, 8, 9, 10, 11, 12

....   *8.   Listen and Read—JKL
Tape Lesson 6—"Figurative Language in Prose"

....   *9.   Listen and Read—G-L
Tape Lesson 24—"Figurative Language"

....   10.   Basic Reading Skills (Scott Foresman)—"Figurative Language" Lessons 101, 102, 103, 104, 105

....   11.   Word Pacers: Idioms—Skill B

....   12.   Macmillan   Reading   Spectrum—Vocabulary—Level   3 (Yellow)

Lesson 27—"Idioms"
Lesson 28—"More Idioms"
Lesson 29—"More About Idioms"
Lesson 30—"Where Did You Get That Expression?"
Lesson 31—"A Short Review of Idioms"

....   13.   Macmillan   Reading   Spectrum—Vocabulary—Level   4 (Green)

Lesson 1—"Up We Go"
Lesson 2—"Heads, Eyes and Fingers"
Lesson 3—"When Words Don't Mean What They Say"
Lesson 4—"Watching for What Words Say"

Application-Transfer. (Choose one of the following to do and then share with your classmates.)

1.   Write a poem or story using figurative language. Record the poem or story.
2.   Make an "Idiom Tree." Each leaf made of colored paper will contain a different idiom.
3.   Make a collection of examples of figurative language that you hear used by people during a one-week period. Give the name of the person who used each example.
4.   Develop and construct a figurative language game and teach your classmates how to play it.

INSERVICE TRAINING
LEARNING CENTER CONTRACT

Contract No. ———— *Supervision of Reading for Administrators: Developing Reading Comprehension Skills—Evaluating Teaching Strategies*

Objectives:
1. To be able to list the cognitive levels.

2. To be able to formulate at least two questions at each of the cognitive levels.

3. To be able to categorize questions according to thinking—literal, interpretive, and creative reading comprehension levels.

4. To be able to evaluate the questioning strategies used by a teacher during an individual teacher-pupil conference and/or a reading lesson.

5. To be able to explain the values and limitations of certain types of programmed instruction to reading instruction aimed at developing comprehension skills.

6. To be able to list two significant problems with instruction that can impede a student's developing adequate reading comprehension skills.

Resources: Cassette program entitled "Developing Reading Comprehension Skills: Workshop for Administrators" by Dr. Frances Bennie.

Accompanying Worksheets
"Kinds of Comprehension Questions Based on Sanders' Taxonomy"

"The Teacher's Role in the Development of Reading Comprehension Skills"

"Activities Using Stories and Related Questions"

"Mike's Story" and Answer sheet for "Mike's Story"

Answer sheet to accompany filmloop entitled "Eskimo Family Meal" (Doubleday Multi-Media)

"The Art of Questioning" from *How to Teach Reading* by Morton Botel, Follett Publishing Co.

Information Please: Reading in Social Studies "Eskimo Family Meal" (filmloop with study cards), Doubleday Multi-Media

"Key for Writing Performance Objectives" by Carter and Mayo

Involving Students in Questioning by Francis Hunkins

Equipment: Filmstrip-Making Kit (AV Do and Learn Lab)
Filmloop Projector and Table Top Screen
Cassette Player
Pencils, Paper, Oak Tag

Activities and Experiences:
1.   *Knowledge and Comprehension Levels*
Listen to the cassette entitled "Developing Reading Comprehension Skills: Workshop for Administrators." The cassette will direct you to use the worksheets entitled "Kinds of Comprehension Questions Based on Sanders' Taxonomy" and "The Teacher's Role in the Development of Reading Comprehension Skills," Part A ("How Students Have Learned to Beat The Game").

2.   *Interpretation Level*
Worksheet entitled "The Teacher's Role...", Part B is intended to assist you in interpreting the information or knowledge that you acquired during the first activity.

3.   *Application Level*
The cassette will direct you to the following activities which are intended to help you to apply the knowledge gained during Activity No. 1:
"Activities Using Stories and Related Questions." (Categorize only the number of questions that are necessary for you to feel that you can apply the Sanders' criteria.)

4. *Analysis*

The following problems are intended to assist you in being able to make an analysis of situations/problems using the knowledge gained in Activity No. 1.

    a.   Several intermediate teachers wish to know why they need a basal reader if they are already using multi-level skills kits and booklets to teach reading. Pupils use these types of programmed materials independently, for the most part. Using the knowledge gained in Activity No. 1 and interpreted and applied in Activities 2 and 3, formulate a response that you would give to these teachers, including a rationale for your response.

    b.   Several teachers of the sixth, seventh, and eighth grades feel that pupils should not have to be taught reading after grade 3 or 4. At that point, they feel, students should be reading to learn instead of learning to read. Formulate a response.

    c.   One of your primary teachers believes that only phonics should be taught in the first two grades and spends very little time attempting to develop comprehension skills. What do you think about this and why?

5. *Synthesis*

Do one of the following:

    a.   Make a filmstrip that you could use to describe to teachers the various levels of comprehension, providing examples of questions at each level.

    b.   Prepare a chart with an accompanying cassette or filmstrip explaining to teachers the concepts of "reading the lines, reading between the lines, and reading beyond the lines." Focus upon how appropriate teacher questioning strategies can help students to develop literal, interpretive, and creative levels of comprehension.

    c.   Write an article for a professional educational journal describing how teachers can improve the reading comprehension skills of their pupils through improved questioning strategies.

    d.   Tape an individual teacher-pupil conference discussing a book from the Xerox Personalized Reading Center or the Scholastic Individualized Reading Center, and categorize the questions asked by the teacher. Make recommendations for improving questioning strategies, if any are required.

6.   *Evaluation*
      Observe a classroom reading lesson using the learning acquired in
      completing this contract to evaluate the lesson and the classroom
      reading program as a whole. List strengths and weaknesses of the lesson,
      and make recommendations to improve the development of compre-
      hension skills of students.

LEARNING CENTER
Group Prescription

Program: ....
Prescribed Lesson No.. .... Date: .... Grade: ....
Teacher: ....

Pupils:	Reading Specialist or Learning Center Aide Comments
1.	
2.	
3.	
4.	
5.	
6.	
7.	
8.	

Teacher Comments ....
....

LEARNING CENTER
Individual Prescription

Program: ....
Lessons: ....
Teacher: .... Grade: .... Date: ....

Teacher's Directions/Comments	Learning Center Teacher's Comments

ASSIGNMENT SCHEDULE

Student: .... Class/Grade: ....
Areas of Concentration: ....
....

Date	Material	Skill	Comments

MASTER ANSWER SHEET

Student: .... Date: ....
Teacher/Instructor: .... Class: ....
Material:..
Page/Cassette/Filmstrip Number: ....
Exercise/Lesson Number: ....
Color or Level: ....
....
....
....
....
....
....
....
....
....
....
....
....
....
....
....
....
....
....
....
....
....

INDIVIDUAL TEACHER-PUPIL
CONFERENCING RECORD

Pupil: .... Grade: ....
Teacher/Instructor: ....

Reading Achievement Stanine   1 2 3 4 5 6 7 8 9

Mathematics Achievement Stanine   1 2 3 4 5 6 7 8 9

Conference Date	*Summary of Conference* (Include topics/work discussed, problems, achievement, skills deficiencies, contracts completed, etc.)	*Recommendations and Work Assignments* (specify due dates agreed upon, if it applies)

Appendix C

Producers of Media Materials

Criteria for Selection of
Commercially Prepared
Instructional Materials

Some Recommended Commercially Available
Learning Center Materials for the
Elementary and Junior High School Levels

Suggestions for Preparation of
High School or College
Learning Center Materials
in Reading, Language Arts, and Study Skills

PRODUCERS OF MEDIA MATERIALS

1. ACI Media, Inc.
   35 West 45th Street
   New York, New York 10036

2. Addison Wesley Publishing Co.
   Jacob Way
   Reading, Massachusetts 01867

3. Adwell Audio-Visual Co., Inc.
   247-40 Jericho Turnpike
   Bellerose, New York 11426

4. Aims Instructional Media
   Services, Inc.
   626 Justin Avenue
   Glendale, California 91201

5. Allyn & Bacon, Inc.
   Rockleigh, New Jersey 07624

6. American Guidance Service
   Publishers' Building
   Circle Pines, Minnesota 55014

7. Ann Arbor Publishers
   Box 388
   Worthington, Ohio 43085

8. A/V Concepts Corp.
   756 Grand Boulevard
   Deer Park, New York 11729

9. Baker & Taylor Companies
   Audio Visual Services Div.
   P.O. Box 230
   Momence, Illinois 60954

10. Barnell Loft, Ltd.
    958 Church Street
    Baldwin, New York 11510

11. Bear Films, Inc.
    P.O. Box R
    Baldwin, New York 11510

12. Bell & Howell
    7100 McCormick
    Chicago, Illinois 60645

13. Benefic Press
    10300 W. Roosevelt Road
    Westchester, Illinois 60153

14. Benziger Bruce & Glencoe, Inc.
    8701 Wilshire Boulevard
    Beverly Hills, California 90211

15. Channing L. Bete Co., Inc.
    45 Federal Street
    Greenfield, Massachusetts 01301

16. BFA Educational Media
    2211 Michigan Avenue
    P.O. Box 1795
    Santa Monica, California 90406

17. Book-Lab, Inc.
    1449 37th Street
    Brooklyn, New York 11218

18. Borg Warner Educational
    Systems
    600 W. University Drive
    Arlington Heights, Illinois 60004

19. Stephen Bosustow Productions
    1649 Eleventh Street
    Santa Monica, California 90404

20. Bowmar, Inc.
    622 Rodier Drive
    Glendale, California 91201

21. Milton Bradley Co./Playskool
    Inc.
    Springfield, Massachusetts 01101

22. Brunswick Productions
    157 Chambers Street
    New York, New York 10007

23. Cambridge Book Co.
    488 Madison Avenue
    New York, New York 10022

24. Centron Educational Films
    1621 West Ninth Street
    Lawrence, Kansas 66044

25. Childcraft Education Corp.
    20 Kilmer Road
    Edison, New Jersey 08817

26. Children's Press
    1224 West Van Buren Street
    Chicago, Illinois 60607

27. Charles W. Clark Co., Inc.
    564 Smith Street
    Farmingdale, New York 11735

28. Cleo Learning Aids
    3957 Mayfield Road
    Cleveland, Ohio 44121

29. The Continental Press, Inc.
    Elizabethtown, Pennsylvania
    17022

30. Coronet Instructional Media
    65 E. South Water Street
    Chicago, Illinois 60601

31. Creative Learning, Inc.
    19 Market Street
    Warren, Rhode Island 02885

32. Croft-Nei Publications
    24 Rope Ferry Road
    Waterford, Connecticut 06386

33. Current Affair Films
    24 Danbury Road
    Wilton, Connecticut 06897

34. Curriculum Associates, Inc.
    94 Bridge Street
    Chapel Bridge Park
    Newton, Massachusetts 02158

35. DLM, Inc.
    7440 Natchez Avenue
    Niles, Illinois 60648

36. Demco Educational Corp.
    2120 Fordem Avenue
    Madison, Wisconsin 53704

37. T.S. Dennison & Co., Inc.
    5100 West 82nd Street
    Minneapolis, Minnesota 55437

38. Denoyer-Geppert Co.
    5235 Ravenswood Avenue
    Chicago, Illinois 60640

39. Disney Educational Media
    500 S. Buena Vista Street
    Burbank, California 91521

40. Doubleday Multi-Media
    Doubleday & Co., Inc.
    1371 Reynolds Avenue
    Santa Ana, California 92705

41. Eastman Kodak Co.
    Audio-Visual Library
      Distribution
    343 State Street
    Rochester, New York 14650

42. The Economy Co.
    P.O. Box 25308
    Oklahoma City, Oklahoma
      73125

43. EDL/McGraw Hill
    1221 Avenue of Americas
    New York, New York 11768

44. Education Representatives
    4 Godwin Avenue
    Fairlawn, New Jersey 07410

45. Educational Activities, Inc.
    1937 Grand Avenue
    Baldwin, New York 11510

46. Educational Dimensions Corp.
    P.O. Box 126
    Stamford, Connecticut 06904

47. Educational Noises & Sounds
    Box 591
    San Clemente, California 92672

48. Educational Progress Corp.
    4900 South Lewis Avenue
    Tulsa, Oklahoma 74145

49. Educational Programmers, Inc.
    P.O. Box 332
    Roseburg, Oregon 97470

50. Educational Reading Service
    320 Route 17
    Mahwah, New Jersey 07430

51. Educational Teaching Aids
    Div. of A. Daigger & Co.
    159 West Kinzie Street
    Chicago, Illinois 60610

52. Educational Technology, Inc.
    2224 Hewlett Avenue
    Merrick, New York 11566

53. Educational Technology
      Publications, Inc.
    140 Sylvan Avenue
    Englewood Cliffs, New Jersey
      07632

54. EMC Corporation
    180 East Sixth Street
    St. Paul, Minnesota 55101

55. Encore Visual Education, Inc.
    1235 South Victory Boulevard
    Burbank, California 91502

56. Encyclopaedia Britannica
    Educational Corp.
    180 East Post Road
    White Plains, New York 10601

57. Eye Gate Media
    146-01 Archer Avenue
    Jamaica, New York 11793

58. Follett Library Book Co.
    4506 N.W. Highway
    Crystal Lake, Illinois 60014

59. Gamco Industries, Inc.
    Box 1911
    Big Spring, Texas 79720

60. Garrard Publishing Co.
    Champaign, Illinois 61820

61. Ginn & Co.
    191 Spring Street
    Lexington, Massachusetts

62. Globe Book Co., Inc.
    175 Fifth Avenue
    New York, New York 10010

63. Great Ideas, Inc.
    40 Oser Avenue
    Hauppauge, New York 11787

64. Grolier Educational Corp.
    845 Third Avenue
    New York, New York 10022

65. Guidance Associates
    757 Third Avenue
    New York, New York 10017

66. Harper & Row Media
    10 East 53 Street
    New York, New York 10022

67. Hoffman Educational Systems
    4423 Arden Drive
    El Monte, California 91734

68. Holt, Rinehart and Winston
    383 Madison Avenue
    New York, New York 10017

69. Houghton Mifflin Co.
    Pennington-Hopewell Road
    Hopewell, New Jersey 08525

70. Imperial Educational Resources

Div. of Educational
    Development Corp.
    P.O. Box 7068
    Tulsa, Oklahoma 74105

71. Imperial International
    Learning Corp.
    P.O. Box 548
    Kankakee, Illinois 60901

72. Jamestown Publishers
    P.O. Box 6743
    Providence, Rhode Island
    02940

73. Thomas S. Klise Co.
    P.O. Box 3418
    Peoria, Illinois 61614

74. Learning Tree Filmstrips
    Box 1590
    Boulder, Colorado 80302

75. Listener Educational Corp.
    6777 Hollywood Boulevard
    Hollywood, California 90028

76. Listening Library, Inc.
    One Park Avenue
    Old Greenwich, Connecticut
    06870

77. Litton Educational Publishing,
    Inc.
    300 Pike Street
    Cincinnati, Ohio 45202

78. Lowell & Lybwood, Ltd.
    965 Church Street
    Baldwin, New York 11510

79. C.F. McCabe Inc.
    Educational Systems
    94 North Woodhull Road
    Huntington, New York 11743

80. Macmillan Library Services
    866 Third Avenue
    New York, New York 10022

81. Media Materials, Inc.
    2936 Remington Avenue
    Baltimore, Maryland 21211

82. Modern Curriculum Press
    13900 Prospect Road
    Cleveland, Ohio 44131

83. National Geographic Society
    17th & M Streets, N.W.
    Washington, D.C. 20036

84. National Microfilm Library
    8090 Engineer Road
    San Diego, California 92111

85. New Dimensions in Education,
    Inc.
    83 Keeler Avenue
    Norwalk, Connecticut 06854

86. Noble & Noble Publishers, Inc.
    1 Dag Hammarskjold Plaza
    New York, New York 10017

87. Nystrom Co.
    175 Fifth Avenue
    New York, New York 10010

88. Oddo Publishing Inc.
    Storybook Acres
    Box 68
    Fayetteville, Georgia 30214

89. Pathescope Educational Media,
    Inc.
    71 Weyman Avenue
    New Rochelle, New York 10802

90. Prentice-Hall Media, Inc.
    150 White Plains Road
    Tarrytown, New York 10591

91. RPL Educational Aids &
    Materials
    36 Hillside Avenue
    Williston Park, L.I., New York
    11596

92. Q-ED Productions, Inc.
    P.O. Box 1608
    Burbank, California 91507

93. Rand McNally & Co.
    P.O. Box 7600
    Chicago, Illinois 60680

94. RCA Records
    Educational Dept.
    1133 Avenue of the Americas
    New York, New York 10036

95. Reader's Digest Services, Inc.
    Educational Division
    Pleasantville, New York 10570

96. The Reading Laboratory, Inc.
    55 Day Street, South
    Norwalk, Connecticut 06854

97. Salenger Educational Media
    1635 12th Street
    Santa Monica, California 90404

98. Society for Visual Education Inc.
    1345 Diversey Parkway
    Chicago, Illinois 60614

99. Spellbinder, Inc.
    33 Bradford Street
    Concord, Massachusetts 01742

100. H.M. Stone Productions, Inc.
    6 East 45th Street
    New York, New York 10017

101. Teaching Resources Corp.
    100 Boylston Street
    Boston, Massachusetts 02116

102. Teaching Resources Films
     2 Kisco Plaza
     Mt. Kisco, New York 10549

103. Union School Products
     561 South Broad Street
     Elizabeth, New Jersey 07202

104. United Learning
     6633 W. Howard Street
     Niles, Illinois 60648

105. Universal Education & Visual
     Arts
     100 Universal City Plaza
     Universal City, California 91608

106. University Microfilms
     International
     300 N. Zeeb Road
     Ann Arbor, Michigan 48106

107. Urban Media Materials, Inc.
     212 Mineola Avenue
     Roslyn Heights, New York 11577

108. Valiant Instructional Materials
     Corp.
     195 Bonhomme Street
     Hackensack, New Jersey 07602

109. Viking/Penguin, Inc.
     625 Madison Avenue
     New York, New York 10022

110. Webster/McGraw Hill
     Princeton Road
     Hightstown, New Jersey
     08520

111. Westinghouse Learning Press
     770 Lucerne Drive
     Sunnyvale, California 90804

112. Weston Woods
     Weston, Connecticut 06880

113. H. Wilson Corp.
     555 W. Taft Drive
     South Holland, Illinois 60473

114. Winston Press
     25 Groveland Terrace
     Minneapolis, Minnesota 55403

115. Workshop for Learning Things,
     Inc.
     5 Bridge Street
     Watertown, Massachusetts
     02172

116. Xerox Education Publications/
     Xerox Films
     245 Long Hill Road
     Middletown, Connecticut
     06457

CRITERIA FOR SELECTION OF
COMMERCIALLY PREPARED
INSTRUCTIONAL MATERIALS

Materials selected should:

A. be consistent with the educational philosophy that children learn in different ways and at different rates; therefore, materials selected should facilitate individualizing instruction, and should afford children opportunities to learn through a variety of modalities in several social contexts.

B. be appropriate to the maturity level and interest areas of the learners for whom they are intended.

C. be consistent with the philosophy that instruction, to be relevant, must (a) be related to and use as a point of departure the experiential background of the learners; and (b) through the instructional process, learning must satisfy some self-perceived needs of the learner.

D. be consistent with the philosophy that learning is most meaningful when integrated across curricular/information areas rather than fragmented into separate disciplines.

E. be consistent with the philosophy that language development occurs as a result of experience and that reading, writing, speaking, and listening skills are all integrally related to the learner's experiences.

F. support the general project goals as they are translated into behavioral outcomes.

G. instructional materials should be selected to support the following categories of outcome-related learning objectives:

1. *Reading Skills Development*
    a. Multi-Sensory Readiness
    b. Decoding
    c. Vocabulary
    d. Comprehension
    e. Location and Study Skills
    f. Reading in the Content Areas
    g. Development of Positive Attitudes Toward Reading, Reading Motivation, and Literature Appreciation.

2. *Language Arts Skills Development*
    a. Speaking and Listening
    b. Creative Writing
    c. Mechanics of Writing and Organization
    d. Functional Grammar and Usage
    e. Spelling

3. *Humanities*
    a. Poetry and Drama
    b. Visual Arts
    c. World Cultures
    d. Music and Performing Arts
    e. Creative Modes of Expression Using the Above
    f. Development of Positive Self-Concept, Values, and Appreciations

4. *Career Education and Language Arts Development. Development of Self-Awareness and Positive Self-Concept.*

5. *Social Sciences and Reading and Language Arts Development; Development of Positive Self-Concept.*

6. *Science and Reading and Language Arts Development.*

H. not stigmatize the child by using ability groupings, but rather allow for continuously changing combinations of independent study, learner pairs/teams, specific skill groupings, and interest groupings.

I. engage modalities appropriate to the particular learning objectives of the material.

J. have an attractive, usable format, and good technical qualities if the material is audio or audio-visual.

K. sequence learning logically, and from simplest to gradually increasingly complex concepts or applications.

L. not stereotype or portray as inferior any persons due to race, religion, sex, ethnic group, or socioeconomic level.

SOME RECOMMENDED COMMERCIALLY AVAILABLE LEARNING CENTER MATERIALS FOR THE ELEMENTARY AND JUNIOR HIGH SCHOOL LEVELS

This list is not intended to be exhaustive of all the media materials presently available. It is, indeed, a very small sampling of materials which focus upon the development of reading and language arts skills—in many instances through the content areas—with which this writer and classroom teachers have had experience and have found to be of some merit. It is hoped that this list will provide a point of departure for the educator seeking to equip a learning center, or seeking particular types of material which must be selected in a short amount of time.

Artifacts
    Inter-Culture Assoc., Desk E, Box 277, Thompson, Conn. 06277*

Audio-Card Reader Programs
    Adwell
    Bell & Howell

Cassette, Individualized Programs
    Coronet
    Doubleday Multi-Media
    Educational Developmental Laboratories
    Educational Progress Corporation
    Learning Resources
    Media Materials
    Modern Curriculum Press
    Reader's Digest
    Society for Visual Education (SVE)

*Addresses not listed previously are given here.

299

Cassettes, Other Types of Programs
    Bowmar
    Spoken Arts, 310 North Avenue, New Rochelle, N.Y. 10801
    SVE

Composition Starters (See Study Prints)

Controlled Reader Programs
    Educational Developmental Laboratories (EDL)

Filmloops
    Disney
    Doubleday Multi-Media

Games and Manipulatives
    Baker and Taylor
    Childcraft Education Corp.
    Charles W. Clark Co., 564 Smith Street, Farmingdale, N.Y. 11735
    Denoyer-Geppert
    Developmental Learning Materials, Inc., 7440 Natchez Avenue, Niles, Illinois 60648
    Educational Teaching Aids, Div. of Daigger Co.
    McGraw-Hill (KELP and other kindergarten, grade 1 material), 1221 Avenue of the Americas, N.Y., N.Y. 10020
    Milton Bradley Co.
    Reader's Digest
    Viking
    Xerox Education Publications

Individualized Reading Programs
(with paperback books and teacher
management system)
    Scholastic Book Services
    Xerox Education Publications

Manipulatives (See Games)

Models
    Milton Bradley

Multi-Level Skills Books
    Barnell-Loft (Specific Skills Series)
    Reader's Digest

Multi-Level Skills Kits
(Laminated Cards, Self-directing,
Self-Correcting)
    BFA
    Educational Progress Corp.
    Random House, 201 E. 50th Street, N.Y., N.Y. 10022
    Science Research Associates, 259 E. Erie St., Chicago, Illinois 60611

Multi-Media Kits
    Benefic (Thinking Skills Development Programs)
    Bowmar
    Children's Press
    Disney
    Educational Progress Corp.
    Random House
    Salenger Educational Media
    Spoken Arts
    Viking

Programmed Learning Devices
    Benefic (Study Scope)
    Field Enterprises/Childcraft/World Book (Cyclo-Teacher), 609 Mission
        Street, San Francisco, California 94105

Simulations
    Interact, P.O. Box 262, Lakeside, Calif. 92040
    Educational Manpower, Inc., Box 4272-E, Madison, Wis. 53711

Slides
    Coronet
    SVE
    Western Psychological Service, 12031 Wilshire Blvd., Los Angeles,
        California 90025

Sound Filmstrip Programs
    Bowmar
    Coronet
    Disney
    Doubleday Multi-Media
    Educational Progress Corp.

Study Prints/Composition
Starters/Task Cards
  Addison Wesley
  Bowmar
  Educational Insights
  Ginn
  Singer/SVE
  Winston Press

Talking Books
  Bowmar
  Children's Press
  Disney
  Garrard
  Random House
  Reader's Digest

Task Cards (*See* Study Prints)

Teaching Machines (sound-slide, automated)
  Borg Warner (System 80)
  Hoffman Educational Systems (Hoffman Readers)

SUGGESTIONS FOR PREPARATION OF
HIGH SCHOOL OR COLLEGE LEARNING CENTER
MATERIALS IN READING, LANGUAGE
ARTS, AND STUDY SKILLS

1. Videotape or audiotape a lecture in each of the college freshman required courses. Prepare model notes for the lecture, a model summary, and a statement of the main idea. Students may then view and/or listen to the lecture, preparing their own notes, summaries, and main idea statements; afterwards, they can compare theirs to the models.

2. Secure copies of the basic texts for each of the required freshman courses. Prepare a model outline of a chapter. Pupils may then attempt to outline the same chapter and compare their outlines to the model outlines. The outline may be recorded on audio cassettes to be used by the legally blind.

3. Prepare a sound-slide program on "How to Listen to and Take Notes on a Lecture."

4. Prepare a videotape training course on research papers.

5. Prepare videotapes or use commercially prepared programs to develop interpretive and critical thinking skills. (The Time-Life videotape cassette programs such as *The Glorious Game* and *Mind Over Body* would be examples of commercially prepared programs of this type.)

6. Prepare a sound-slide program on "How to Take Tests."

7. Prepare a sound-slide or videotape cassette program on propaganda techniques.

8. Prepare audiotape cassettes of lectures in freshman required courses. Develop model questions at the literal, interpretive, and creative thinking levels based upon the content of each lecture. Students listen to lecture and develop questions based upon it.

9. Develop a sound-slide or audiotape cassette program on questioning strategies at the various cognitive levels. Apply this to reading.

10. Develop sound-slide programs on interesting and thought-provoking themes along with model outlines, summaries, and bibliographies, focusing upon developing organizational skills for writing.

11. Develop sound-slide presentations to teach understanding of the various types of writing (e.g., narrative, expository, etc.).

12. Develop audiotape cassette and/or sound-slide programs on descriptive language, figurative language, emotionally-charged words.

13. Develop sound-slide presentations of various writing techniques and styles of writing using samples from published writers and providing guided opportunities for students to experiment with each technique.

14. Prepare sound-slide or audiotape cassette lessons on sentence structure and on the mechanics of writing.

15. Prepare slides or silent filmloops and have pupils provide literal, interpretive, and creative responses to the visuals.

16. For the bilingual student, audio card-reader word-picture programs, idioms, and figurative expressions, as well as various structure patterns, may be prepared. In addition, audiotape cassette dictation exercises and listening comprehension exercises may be developed.

Appendix D

Volunteer and Tutorial
Program Forms

LETTER FOR PARENTS

Dear Parents:

The .... School Language Arts Learning Center is going to institute a training program to train persons to serve as volunteer Learning Center aides. The participants will be taught the role and function of the Learning Center's program and how to assist children in the individualization of instruction, as well as scheduling, distribution, preparation, and production of materials and operation of equipment.

The participants will be given training in such activities as scheduling and distribution of teaching materials and equipment; preparation and production of print materials, simple displays, transparencies, and audio tape recordings; operation of audio-visual and other equipment; and library skills, such as shelving books, clerical tasks, technical processing, repair of books, films, tapes and other materials, and simple maintenance of equipment.

If you can give a half-day a week to the program and would like to make a positive contribution to our Learning Center, we need you! Anyone wishing to participate as a volunteer aide should complete the bottom half of this notice and return it to the .... School front office.

Sincerely,

Principal, ... School

— —

NAME ....
ADDRESS ....
PHONE ....
DAYS AVAILABLE ....

307

VOLUNTEER PROGRAM
LANGUAGE ARTS CENTER

Data Form

NAME ....

ADDRESS ....

                 street   town   zip

DATE   ....   TELEPHONE ....

1. I am a high school graduate. Yes ...... No ......
2. If "yes" to above, my diploma was obtained at

   ....

           (high school)   (town)   (state)

3. In addition to having graduated from high school, I have completed the number of years checked of formal education in an educational institution beyond high school.

            One year   ......

            Two years   ......

            Three years ......

            Four years   ......

            More than

            Four years   ......

4. The education referred to in No. 3 was obtained at ....

   ....

5. Although I am not a high school graduate, I have had the following experiences which I consider to be equal to a high school education. (Please be sure to list every experience which you feel has been valuable to you educationally.) ....

   ....

6. I have been employed by a school or school system. Yes ...... No ......
7. If "yes" to No. 6, the position(s) I held was (were) ....

   ....

   ....

8.   Other work experience which I have had is as follows: ....
....
....

9.   Please list any experience you have in any of the following:
        Typing ......   Cameras ......
        Mimeograph ......   Cataloging of Books-Materials ......
        Ditto ......   Filing ......
        AV Equipment ......   Other ......

10.   Present occupation ....
....
....

11.   List any employment you have had which involved working with children. ....
....
....
....

VOLUNTEER TRAINING PROGRAM

Check off as you
a c h i e v e   each
objective

Objectives for Volunteers
As a result of this orientation and training program,
the parent volunteer will be able to do the following:

....   1.   Describe the philosophy and goals of the
learning center approach.

....   2.   Describe his/her role and functions in the
learning center.

....   3.   Explain the lines of authority and channels of
communication with respect to reading special-
ist, teacher aides, principal, classroom teachers,
and language arts coordinator.

....   4.   Describe the learning center schedule for volunteers and procedures to follow when the vol-
unteer will be absent during an assigned day.

....   5.   Identify and operate the following audio-visual
equipment and manipulatives:

....   Hoffman Reader

....   System 80

....   Cassette Players

....   Cassette Player-Recorders

....   Filmloop Viewer

311

....   Filmloop Projector

....   Filmstrip Previewer

....   Caramate Sound Slide Viewer

....   Dukane Sound Filmstrip Viewer

....   Phonograph

....   Slide Previewer

....   Master Carrel Panel

....   Carrel Station Selectors

....   Audio Card-Readers (Tutorette and Califone)

....   Cyclo-teacher

....   Television and Wireless Headsets

....   6.   Operate the following duplicating equipment:

....   Ditto machine

....   Mimeograph machine

....   Laminating machine

....   7.   Locate, at minimum, the following instructional materials in the learning center:

....   Imperial Intermediate Reading Program

....   Hoffman Reading Program

....   System 80 Lessons

....   Reading for Understanding Kit

....   Spelling Mini-Systems

....   Random House Tell Me A Story Series

....   Audio Card Reader Programs

....   Filmloops

....   Slides

....   EPC Audio Reading Program

....   8.   Assist pupils in locating materials and in operating audio-visual equipment.

....   9.   Handle effectively common situations that might arise while assisting pupils in the learning center.

....   10.   Be familiar with and adhere to rules of dress, conduct, school safety and fire regulations, and other basic modes of school operation.

....   11.   Catalog and file materials for learning center and library. Be able to assist children in location and use of library type materials.

TUTORIAL SESSION EVALUATION

Pupil:.. Date:............................
Tutor:................................... Time: .... Session No.: ....
Length of Session: .... Subject: ....

Materials/Activities	Success/Achievement	Pupil Response

Assignment ....
....
....

Observations/Comments ....
....
....

Appendix E

Learning Center Evaluation
Attitudinal Assessment Questionnaires

PUPIL ATTITUDINAL ASSESSMENT
GRADES K-2

Teacher: .... Grade: ....
Date: .... School: ....

Direction to the Teacher:
Please ask your pupils the following questions and record their responses. (Indicate number of pupils giving response.)

1. Did you enjoy visiting the Learning Center this year?
    ...... Yes   ...... No   ...... Most of the time

2. What did you enjoy doing most in the Learning Center?
    ....
    ....
    ....

3. Would you like to visit the Learning Center again next year?
    ...... Yes   ...... No   ...... Maybe

4. Would you like to be able to go to the Learning Center more than once a week?
    ...... Yes   ...... No   ...... Maybe

5. Was there anything you didn't like about the Learning Center? What?
    ...... Yes   ...... No

PUPIL ATTITUDINAL ASSESSMENT
GRADES 3-5

Name: .... Grade: ....
Teacher: .... Date: ....

Directions: Check the column that best describes your response to each
question.

	YES	NO	NOT SURE
1. I enjoy working in the Learning Center.			
2. I would like to be able to visit the Learning Center more often.			
3. I am able to find what I need and I can operate the equipment in the Learning Center.			
4. The materials I used in the Learning Center were interesting.			
5. I am learning through my work in the Learning Center.			
6. The things I do in the Learning Center are different from those I do in the classroom.			
7. I would like to be able to do some of the things I do in the Learning Center in my classroom more often.			

	YES	NO	NOT SURE
8. I am able to get help from the adults in the Learning Center when I need it.			
9. The things I enjoyed doing most in the Learning Center were: a. .... b. .... c.			
10. I would like to see the following changes made in the Learning Center. If none, write "none."			

TEACHER ATTITUDINAL ASSESSMENT

Teacher: .... Grade: .... Date: ....

	Strongly Agree	Agree	Uncertain	Disagree	Strongly Disagree
	5	4	3	2	1
1. My pupils usually enjoy working in the Learning Center. Comments					
2. The Learning Center provides opportunities for: a. remedial work b. enrichment c. follow-up and extension of classroom activities d. introducing new concepts, new skills or new units in an interesting manner Comments					
3. The Learning Center helps me to accommodate diverse learning styles and learning needs. Comments					

	Strongly Agree	Agree	Uncertain	Disagree	Strongly Disagree
	5	4	3	2	1
4. Pupils seem to have positive attitudes toward the materials and equipment in the Center.					
Comments					
5. The approach used in the Center helps me to meet individual pupil needs more effectively.					
Comments					
6. The resources borrowed from the Center help me to meet individual needs in the classroom more effectively.					
Comments					
7. My pupils' experiences in the Center are helping them to become more independent learners.					
Comments					
8. My pupils look forward to coming to the Learning Center.					
Comments					
9. I have learned about many new in-					

	Strongly Agree	Agree	Uncertain	Disagree	Strongly Disagree
	5	4	3	2	1
structional resources through my experiences with the Learning Center.					
Comments					
10. The Learning Center is a valuable asset to the total instructional program.					
Comments					

Please comment on any of the following that you feel might be improved. Suggestions for improvement are welcomed.

11. Scheduling

12. Staffing and role definitions

13. Planning sessions

14. Materials previews

15. Resources

16. Activities in the Center

17. Resource loan system

18. Equipment

19. Physical facility/design

20. Record-keeping procedures

21. Diagnostic-prescriptive procedures

OTHER:

Appendix F

Pupil Orientation to Media:
Elementary Level

LANGUAGE ARTS LEARNING CENTER
PUPIL ORIENTATION TO THE MEDIA

To the Teacher:

Today it is rare to find a child who has not had some experience with the media. Cameras, television, radios, and phonographs are found in nearly every home. Most children have been to the movies. Many have used cameras themselves or have seen their parents use them to take snapshots, slides, or movies. Many children have had experiences with tape recorders, cassette player-recorders, and typewriters.

It is the aim of this orientation program to (1) increase the learner's awareness of the uses of the media, and (2) to increase awareness and to encourage him or her to respond to his or her own experiences with the media.

The teacher should encourage pupils to describe these experiences. Pictures of the various forms of media may be clipped from magazines. Pupils may point out examples of media found in their classroom, homes, and/or the school. Pupils may be involved in drawing a picture of a scene from a favorite movie or television show. They may list all forms of media that involve "seeing," "listening," "touching," "speaking," or combinations of these.

The learning outcomes that should result from these experiences are as follows:

I. Learner is familiar with each of the various types of media (record discs, movies, slides, cassettes, TV, radio).

II. Learner is familiar with the characteristics and potential functions of each of the various types of media.

III. Learner describes and responds to his experiences with each of the various types of media.

INTRODUCTION TO THE MEDIA
Behavioral Objectives

1. Learner identifies different types of audio-visual media with which he or she had experiences (cassette, TV, radio, phonograph, movies, slides, photography, etc.).

2. Learner describes the characteristics of each type of media with which he or she has had some experience (sound, moving picture, color, no commercials, sound with picture, etc.).

3. Learner describes his or her experiences with the various types of media. (Describe movies, TV programs seen, favorite phonograph records, home movies, slides, photographs, cassette recordings.)

4. Learner compares and contrasts the various types of media.

5. Learner identifies his or her favorite type of media and explains why he or she prefers this one to the others.

6. (Primary) Learner draws a picture of a scene or a character from his or her favorite movie or TV program.

7. Learner describes things he has learned through the media (songs, rhythm, facts about people, letter sounds, science, etc.).

8. Learner identifies the kinds of media available in the learning center.

Appendix G

Observation Guide for Visitations
to Learning Centers

OBSERVATION GUIDE FOR VISITATIONS
TO LEARNING CENTERS

Date of Visitation: .... School: ....
District: ....

1. What is the relationship of the library to the learning center? Role of the librarian? ....
   ....

2. Role definitions and staffing procedures for learning center and library?
   Reading Specialist? ....
   Librarian? ....
   Teacher Aides? ....
   Parent Volunteers? ....
   Other? ....

3. Scheduling procedures?
   Who does scheduling? .... Criteria used?
   ....
   Pupils visit individually? ....
   Class visits as a whole? ....
   Frequency of visits? ....
   Classroom teacher's role? ....
   Length of each visit? ....

4. What kind of feedback to teacher occurs? Types of record-keeping of individual pupil's progress? ....
   ....

5. What diagnostic procedures, techniques, and instruments are used to assist in prescriptive programming? (See next page.)

Level   Instrument/Procedure

....

....

....

....

....

6. Who is responsible for maintaining the learning center—ordering new materials, maintaining equipment, clerical work, keeping materials and worksheets in order and readily available, assisting students, etc.? ....
....
....

7. How were teachers oriented to and trained to use learning center? ....
....

8. How are pupils oriented? ....

9. What materials are available in the learning center and what are the criteria used for selection of these materials? ....
....

10. Evaluation procedures? ....
....

Index

Learning centers

DATE DUE		
MAR 1 0 1980		
AUG 1 8 1981		
MAY 1 9 1982		
APR 2 7 1984		
APR 2 3 1985		
JUL 1 7 1985		
JUL 1 1 1991		